Serious Performance Consulting

According to Rummler

Geary A. Rummler, CPT

A publication of the International Society for Performance Improvement

Pfeiffer™

1807
WILEY
2007

John Wiley & Sons, Inc.

Published by Pfeiffer
An Imprint of Wiley
989 Market Street, San Francisco, CA 94103-1741
www.pfeiffer.com

For additional copies/bulk purchases of this book in the U.S. please contact 800-274-4434.

Pfeiffer books and products are available through most bookstores. To contact Pfeiffer directly call our Customer Care Department within the U.S. at 800-274-4434, outside the U.S. at 317-572-3985, fax 317-572-4002, or visit www.pfeiffer.com.

Pfeiffer also publishes its books in a variety of electronic formats. Some content that appears in print may not be available in electronic books.

Cataloging-in-Publication data on file with the Library of Congress.

ISBN-13: 978-0-7879-9616-1

Printed in the United States of America
Printing   10   9   8   7   6   5   4   3   2

 **About ISPI**

The International Society for Performance Improvement (ISPI) *is dedicated to improving individual, organizational, and societal performance.* Founded in 1962, ISPI is the leading international association dedicated to improving productivity and performance in the workplace. ISPI represents more than 10,000 international and chapter members throughout the United States, Canada, and 40 other countries.

ISPI's mission is to develop and recognize the proficiency of our members and advocate the use of Human Performance Technology. This systematic approach to improving productivity and competence uses a set of methods and procedures and a strategy for solving problems for realizing opportunities related to the performance of people. It is a systematic combination of performance analysis, cause analysis, intervention design and development, implementation, and evaluation that can be applied to individuals, small groups, and large organizations.

Website: www.ispi.org
Mail: International Society for Performance Improvement
1400 Spring Street, Suite 260
Silver Spring, Maryland 20910 USA
Phone: 1.301.587.8570
Fax: 1.301.587.8573
E-mail: info@ispi.org

Dedication

This book is for Margaret,
in appreciation of her understanding,
patience, tolerance, and support
during 40 years of tilting at windmills.

Table of Contents

According to Whom?..vii

Foreword..ix

Preface xi

Introduction 1

    A Typical Situation 1

    Serious Performance Consulting 2

    Characteristics of a Serious Performance Consultant...7

    Looking Ahead...7

    Introduction Highlights 8

Part One: The NuPlant Case Study..9

1. Welcome to NuPlant...11

    The Request 11

    Responding to the Request...12

    Chapter 1 Highlights 13

2. Performance Analysis Framework and Process..15

    Applying the Anatomy of Performance Framework..16

    The Anatomy of Performance 17

    Making a Diagnosis..33

    Prescribing Changes 35

    The Analysis Process 35

    Chapter 2 Highlights 37

3. The NuPlant Case Study 39

    Phase I: Desired Results Determined and Project Defined..39

    Phase II: Barriers Determined and Changes Specified 45

    Summary of Bert's Findings 59

    Final Report Postscript 74

    Chapter 3 Highlights 75

4. Case Study Debrief 77

    NuPlant Project Review 77

    Top 10 Reasons Why the NuPlant Project is My Favorite...81

A Critique of the NuPlant Project...82

Project Generalizations...82

Scalability of Models...84

The Anatomy of Performance and Culture..87

The Anatomy of Performance and Leadership..89

Wrapping up the Case Study...91

Chapter 4 Highlights...92

Part Two: The Craft of Serious Performance Consulting **93**

5. Performance Analysis and the Internal Consultant...**95**

Serious Performance Consulting on the Inside 95

The Organizational Reality of the Internal Performance Consultant 95

Dealing with Organizational Realities as an Internal Consultant 98

Tools to Assist the Internal Performance Consultant..98

Internal Performance Consulting: An Example..113

Chapter 5 Highlights...116

6. A Path to Becoming a Performance Consultant **117**

Dimensions of Serious Performance Consulting Capability 117

Building Your Serious Performance Consulting Capability 119

The Path Forward 131

How About You?..131

Chapter 6 Highlights...133

Appendix A: NuPlant Project Findings..135

Appendix B: NuPlant Project Recommendations..151

Glossary 163

References 169

Additional Resources 171

According to Whom?

According to Geary Rummler, who has been doing performance consulting for 35 years. He has completed more than 125 successful, significant projects in the areas of sales, service, manufacturing, new product development, strategy implementation, supply chain management, order fulfillment, information technology implementation, and customer service in both the private and public sectors.

Rummler has developed a robust, effective, and proven performance consulting methodology. The initial models were developed in the 1960s with Dale Brethower at the University of Michigan. His models were applied and enhanced at Praxis Corporation with partner Tom Gilbert during the 1970s. During the past 20 years, first with the Rummler-Brache Group and now the Performance Design Lab, he has applied his models at the organization, process, and job levels and has continued refining the models and developing numerous practical analysis tools.

He strives to communicate these models and the consulting methodology by teaching hundreds of individuals through a series of workshops and by publishing the methodologies, most notably in a book co-written with Alan P. Brache entitled *Improving Performance: Managing the White Space on the Organization Chart* (Jossey-Bass, 1995). Having been printed in six languages and having sold more than 150,000 copies, this book has served as a practical guide for tens of thousands around the globe who manage organizations, processes, and jobs.

Among his other accomplishments, he has earned master's and doctoral degrees from the University of Michigan, served as president of the International Society for Performance Improvement, and was elected to the board of directors of ASTD. In 1986, he was inducted into the Human Resource Development Hall of Fame. He has also been awarded the Distinguished Professional Achievement Award from the International Society for Performance Improvement (1992), the Enterprise Reengineering Excellence Award from Enterprise Reengineering Magazine (1996), the Distinguished Contribution Award for Workplace Learning and Performance from ASTD (1999), and the Lifetime Achievement Award from the Organization Behavior Management Network (1999).

Geary Rummler and his wife, Margaret, live in Tucson, Arizona. They have three great sons and daughters-in-law, as well as four fantastic grandchildren.

Readers may contact the author through:

Performance Design Lab
P.O. Box 64640
Tucson, AZ 85728-4640
Telephone: 520.529.1151
email: grummler@performancedesignlab.com
website: performancedesignlab.com

Foreword

Performance consulting has enjoyed rapid growth in the last several years, enticing numbers of professionals from a variety of fields to describe themselves as performance consultants.

Unfortunately, not everyone using the performance consultant designation has the knowledge and skills to do the work of performance consulting; the job requires much more than a business card with a trendy title.

This book invites you to join an accomplished performance consultant on a project journey during which you will discover how the work of performance consulting is done. As experienced travelers know, voyages to unfamiliar locations are enhanced by advance preparations that include learning about what visitors may experience in a new locale.

The Performance Consulting Landscape

Allow me to introduce you to the performance consulting landscape where we will preview the mileposts of the performance consultant's world of work and orient new travelers to what lies ahead (Addison, 2003).

The Performance Consultant's Approach

"Rather than defining performance consulting by the interventions they use, performance consultants take a comprehensive systems view of performance, examining the alignment of the total performance system in every venue where they work. Because workers do not perform in a vacuum, successful performance consultants leverage that systems viewpoint to learn how the workers, processes, and organizational goals are aligned and how the total performance system operates. This system includes the environment, culture, inputs, processes, outputs, feedback, and organizational stakeholders particular to the organization" (Addison, 2003).

The Work of Performance Consulting

The work of performance consulting is rooted in a systematic approach that begins at the end rather than the beginning by asking: What should the results be when the work is done? Performance consultants take a broad, systematic view of the work environment to identify all the systems in the organization that will be affected. They focus on the business and ensure that the client receives added value in the process. And, to further ensure success, performance consultants establish partnerships with both needed experts and the client.

How Performance Consultants Work

The steps performance consultants take in the course of their work usually begin with identification of value to clarify the problem, business issue, or opportunity. Once this is known, they move to the end of the process to establish a definition of results that specifies the requirements for creating the value or closing the gap between existing and desired results. Next, they conduct an analysis of performance to identify factors in the existing performance system that influence the production of results to meet requirements.

At this point, performance consultants have the information needed for the selection of interventions or solutions in which they select from a range of possible solutions those that will best meet the requirements, given the performance information collected in the previous step. Now, they are ready for the design and development of interventions or solutions in which they prepare for execution, including decision making about how to cost-effectively implement the solution and match the organization's cultural environment. At this stage, performance consultants are ready for the deployment of interventions or solutions when they execute the design to meet the specified requirements.

Finally, performance consultants perform an evaluation of effectiveness to measure intervention or solution processes, outcomes, and results to determine how well they met the requirements and what might be required to further improve results for the client.

A Special Invitation

In *Serious Performance Consulting According to Rummler,* Geary extends a rare invitation to travel with him on assignment. He answers the question "What do performance consultants do?" using a case study with thorough annotations and comments. Through a series of data sweeps, he shows us the inner workings of performance analysis as performed by an acknowledged expert. As a bonus, we are given lists of findings and recommendations for this case.

Although the case study is from a manufacturing setting, I was struck by how well it applies to service and financial organizations as well. The same business issues explored in the case study are also concerns faced by the dozens of *Fortune* 500 companies, across all industries, with which I have worked over the years. It is no wonder that when you read the book you may think it is about your organization.

A Final Thought

About 25 years ago, I took my first performance analysis workshop from Geary Rummler when he was at Praxis. Since then, I've used the tools and resources he provided, and I can truly say that by focusing on results, organizations can save millions of dollars each year while providing an environment where people can do their best work.

Roger M. Addison,
Certified Performance Technologist
Director of Human Performance Technology,
International Society for
Performance Improvement
Sausalito, California

Preface

Why This Book, Why Now?

It seems everybody is or wants to be a performance consultant these days. In general this trend is a good one, but it's a little scary when I see some of the things being passed off as "performance consulting."

I consider myself a performance consultant and, along with a small cadre of colleagues, have been practicing this important and noble craft for 35 years. But, I must admit that much of what I have seen published on the topic would have to be characterized as performance consulting "lite" or performance consulting "dabble."

Granted, when people embark on performance consulting as a career, they are necessarily nibbling around the edges of significant opportunities as they earn their stripes. Largely ignored, however, has been *serious performance consulting,* which moves beyond job-level performance improvement to process- and organization-level performance improvement.

That's the level where performance consultants can make a real difference. Hence, this book.

Who Will Benefit from This Book?

A number of audiences may find value in this book. The first includes those identified in the title of the book—performance consultants. Within that audience, there are three possible subgroups:

- *Individuals considering becoming performance consultants:* For them, I hope to provide a helpful look at what a performance consultant does and what an exciting and challenging role performance consulting can be. But this field is not for everyone. If you are uncertain that performance consulting is the field for you, the case study may help you decide.
- *Individuals who are beginning careers as performance consultants:* It is my hope that this book will provide additional incentive to pursue this line of work and will provide some guideposts on the way to *serious* performance consulting—performance improvement that consistently makes a difference.
- *Experienced practitioners of the performance consulting craft:* If you are like me, you're always looking for insights into how to better practice your craft and serve your clients. If this describes you, I hope this book will provide such insights and add to your performance improvement repertoire.

A second general audience is those individuals playing some consulting role by responding to requests for help in improving individual performance and organizational results. This audience includes organization development, organization effectiveness, and Six Sigma specialists, to name a few.

A third audience is managers and supervisors—the individuals charged with delivering results and seeking to improve the performance of their operations. This book provides them a framework for identifying and managing the elusive variables that affect the performance of their work units. *Serious Performance Consulting According to Rummler* also gives managers an idea of what to expect from a performance consultant, should they wish to employ one.

What Is the Purpose of This Book?

The purpose of this book is to illustrate and describe what serious performance consulting is (or should be) and what a serious performance consultant does beyond zapping an occasional performance gap.

I will do that by first presenting a comprehensive conceptual framework for conducting performance analysis, followed by the application of the framework to an extensive case study illustrating the role of a serious performance consultant. The case study is followed by comments on the performance consultant's role and what is required to become one. The core of the book is the performance improvement case study, which the reader has the opportunity to engage at three levels of detail.

In chapter 3, the reader has the opportunity to get a relatively high level overview of the project and see the general project flow and timeline. Also in this chapter, the reader can get a second view of the project by reading my running commentary on how the project is being conducted. All the project findings and recommendations discussed are also linked to detailed descriptions in the appendixes. A review of these detailed findings and recommendations, as they appeared in the project final report to the client, provides the reader with the third view of the case study.

The case study is based on an actual project, which is described here from start to finish. It is not a combination of projects or cases to present some ideal. I have purposely included all the nitty-gritty detail of this project in this book because I want the reader to understand what serious performance consulting looks like—the level of detail that must be systematically uncovered, analyzed, understood, documented, and communicated.

Serious Performance Consulting According to Rummler is also equally appropriate for the internal

and external consultant. The basic framework in chapter 2 applies to *anyone* concerned with obtaining significant results in an organization, whether he or she is a consultant (internal or external) or manager. The case study is seen through the eyes of an external performance consultant. However, chapter 5 presents strategies, tactics, and tools for the internal performance consultant, who faces a number of unique challenges.

What This Book Is *Not*

A colleague asked me if this book was about what I had learned since the second edition of *Improving Performance: How to Manage the White Space on the Organization Chart* was published (Rummler and Brache, 1995).

It is not.

It is, rather, a demonstration and examination of how many of the concepts and principles in *Improving Performance* can and should be applied by a performance consultant to improve organization results. But, it is safe to say there are also a number of new thoughts on improving performance as well as extensions of a number of *Improving Performance* concepts in this book.

It also is not explicitly a how-to book on performance consulting. That is, there are not a large number of tools (there are a few), and there are not guidelines and checklists of how to do performance consulting. It is more of a what-to-do book. The case study illustrates what I think serious performance consultants do and what they produce on their way to delivering valued results to their clients. Nevertheless, you will find a great deal of implicit how-to in the case study and follow-on discussions.

Finally, the central intent of the book is not about building and managing a performance consulting organization; it is about *doing* performance consulting. However, chapter 5 contains strategies and tactics that have proven useful in managing the internal performance consulting organization.

How Is This Book Organized?

This book is divided into several parts. It opens with an introductory chapter, which defines serious performance consulting and identifies the characteristics of the serious performance consultant.

Part One consists of four chapters dedicated to the NuPlant case study:

- Chapter 1 briefly describes the situation leading to this particular performance improvement project.
- Chapter 2 presents the underlying mental model and templates used by the performance consultants in the case study as they go about identifying the barriers to NuPlant's desired results and specifying the changes necessary to obtain those results.
- Chapter 3 is a high-level walk-through of the project, with a week-by-week timeline, from project design to final recommendations. It is structured so you can drill down for more details on any of the project findings (in appendix A) and recommendations (in appendix B). It also contains my running commentary on the project where I point out what I think are particularly relevant points for the performance consultant. You'll see my comments presented in text boxes captioned "According to Rummler."
- Chapter 4 provides a brief recap of the project with comments on the project approach, some project shortcomings, and an explanation of why this is one of my favorite projects of all time. Most important, I have also summarized what I believe you can generalize from this case to most any performance improvement situation.

Part Two of the book covers the profession of performance consulting:

- Chapter 5 provides a discussion of the special challenges the internal performance consultant faces when doing serious performance consulting and presents some strategies and tactics that have proven helpful in meeting those challenges.
- Chapter 6 suggests some things aspiring performance consultants might do to learn and practice their craft.
- Appendix A contains the detailed findings of the NuPlant project as they appeared in the

project final report. They are cross-referenced to the recommendations in appendix B and the project description in chapter 3.
- Appendix B comprises the detailed recommendations of the project as they appeared in the project final report. They are cross-referenced to the findings in appendix A and the project description in chapter 3.
- A glossary of terms is included to help readers recall terms, abbreviations, and acronyms.
- The list of references enumerates the sources cited in this book.
- The additional resources section gives some resources that will be useful to readers who wish to learn more about serious performance consulting.

Why I Am Still a Performance Consultant (After All These Years)

Let me conclude by explaining why I continue to do serious performance consulting after all these years and still love it. There are three reasons:

First, it is important, value-added work—on two levels. The first level is obvious: making organizations more effective, as reflected by the products and services provided to their customers, returns to their shareholders, and a productive work environment for their employees. The second level is also part of organization effectiveness but with a focus on the performer in the system, as personified by the production supervisors in the NuPlant case study you are about to encounter.

Forty years ago I made the observation, "Put a good performer in a bad system, and the system will win every time." The result of this reality is that individuals are frequently falsely accused of being the cause of the "problem," and organizations spend tons of money subjecting the falsely accused to hours of useless, time-consuming, non-value-added "interventions." Several things really upset me about this situation:

- the tremendous amount of money and employee time spent addressing problem's symptoms rather than addressing the true system cause of the gap in results.
- performers getting trapped in situations (i.e., "bad systems") where they are doomed to fail

from the outset. Managers who do that or allow that to happen are incompetent and irresponsible. The most basic responsibility of a manager is to provide a productive work environment for his or her direct reports.

The reality is that no one takes responsibility for these bad systems in organizations. In truth, the managers usually are unaware that there is any such thing. The performers in the system (as you will see in the NuPlant case study) seldom can get the traction to change the system they are in. That leaves the system change up to serious performance consultants whose job it is to liberate the performer from ugly, untenable work situations.

Second, serious performance consulting is rewarding work. What could be more professionally rewarding than improving the performance of an organization and liberating a group of performers at the same time? Not many things, in my experience.

Third, serious performance consulting is interesting and fun. Finding the real cause of poor results is very interesting and exciting work. In many ways, it is detective work. Basically, I want to answer the question "What killed results?" As you will see from the NuPlant case study, there are proven templates for systematically conducting an analysis, not unlike the systematic approach to a homicide investigation.

It is my objective that the case study and the subsequent discussions in this book will encourage you to join the ranks of serious performance consultants in search of "what really killed results."

The Roots of Serious Performance Consulting

The performance analysis and improvement concepts and techniques presented in this book have been evolving since 1956 and have been built on the input of many people, whom I acknowledge here.

I offer thanks to the following individuals who provided me the opportunity to first see organizations as systems at work:

- Carl Anderson, Royce Rivard, and Richard Rummler (my father), formerly of the Mitchell-Bently Corporation (1955–1956).

I gratefully acknowledge the contributions that the following people made to the basic concepts underlying serious performance consulting:

- Dale M. Brethower (Western Michigan University) for starting me on this path, including the General System Model and behavioral analysis (since 1961)
- George S. Odiorne (formerly of the University of Michigan) for making it clear that it was all about results (1960–1990)
- Gus Rath, Len Silvern, and Malcolm W. Warren for teaching me about systems thinking before it was a fad (1965–1966)
- Karen S. Brethower and George L. Geis (formerly of the University of Michigan) for insights into the human performance system (since 1963)
- Thomas F. Gilbert (former partner in Praxis Corporation) for insights into understanding the economics of performance (1967–1979)
- Kai Dozier for insights into the human side (since 1990)
- Carl C. Semmelroth (formerly of the University of Michigan) for help in thinking about behavior and performance (since 1965)

The following people have promoted the continuing development of these ideas and tools through diligent and innovative application:

- Pamela Moulton, Sandra Cowen, Steve Anderson, Rick Rummler (my brother), Michele Smith, and Jim Webber, formerly of Praxis Corporation (1969–1979)
- Saura Morgenstern and Carol Panza, formerly of the Rummler Group (1982–86)
- Paul Heidenreich, Alan Ramias, Alan Brache, Patricia Floyd, Bob Morrow, Alison Burkett, Sean McLernon, Mike Hammer, Roger Proulx, Paul Fjelsta, Patrick Murphy, Marty Smith, Rick Rummler (my son), Bernie Miller, and Cherie Wilkins of the Rummler-Brache Group (1987–1997)
- Jaime Hermann (formerly of Ford Motor Company), Kenneth Massey (formerly of Grupo Alfa), Roger Addison (formerly of Wells Fargo Bank), John Swinney (formerly of Eckerd Drug), and Ron Mathos (DuPont)

Thanks are due to the following people who gave me opportunities to apply and expand this thinking:

- Malcolm W. Warren (formerly of AP Parts) for the opportunity to perform the first performance audit (1967)
- C.C. Schmidt (formerly of Ford Motor Company) for the opportunity to apply these ideas to manufacturing productivity (1971)
- Kathryn Breen (formerly of Montgomery Ward) and Art Maine (formerly of Sherwin-Williams) for the opportunity to apply these ideas to retailing (1973–1977)
- John R. Murphy (formerly of McGraw-Hill and GTE) for the opportunity to apply these ideas to publishing and telecommunications
- Bill Wiggenhorn, Carlton Braun, Steve Hanson, and Alan Ramias (Motorola) for the opportunity to influence the thinking and productivity of a global company (1982–1993)
- Lawrence McLernon (formerly of Litel) for the opportunity to apply these ideas in an entrepreneurial setting
- Thomas Schnick (Commonwealth Insurance Company) for the opportunity to apply these ideas to the insurance industry
- Richard Rummler (brother, and formerly of Steelcase) for the opportunity to apply these ideas to the design of a management system
- Denny Taylor (Shell) for the opportunity to apply these ideas in the petroleum industry
- Steve Hassenfelt (North Carolina Trust Company) for the opportunity to apply these ideas to the management of a financial institution
- Barry Owens and Ron Mathos (DuPont) for the opportunity to apply the Performance Logic notion
- Charlie Bishop (formerly of Baxter-Travenol) for the opportunity to introduce the systems view into management training
- Bob Moore for the opportunity to see the "perfect system for losing money"
- Yvette Montagne (formerly of Louisiana Pacific and Tektronix) and Ken Sperling (formerly of Warner-Lambert) for demonstrating how OD professionals can have a significant impact on organization results using this methodology
- Carroll Nelson (formerly of Sematech and VLSI Technologies) and Mark Munley (formerly of AG Consulting) for the opportunity to apply these ideas to organization design
- My colleagues in the "Tucson Seven"—Dale Brethower, Bob Carleton, Roger Kaufman, Danny Langdon, Claude Lineberry, and Don Tosti who engaged me in insightful and challenging interchanges

Acknowledgments

I am indebted to several individuals who encouraged me along the journey to write this book.

My brother, Rick Rummler, was instrumental to the project described herein and helped get this important performance improvement project communicated. Dale Brethower continually reassured me there was a need for a book such as this and offered helpful comments and guidance during its development. Kimberly Morrill, Performance Design Lab partner, served as a role model for what the next generation of performance analysts should be, and provided invaluable assistance in getting the words from thin air to paper.

Performance Design Lab partners Cherie Wilkins and Rick Rummler, both master performance analysts, offered their support and helpful suggestions in bringing this writing project to a close. Roger Addison, who during his 17 years at Wells Fargo formed and managed one of the premier internal consulting organizations in the world, provided the foreword for the book. Timm Esque, Pat Galagan, Mike Hammer, Jaime Hermann, Roger Kaufman, Sally Lanyon, Mark Munley, Joe Sasson, Karloyn Smalley, Debbie Titus, and Klaus Wittkuhn all encouraged me and offered helpful comments on the manuscript. Roger Chevalier and April Davis oversaw the project from initial manuscript to published book. And, finally, I thank my editor Karen Eddleman, literary alchemist extraordinaire, who succeeded in converting my good intentions into helpful prose.

Geary A. Rummler
Tucson, Arizona
April 2004

Introduction

A Typical Situation

Figure I-1 represents some of the dynamics that characterize a typical consulting situation.

It works like this: The majority of consulting work begins with a request from an executive or manager of some operation who sees or hears something (A) that causes the person to believe a "problem" exists. Moreover, in many instances the requestor also reaches a conclusion as to what an appropriate "solution" should be (e.g., team building, training, ropes course). The requestor (or worse yet, an intermediary, with his or her own interpretation of the problem and solution) then contacts (B) a resource and requests that particular "solution," seldom mentioning any gap in job performance or organization results (C) that might have occurred because of (A). Now the scenario gets interesting—what will the receiver of the request (B) do?

Performance consulting (and this book) addresses what might happen next in this scenario. Usually, the resource has two options at this point. The first option is to follow path (D) and just say yes to the request and faithfully deliver the requested "solution." Alternatively, the resource could follow path (E) and

1. Examine the situation (A) for himself or herself.
2. Determine if the apparent problem can be linked to a gap in results (C).
3. Employ a sound analysis methodology and arrive at independent conclusions regarding the problem and solution.
4. Work with the requestor to define a project that will solve the problem as perceived by the requestor and deliver measurable results (C).

A possible outcome of path (E) is the confirmation of the stated problem and the proposed solution. The value added of taking this path versus path (D) is the establishment of criteria for subsequent evaluation of the solution.

If the resource described in this scenario is a performance consultant, then he or she likely will follow path (E), at least under ideal circumstances. Many times, though, reality intervenes.

Figure I-1. Typical performance consulting situation.

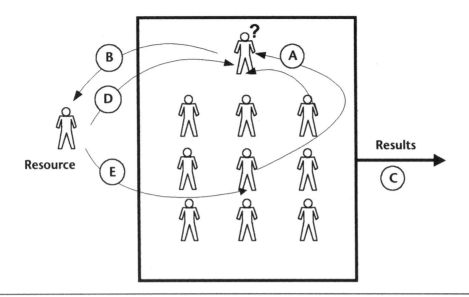

For example, sometimes the resource is perceived to be a mere "solution provider," who damn well better deliver the requested solution, be it training, team building, or process improvement.

Few individuals are in a position to always pursue path (E). Most aspiring performance consultants occupy roles within their organizations in which they are sometimes called upon to deliver "solutions," but they must be able to pursue either path (D) or path (E). In many cases, being a performance consultant is a role to play, not a full-time job. This book is about how to perform that role or wear the performance consultant hat. Furthermore, this book outlines some strategies to help the resource move a request from path (D) to path (E).

One final observation on the typical performance consulting situation presented in figure I-1: Most of the time the performance consultant is going to be in a reactive mode—responding to a request for help. Nevertheless, to be truly successful, the internal performance consultant must also work in active ways to identify opportunities to improve performance and demonstrate the value of performance improvement to the organization. The case study revealed in Part One illustrates how to be proactive in a reactive situation. Part Two discusses other reactive and proactive strategies.

Serious Performance Consulting

As described in *Improving Performance: How to Manage the White Space on the Organization Chart* (Rummler and Brache, 1995), three levels of performance exist in any organization:

- *The organization level:* the performance desired by the institution
- *The process level:* the performance required of all processes in order to achieve the organization-level performance
- *The job level:* the performance required of all jobs in order to achieve the process-level performance

Ideally, the performance goals of all three levels are aligned. If you are not familiar with this concept of the three levels, hold on, because they are explained in chapter 2.

Within the context of the three levels and within the constraints of the real world, three beliefs form the basis of serious performance consulting.

Belief 1: Performance Consulting Is About Improving Results

Performance equals results. Performance consulting is about closing the gap between "is" results (what exists now) and "should" results (what the client desires). The objective of performance consulting, then, is to improve results. Table I-1 offers a few examples of "is" and "should" results as seen from the three levels of performance.

Every request should be tied to a measurable gap in results. A corollary is that the serious performance consultant pursues *significant* issues or gaps in results. Therefore, it is necessary to move beyond improving job-level performance to process- and organization-level performance, primarily because improvements at the job level alone very seldom impact organization results, a major requirement of this work.

The various levels of performance (job, process, and organization) will be discussed in some detail in chapter 2. Additionally, the case study in chapter 3 illustrates how to move from a job-level request to the organization level.

Belief 2: Performance Consulting Follows a Systematic Process

Figure I-2 demonstrates how the serious performance consultant follows some approximation of the results improvement process (RIP), shown at the top of the matrix.

You may encounter numerous depictions of results/performance improvement processes, running from four to 10 boxes, but at some level of detail, they are all consistent with this diagram. Basically this figure is a detailed look at the ideal path (E) followed by the resource in figure I-1.

The first row in figure I-2 summarizes the objectives the performance consultant is trying to accomplish in each phase of RIP. The second row describes the outputs that are typically produced during each phase. These four phases represent "what" a performance consultant must accomplish.

There are four major approaches, or engagement models, that a performance consultant might use for the four-phase RIP. They are shown in the bottom four rows on the table in figure I-2. Whether the performance consultant is an internal or external consultant, the basic engagement models are

A. The work in all four phases is done primarily by the performance consultant with input from members of the client organization.

B. The work in the first two phases is done primarily by the consultant with input from members of the client organization, and the last two phases are carried out by the client organization with little or no input from the consultant.

C. The work in the first two phases is done primarily by the consultant with input from members of the client organization, and the last two phases are carried out primarily by the client organization under the leadership of the consultant.

D. The work in all four phases is led by the consultant working with employees of the client organization, who usually are organized in teams or taskforces.

Table I-1. Examples of performance expressed as results.

Level	Results Area	"Is" Result	"Should" Result
Organization	Market share	38%	60%
Process	Time to receive orders	30 days	5 days
Job	Incomplete sales order forms	13%	0%

Figure I-2. The results improvement process.

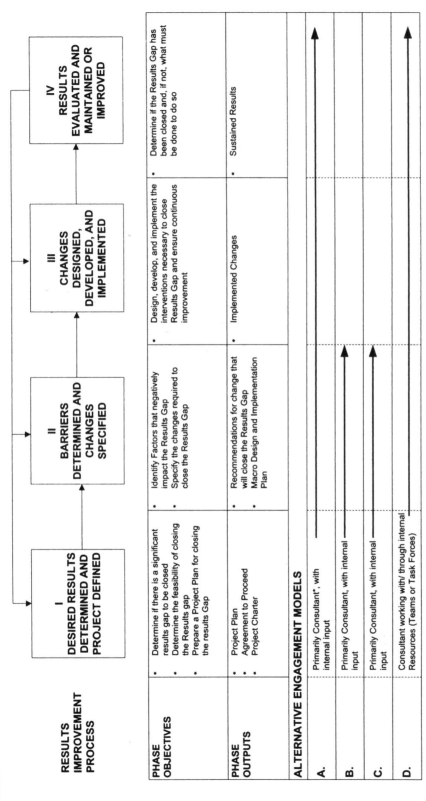

RESULTS IMPROVEMENT PROCESS	I DESIRED RESULTS DETERMINED AND PROJECT DEFINED	II BARRIERS DETERMINED AND CHANGES SPECIFIED	III CHANGES DESIGNED, DEVELOPED, AND IMPLEMENTED	IV RESULTS EVALUATED AND MAINTAINED OR IMPROVED
PHASE OBJECTIVES	• Determine if there is a significant results gap to be closed • Determine the feasibility of closing the Results gap • Prepare a Project Plan for closing the results Gap	• Identify Factors that negatively impact the Results Gap • Specify the changes required to close the Results Gap	• Design, develop, and implement the interventions necessary to close Results Gap and ensure continuous improvement	• Determine if the Results Gap has been closed and, if not, what must be done to do so
PHASE OUTPUTS	• Project Plan • Agreement to Proceed • Project Charter	• Recommendations for change that will close the Results Gap • Macro Design and Implementation Plan	• Implemented Changes	• Sustained Results

ALTERNATIVE ENGAGEMENT MODELS

A.	Primarily Consultant*, with internal input			
B.	Primarily Consultant, with internal input			
C.	Primarily Consultant, with internal input			
D.	Consultant working with/ through internal Resources (Teams or Task Forces)			

*In all cases, consultants can be either internal or external to the organization.

The appropriate engagement model for conducting the four phases of RIP varies with scope of the project, time and resources available, project urgency, change management challenges, and, truthfully, what the performance consultant is comfortable doing. The case study presented in chapter 3 follows the RIP shown in figure I-2 and also demonstrates engagement model alternative B (the work in the first two phases was done by an external consultant with input from members of the client organization and the last two phases were carried out by the client organization, with no input from the consultant). The rationale for the selection of this model will be examined in chapter 4, which consists of a project debrief for the case study.

According to Rummler

The methodology for performance analysis as described in this book has been evolving over a period spanning 35 years. It has its roots in conceptual work I did in collaboration with Dale Brethower at the University of Michigan in the 1960s and application work done with Tom Gilbert at Praxis in the 1970s. I've acknowledged in the preface many others who also contributed to the development and application of this methodology.

Belief 3: Performance Analysis Is the Heart of Serious Performance Consulting

Figure I-3 shows how the performance analysis methodology is basic to conducting effectively phases I and II of RIP. Performance analysis involves determining the *specific* gaps in results that are to be closed, the *precise* barriers to desired results, and the specification of the *exact* changes necessary to close the gap in results. Stated otherwise, performance analysis is at the center of performance consulting.

Performance consulting, of course, involves much more than performance analysis. In phase III, performance consultants design and develop (or oversee the design and development of) various solutions to achieve the desired results. They manage or oversee the implementation of the

solutions. They may deliver some of the solutions, including coaching of managers or executives. In phase IV, they guide the evaluation of results. They manage the relationship with the client throughout the engagement and, depending on the engagement model used, performance consultants may guide client teams or work groups.

Notwithstanding the critical significance of other activities undertaken by performance consultants, the results of a performance improvement project are only as good as the underlying performance analysis. If a proper performance analysis has not been done, performance consultants will

- not have identified or validated a significant gap in results that is to be closed
- be unable to uncover the root cause of the gaps in results
- be unable to specify the critical changes required to close the gap in results
- be unable to evaluate the effect of any changes they made even if they did close a results gap

It is performance analysis that separates performance consulting "lite" from *serious* performance consulting. The case study in chapter 3 is a grand example of performance analysis and illustrates how a performance consultant can

- go beyond the initial request for help to find a viable critical business issue and a gap in results and to establish how success of the project will be evaluated
- use a conceptual performance analysis framework to generate hypotheses for possible causes of the gaps in results
- follow an effective, systematic process for conducting the analysis (i.e., test the initial hypotheses)
- determine through interviews and observation the detailed reality of the human performance systems for key positions that have been identified, so that the root causes of undesired behavior can be understood and corrected
- identify exemplary performance to establish the differences between "is" and "should"

Figure I-3. The results improvement process with performance analysis highlighted.

RESULTS IMPROVEMENT PROCESS			
I DESIRED RESULTS DETERMINED AND PROJECT DEFINED	**II** BARRIERS DETERMINED AND CHANGES SPECIFIED	**III** CHANGES DESIGNED, DEVELOPED, AND IMPLEMENTED	**IV** RESULTS EVALUATED AND MAINTAINED OR IMPROVED

| PHASE OBJECTIVES | • Determine if there is a significant results gap to be closed
• Determine the feasibility of closing the Results gap
• Prepare a Project Plan for closing the results Gap | • Identify Factors that negatively impact the Results Gap
• Specify the changes required to close the Results Gap | • Design, develop, and implement the interventions necessary to close Results Gap and ensure continuous improvement | • Determine if the Results Gap has been closed and, if not, what must be done to do so |
| PHASE OUTPUTS | • Project Plan
• Agreement to Proceed
• Project Charter | • Recommendations for change that will close the Results Gap
• Macro Design and Implementation Plan | • Implemented Changes | • Sustained Results |

ALTERNATIVE ENGAGEMENT MODELS

A.	Primarily Consultant*, with internal input
B.	Primarily Consultant, with internal input
C.	Primarily Consultant, with internal input
D.	Consultant working with/ through internal Resources (Teams or Task Forces)

*In all cases, consultants can be either internal or external to the organization.

performance and the cause behind such differences.

- use "hard" performance data to test hypotheses and support conclusions and recommendations
- conduct a comprehensive analysis of all factors that may be contributing to the gap in results
- specify a solution set that addresses all significant factors that affect the gap in results
- develop prototypes of key recommended solutions to illustrate their scope and value
- organize recommended changes to meet various client needs and priorities
- follow the implementation of recommendations and evaluate the success of the project

Characteristics of a Serious Performance Consultant

If you're going to call yourself a performance consultant (as opposed to a training consultant, a media consultant, an organization development consultant, etc.), then you should possess these key characteristics:

- You are *committed to improving performance and results*, not to implementing some pat, predetermined, single solution such as training, team building, performance support software, and the like. You are basically

solution-neutral. If you are the resource in figure I-1, you don't hear the request with a preconceived solution in mind. You challenge all proposed solutions attached to requests for help and drive toward path (E).

- You employ a validated, robust methodology for determining desired results, identifying barriers to the desired results, specifying the changes necessary to achieve the desired results, and evaluating the impact of the specified changes on results.
- You command a *broad repertoire of results improvement strategies and tactics*, enabling you to recommend appropriate solution sets to address significant gaps in results. (You don't need to be able to design or develop each of them, but you know what they can do and when to recommend them.)

Looking Ahead

That's enough "tell" for the moment; let's look at the NuPlant case study. The focus of the case and commentary is on the performance analysis aspect of RIP (figure I-3), specifically phase I (Desired Results Determined and Project Defined) and phase II (Barriers Determined and Changes Specified). Why? Because performance analysis is largely overlooked in today's instruction and writings about performance consulting. Would-be

---

According to Rummler

With a nod to Tom Wolfe, I label these three key characteristics serious performance consultant "right stuff." You'll find that there is a high degree of correlation between these characteristics and the standards for the Certified Performance Technologist program sponsored by the International Society for Performance Improvement (ispi.org) and ASTD (astd.org). Throughout the book, the term serious performance consultant (SPC) means a performance consultant who not only closes the gap between "is" and "should" results and follows a results improvement process such as that depicted in figures I-2 and I-3, but also—and most important—conducts a rigorous, sound performance analysis as part of performance improvement efforts.

A note for those individuals who have a background in human resources, training, teaching, social work, counseling, or some other helping profession and who are making the transition to performance consulting: You must understand that factors that impact results go far beyond the individual performer. In serious performance consulting, the performer is frequently a small piece of the ultimate formula required to improve results. In short, the focus here is on performance, not on the performer. Improvement of performance and results can come from many different opportunities beyond people, including information technology, tools, materials, and so forth.

performance consultants must see what serious analysis, findings, and recommendations look like, and that's what this case study offers.

The case illustrates engagement model B (figures I-2 and I-3). Phases I and II were conducted by an external consultant with significant client input. Phases III (Changes Designed, Developed, and Implemented) and IV (Results Evaluated) were executed by client resources, with no input from the external consultant. Other engagement models could have been used, but for various reasons they were not. Although the choice of engagement model will be discussed later, that decision is not the focus of this book. Rather, the emphasis is on the results of the analysis.

Now, on to Part One and the NuPlant case study.

INTRODUCTION HIGHLIGHTS

1. In many cases, being a performance consultant is a role one plays, not a full-time job. This book is about what should be done when performing that role or wearing the performance consultant hat.

2. Serious performance consulting is distinguished from performance consulting "lite" by the following:

- the objective of closing the measurable gap between "is" and "should" results
- the application of a systematic results improvement process
- sound, rigorous performance analysis

3. Performance consultant "right stuff" includes

- being committed to improving measurable results
- remaining solution-neutral
- being capable of using a validated, robust methodology for (1) determining desired results; (2) systematically identifying barriers to desired results; (3) specifying changes necessary to achieve the desired results; and (4) evaluating the impact of the specified changes on results
- having a broad repertoire of results improvement strategies and tactics

4. Most times, performance consultants are in a reactive mode, responding to requests for help. To be successful, however, performance consultants must also learn to be proactive, finding opportunities for results improvement.

Part One

The NuPlant Case Study

This part of the book is dedicated to the NuPlant case study. Chapter 1 briefly describes the situation leading to this particular performance improvement project, and chapter 2 presents the underlying mental model and templates used by the performance consultants in the case study as they identified the barriers to NuPlant's desired results and specified the changes necessary to obtain those results. Chapter 3 is a high-level walk-through of the project, including a week-by-week timeline spanning project design to final recommendations.

The case study is the story of Bert, a performance consultant, and how he changed the attitude of production supervisors and turned around the performance of NuPlant, all in a matter of months. Well, maybe that's a slight overstatement: The case study actually covers the performance analysis conducted by Bert and his team to determine the cause of poor supervisory and plant performance and his prescription for change.

The idea of this case study is to take you along on the performance analysis, to describe in detail what Bert does and why, and to see what he learns along the way.

Let's start the story of Bert and NuPlant at the beginning.

1

Welcome to NuPlant

"They did WHAT?" Bert asked incredulously.

"Yup, last week someone put a dead rat in a supervisor's lunchbox and then welded the box to one of the steel girders out in the production area," the plant's human resources manager answered. "I'd say that things have been going from bad to worse. Every day there's more tension between production supervision and hourly personnel. The supervisors just have a generally bad attitude toward the hourly workers. That attitude is one reason we can't get our local union agreement signed. We need human relations training for our production supervisors—no doubt about it!"

The Request

The project began when Bert received a call from an acquaintance who headed the corporate training organization of Big Auto, a major U.S.-based automobile manufacturer. During this call, Bert learned the following:

- The human resources (HR) manager of Big Auto's newest and largest stamping plant (called NuPlant in this case study) had requested human relations training for first-line production supervisors from the stamping division's training organization.
- The division's training organization did not have the resources to respond to the request, so the request was referred to Big Auto's corporate training department.

- The director of corporate training was not convinced training was the solution and was interested in an outsider's view and opinion.

Key to this and any performance consulting project is having a contact or sponsor who understands that whatever is requested (in this case, training) is not always the solution to the problem. In this case, it was impolitic for the corporate training director to ignore the request for training even though she suspected this was not a training problem. She decided to use an outsider to present what would be seen as an objective view. Her choice of Bert was no accident because she knew he shared her view of training and performance.

The director of corporate training wondered if Bert and his organization would be interested in looking at this opportunity. If so, would Bert like to join her at NuPlant to take a closer look at the situation?

Bert said yes to both questions. His experience and belief in a model he called the anatomy of performance roused his curiosity about the perceived problem that caused the HR manager to conclude that training in human relations would benefit the plant's first-line production supervisors. Bert thought it was definitely worth a look.

Bert was a believer in the following performance consultant rule: You should never trust anyone's (particularly management's) description of

11

an apparent problem, probable cause, or preferred solution. The requestor is usually

- too far removed from the situation (and responding to "hearsay")
- not trained in observation and analysis
- heavily biased as to the probable cause and solution

Although the initial request to Bert was for human relations training for the first-line supervisors, Bert knew that he had to go see for himself what was going on at NuPlant.

Responding to the Request

The request from the client is a critical point in this or any project. It is the critical juncture depicted in figure 1-1. Will the resource take path (D) or path (E)?

The response to a request such as, "We need human relations training for our first-line supervisors," can go in a variety of different directions, depending on the viewpoint, model, assumptions, and capability of the receiver of the request. If the resource takes path (D), likely "interventions" in response to this particular request could include the following:

- human relations training, with "human relations" being interpreted as any number of human relations knowledge and skill areas
- training in communications
- installation of a 360-degree feedback system
- changes in the performance management system
- an employee attitude survey
- team building
- a ropes course
- an analysis of the organization's culture

In reality, the proposed "intervention" will depend entirely on what the resource/consultant is capable of delivering. His or her capability influences the definition of the "problem" and the selection of an intervention. Unfortunately, in most cases, this approach via path (D) leads to a "buyer beware" situation for the client.

Figure 1-1. Typical performance consulting situation.

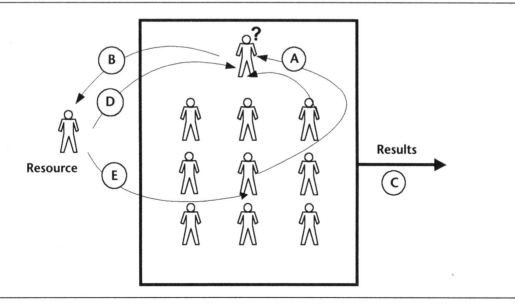

In contrast, the serious performance consultant remains solution-neutral. Bert's focus in a situation like this (indeed, in any situation) is to trace the symptom back to desired organization results to determine the performance context of the symptom/request and work from there (path E). To do this, he applies a conceptual framework called the anatomy of performance (AOP) and follows the results improvement process presented in the Introduction (According to Rummler [ATR] 1-1).

According to Rummler 1-1

Before we continue with the case study, I'd like to acquaint you with Bert's mental model for improving performance and the process he will be following on this project. Those items are discussed in the next chapter. Read on to see that, indeed, there is a method to his madness.

CHAPTER 1 HIGHLIGHTS

1. Performance problems in organizations tend to be defined by the solutions available.

2. Managers and executives need to be very careful when seeking help to solve a performance problem because the resource/consultant will tend to define the problem in terms of the solutions he or she is most comfortable with or capable of delivering.

3. A serious performance consultant must remain solution-neutral, take a good look for him- or herself, and trace the problem symptoms back to desired organization results.

Performance Analysis Framework and Process

As Bert fields the request for help at NuPlant, he finds himself in a typical performance consulting situation (figure 2-1).

In this case, the HR manager of NuPlant has identified (A) a problem labeled "production supervisor attitudes" and concluded that "production supervisors need training in human relations." The HR manager contacted (B) various training organizations in Big Auto, and the request has finally reached Bert. In the process, there has been no mention of a gap in results (C) by the HR manager or anyone else, for that matter.

Now Bert is at that critical juncture in the life of a request for help. Does he follow path (D) and deliver the requested solution (training in human relations), or does he pursue path (E) and take a firsthand look at what is happening or not happening on the job? Bert, being a serious performance consultant (and our hero), is about to embark on path (E) and go look for himself.

Figure 2-1. Typical performance consulting situation.

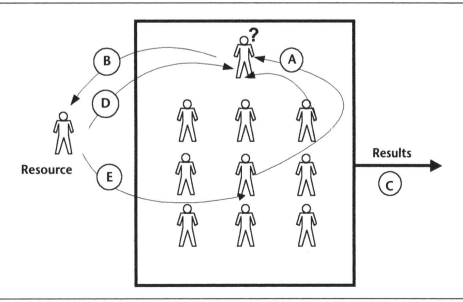

Reprinted with permission of Geary A. Rummler, Performance Design Lab, 2004.

Applying the Anatomy of Performance Framework

As Bert pursues path (E), the process he will follow is the results improvement process described in the Introduction and depicted here in figure 2-2.

What Bert will be looking for as he pursues path (E) is guided by his mental model or framework that identifies the factors or variables affecting individual performance and influencing the organization's results. When Bert looks at or thinks about NuPlant, or any organization, what he envisions is the anatomy of performance, shown in figure 2-3.

The anatomy of performance boils down to these two points:

- An organization is a complex system of individuals, jobs, processes, functions, and management.
- Organizational performance or results are a function of how well these interdependent components are aligned and working toward clearly specified results.

In the eyes of a serious performance consultant, every performance issue—individual, job, or process—must always be seen in the overarching organizational context: the anatomy of performance (AOP).

The AOP is to Bert what knowledge of the human anatomy is to a physician. Knowledge of human anatomy provides the physician with an understanding of how components of the human body interact. Every physician knows the factors that determine good health, the consequences of a failure in any of those factors, and what must be done to correct a failed factor and return the patient to good health. Physicians also know that symptoms in one area may result from problems in another; this understanding requires them to take a systems view of the problem. Even though patients come in different sizes and colors, physicians know that inside, they all have the same parts, located in basically the same physical area, and that they are supposed to perform the same function within the system. The same is true with a business.

The AOP provides a similar framework for Bert. As you will see, the AOP identifies the basic factors or variables that affect individual performance and organization results. Although organizations are very different on the outside (big or small, public or private, products or services), inside they all have a common anatomy. This knowledge of the underlying organizational anatomy is very helpful in the initial discovery stage of Bert's analysis. He knows what he is looking for as he starts to understand an organization. He knows that all organizations contain the components of the AOP; he just needs to find the specifics for NuPlant in this case.

Figure 2-2. Bert's path through the results improvement process.

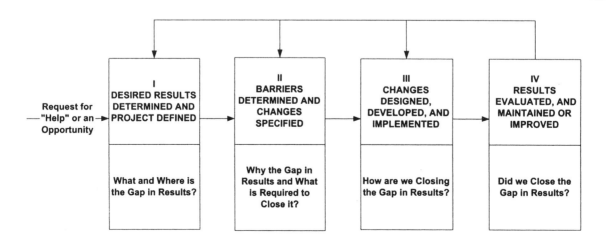

Reprinted with permission of Geary A. Rummler, Performance Design Lab, 2004.

Figure 2-3. The anatomy of performance of organizations.

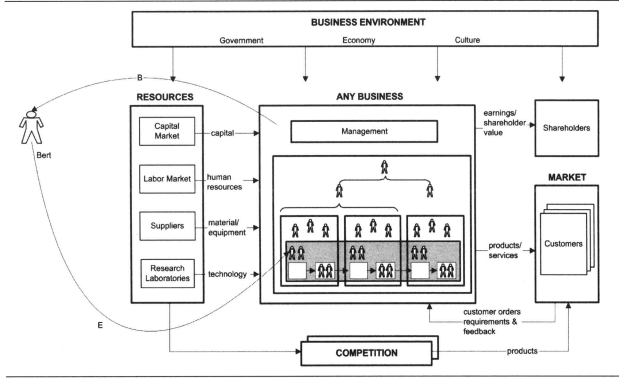

Reprinted with permission of Geary A. Rummler, Performance Design Lab, 2004.

Knowledge of the underlying anatomy—whether for a human being or for an organization—is critical for arriving at an accurate diagnosis. The physician knows what a healthy human anatomy looks like. So, as physicians examine X-ray results, for example, they are comparing the "is" X-ray of a patient against the "should" model they have in their head or medical references. The same is true for Bert. He knows the requirements of an effective (i.e., "healthy") AOP for an organization. His diagnostic phase or analysis is comparing the "should" AOP against the "is" reality he sees in an organization such as NuPlant.

 ## The Anatomy of Performance

1. Organizations are systems.
2. Organizations are processing systems.
3. Organizations are adaptive systems.
4. Jobs or roles and functions exist to support the processes of the organization.
5. All performers are part of a human performance system (HPS).

6. Management must keep the organization system aligned.
7. The results chain must link to a critical business issue.

The following sections delve into some details behind the key points of AOP. The discussion will move from macro to micro, from organization to process to job to individual, peeling the organization like an onion. Subsequent sections will address the analysis sequence that Bert will follow at NuPlant.

AOP Key Point 1: Organizations Are Systems

What Bert Knows. Bert knows that NuPlant, like every organization, is a system (figure 2-4) that exists to produce two types of system outputs:

- Desired products or services for some "receiving system" or customer
- An economic return to shareholders who have underwritten the existence of the organization entity

Figure 2-4. Viewing the organization as a system.

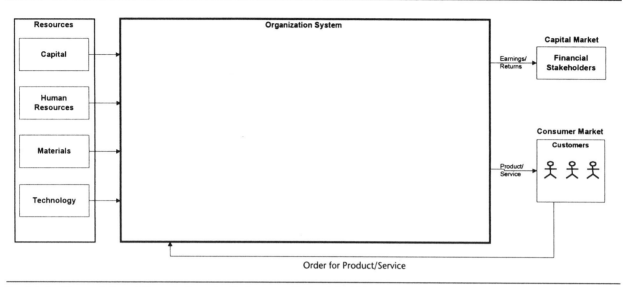

Reprinted with permission of Geary A. Rummler, Performance Design Lab, 2004.

Bert also understands the relationship between these two primary system outputs: If the organization fails to meet its customer needs through appropriate products or services, it will only be a short time before the earnings output will begin to fail to meet the capital market expectations. Trying to bolster the earnings output by cutting corners on the product or service output simply does not work over the long haul.

What Bert Is Looking for and Why. Bert wants to understand the products and services of NuPlant, NuPlant's customers, and what is important to the customers about the delivery of those products and services in terms of cost, quality, timeliness, and so forth. Why? The quickest introduction to a client organization is to get a fix on its products or services and its customers.

Bert also wants to learn what he can about the economic performance expectations of NuPlant and how well it is performing against those expectations. Why? The economic demands on an institution are likely to be an underlying factor in any performance issue. If this is a variable that cannot be changed, it is still necessary to understand it as a major constraint on any changes Bert might subsequently want to make. Likewise, if the client

were an internal department, a performance consultant would want to learn about the economic expectations and the funding or budget of the unit for the same reason.

AOP Key Point 2:
Organizations Are Processing Systems

What Bert Knows. As shown in figure 2-5, Bert knows that every organization, including NuPlant, is a processing system of primary and support processes. In a sense, every organization is a machine that receives inputs and then converts or transforms them into *valued* outputs. In so doing, the organization consumes or utilizes key resources such as capital, technology, human resources, materials, and equipment.

An organization is a value machine, producing value for both its customers and investors. The organization produces a valued product or service through a value chain of primary processes having to do with inventing, developing, selling, and delivering products or services that directly impact the customer. Support processes are those that buttress the primary processes and are typically related to HR, finance, information technology (IT), and so forth.

Figure 2-5. Viewing the organization as a processing system.

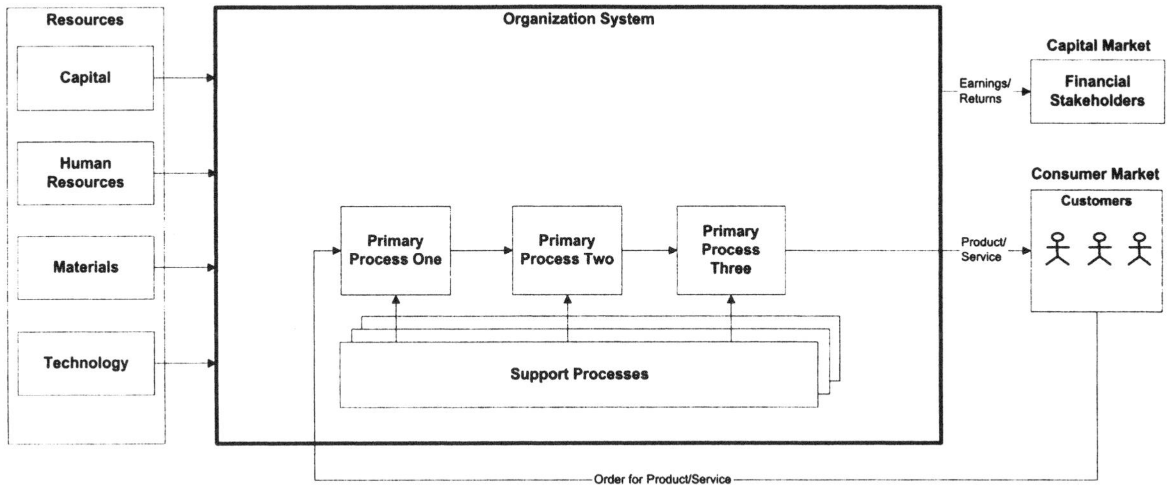

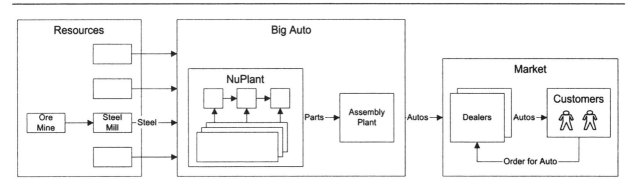

Reprinted with permission of Geary A. Rummler, Performance Design Lab, 2004.

Bert understands that this basic notion of a processing system applies to *any* organization, including

- call centers, which convert customers with questions or complaints into satisfied customers
- HR departments, which, among other things, convert staffing requests into filled positions
- bank branches, which convert payroll checks into cash, cash into certificates of deposits, and so forth

Based on his general business knowledge and his specific understanding of organizations as value machines and processing systems, Bert

hypothesizes that NuPlant converts sheet steel into automobile parts. He'll be able to confirm this hypothesis with just one or two quick questions. Bert also knows that not only is NuPlant itself a processing system, it is also part of a larger processing system—Big Auto.

Although he doesn't know for sure, he can hypothesize (again based on his general knowledge of business and casual reading about the automobile industry) that the larger processing system looks something like figure 2-6.

What Bert Is Looking for and Why. Bert will be seeking the answers to such questions as these: What are the primary processes in NuPlant that

Figure 2-6. The NuPlant/Big Auto processing system.

Reprinted with permission of Geary A. Rummler, Performance Design Lab, 2004.

produce the parts? How well are these processes performing? Where and why are they not performing well? Then, he'll ask the same questions about the support processes critical to the primary processes producing the parts.

Why? In general, because after identifying the products or services of a client entity, the quickest and most reliable way to understand the organization is to identify the primary processes that create, sell, and deliver those products or services. Knowledge of these basic processes provides a blueprint for how the organization delivers value to the customer. And, virtually all performance improvement ultimately is about increasing value to customers.

Specifically for NuPlant, Bert wants to understand the processes that produce the plant output—the parts. Eventually, he wants to establish a link between the job performed by production supervisors (the ones with the "bad attitudes") and process and plant performance.

Additionally, Bert wants to know more about the larger system (the super-system) of which NuPlant is a part. Why? Because NuPlant is part of a system, it must be affected by other parts of that system, including Big Auto.

Bert wants to identify as quickly as possible factors external to NuPlant that influence its poor performance. An obvious source of such factors or variables would be upstream operations or suppliers. Knowledge of downstream components of the larger processing system may be important to a performance consultant when establishing or validating the significance of a performance gap a client organization is experiencing. In the case of NuPlant, understanding the impact of poor productivity on the downstream automobile assembly plants will be helpful when making the case for recommended changes.

AOP Key Point 3: Organizations Are Adaptive Systems

What Bert Knows. As noted earlier, NuPlant exists within the larger system of Big Auto. Bert knows that Big Auto, in turn, exists in a larger business system or what Bert refers to as a super-system

(figure 2-7). The organization system depicted in the center of the figure is Big Auto. All components outside that box—the consumer and capital markets; the resources/supply chain; the competition; and the general business environment—are considered part of the super-system.

Note that the entire organization system plus its resources, competition, customers, and shareholders are all under the same umbrella of business environment and are, therefore, subject to the same influences of economy, legislation, and culture.

Bert also knows that the bottom-line reality faced by every business (and most every organization) is that it must adapt or die. The organization must be able to accommodate changes—large or small, rapid or gradual—in the larger super-system in which it operates. For example, Bert hypothesizes that Big Auto must be able to adapt to such things as

- Big Auto's competition cutting its prices
- customers expecting new product features now being offered by a competitor
- the general economy experiencing a slump
- labor union demanding higher wages
- interest rates rising for the capital required for expansion
- supply of raw materials being disrupted

Likewise, NuPlant must adapt to changes within Big Auto (e.g., lower demand for its products, more efficient competing plants in the division) as well as such external, super-system factors as labor availability, steel quality, and cost of energy (According to Rummler [ATR] 2-1).

According to Rummler 2-1

For an organization to succeed on any level requires that it be able to adapt, but an organization can adapt at two speeds: low gear or high gear. In low gear, the organization adapts to changes in the super-system as necessary to survive. In high gear, the organization views changes in the super-system as opportunities upon which it can capitalize by taking aggressive action to not only survive but to thrive.

Figure 2-7. Viewing the organization as an adaptive super-system.

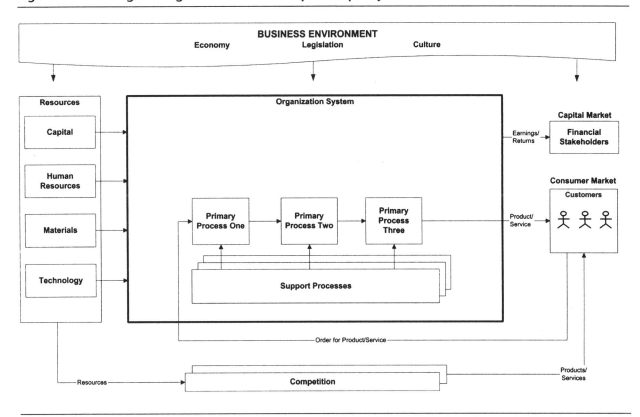

Reprinted with permission of Geary A. Rummler, Performance Design Lab, 2004.

What Bert Is Looking for and Why. Bert will try to identify the factors in NuPlant's super-system that are affecting its current performance. In addition, he recognizes that there may be factors in the super-system that may constrain or support changes that he is likely to recommend.

Why? In general, knowledge of a client's super-system can assist you as a performance consultant or analyst in several ways:

- It may explain the current pressures you see inside the organization.
- It could provide insight into potential challenges your client will be facing, suggesting ways in which you can proactively assist them in the future.
- It may allow you to link inside issues to outside realities that will lead to necessary management support for change (ATR 2-2).

According to Rummler 2-2

Note that the super-system components of the AOP framework act as a template for gathering data on a client's super-system. You can ask yourself, "What do I know about my client's customers and their customers and those customers' competition? What do I know about my client's critical resources? My client's competition? The impact of pending legislation on my client?"

AOP Key Point 4:
Jobs or Roles and Functions Exist to Support the Processes of the Organization

What Bert Knows. Bert knows that all the tasks that make up the primary and support processes in NuPlant are performed by a combination of individuals, machines, and computers. The tasks performed by individuals are usually organized into jobs, roles, or positions, which make up functions or departments. Furthermore, Bert believes that jobs or roles exist solely to perform, support, and manage the primary and support processes in any organization.

Functions and jobs represent non-value-added costs until they are linked to primary processes that add value to customers (figure 2-8). Bert knows that NuPlant has dozens, probably hundreds of jobs performed by several hundred individuals in a number of functions or departments. But, as he begins his data gathering and analysis, he is always going to be trying to understand each job in a process context; that is, to learn how each job contributes to the primary processes that produce NuPlant's outputs.

What Bert Is Looking for and Why. Bert wants to find out which jobs affect primary and key support

processes and how those jobs affect those processes. Additionally, he'd like to know how well current job expectations meet the requirements of the primary and key support processes.

Why? The link between job and process is critical and very often a major issue impacting organization results. Bert knows that jobs and departments are highly visible compared to processes, which tend to be invisible in most organizations. That reality leads to jobs evolving in ways that don't efficiently or effectively support the processes that are supposed to be delivering value to customers. In effect, jobs take on a life of their own.

Too frequently, processes that deliver value to customers are suboptimized by departmental goals and job convenience. An example of this phenomenon is the case of an employee in the finance department who has the task of performing credit checks on prospective new customers. This task is one of many tasks making up this job, and the employee decides it is less disruptive if

Figure 2-8. Getting work done in the organization system.

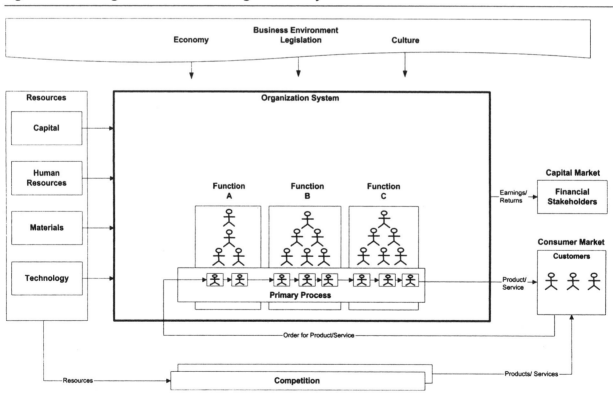

Reprinted with permission of Geary A. Rummler, Performance Design Lab, 2004.

these credit checks are performed in one big batch at the end of the week. Because of this subtle change in job priorities, the process of filling a new customer's order (a process that delivers value to the customer) is delayed as much as four days, pending the credit check. The predictable result of that delay is an unhappy customer.

Bert hypothesizes that a significant contributor to NuPlant's productivity woes is departments and jobs putting their interests ahead of those of the plant.

AOP Key Point 5:
All Performers Are Part of a Human Performance System

What Bert Knows. Bert knows an organization is a system. He further knows that each individual performer in any organization is also part of a unique personal system—what Bert calls the human performance system (HPS) (ATR 2-3).

According to Rummler 2-3

Way back in 1964 at the University of Michigan, I first articulated the conceptual model known as the human performance system. It is an amalgam of B.F. Skinner's pioneering work in reinforcement theory, cybernetics, and basic industrial engineering practices. The development of the model was heavily influenced by Dale M. Brethower and George L. Geis, colleagues of mine at the University of Michigan. The HPS is distinguishable from other cause analysis models because it conceptually and graphically recognizes a critical underlying principle: The variables impacting human behavior and performance are part of a system.

Bert knows that every performer at NuPlant from the plant manager to the hourly workers functions in an HPS, which consists of the five components shown in figure 2-9.

The performer (1) is required to process a variety of inputs (2), such as a metal part, form, or

Figure 2-9. The human performance system.

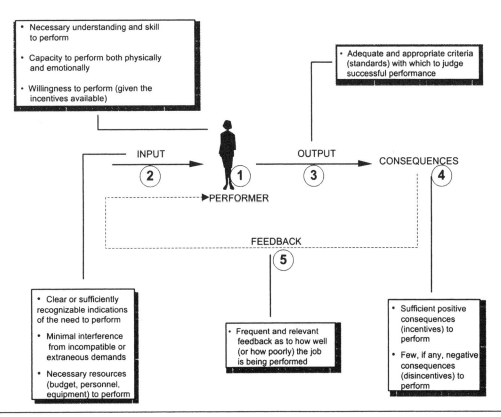

phone call. For each such input, there is a desired output (3), such as a part welded, form processed, or decision made. For every output produced (as well as the action required to produce an output), there is a resultant set of consequences (4)—some event that affects the performer. In general, this event is uniquely interpreted by the performer as either positive or negative.

Bert understands the behavioral law dictating that people's behavior is influenced by consequences; people will do things that lead to positive consequences and avoid things that lead to negative consequences. A corollary to this law is that what is deemed positive or negative under these circumstances depends entirely on the perception of each individual. The last component of the performance system is feedback (5) to the performer on the output. The feedback needs to be accurate, timely, delivered frequently, and on performance that is under the performer's control.

Corresponding to numbers in figure 2-9 are the basic requirements of each component of the HPS. All components of the HPS must be in place at some minimal level if NuPlant is to get the desired performance from an individual on a consistent basis. If an individual fails to produce a desired output in NuPlant, it is a function of a failure of one or more of the components in the HPS (ATR 2-4).

Just as the AOP framework acts as a template for identifying and understanding the components impacting organization performance, the HPS framework in figure 2-10 can be used as a template for troubleshooting poor individual performance and for designing an effective performance environment for an individual.

When an individual is not performing as required, Bert uses the diagram in figure 2-10 to systematically test the condition or state of each component of the HPS to see if and where there is a breakdown or deficiency. Frequently, more than one component is deficient. Based on his experience, Bert has alphabetized the HPS components to reflect the likelihood of that component being deficient. As you can see, performance specification is the most likely trouble spot, and individual capacity is the least likely.

Bert can also use the questions in figure 2-10 as a checklist for designing an improved work environment. If Bert wishes to get performance *X* from performer *Y*, he can systematically use the framework to ask, "Are the performance specifications clear?" "Does the balance of consequences support getting *X*?" "Does *Y* receive information about his or her performance?" "Does *Y* have the necessary skill and knowledge to perform?"

What Bert Is Looking for and Why. If an individual is not performing as required by NuPlant, Bert must ask himself where the HPS of that individual is deficient and what must be changed in the HPS to get the desired performance. Why? Ninety-nine percent of the time poor performance among a group or class of individual performers is a function of deficiencies in the HPS. The cause of these

---

According to Rummler 2-4

You may recall that in the preface I wrote, "Put a good performer in a bad system (the HPS), and the system will win every time." Consider the implications of this reality. First, the performer is the component in the HPS that is most visible and recognizable to managers. When managers don't get desired job results, they tend to focus on that component almost exclusively, asking the performance consultant to fix it ("They need training") or replace it ("Find me an 'A player.'"). The performer is almost always going to be the default cause of poor performance in the eyes of unenlightened management.

Second, it is a rare organization indeed that recognizes that a bad system exists and that it needs to be fixed. Unfortunately, the performer in the system seldom can get the traction to change the system he or she is in. That reality leads to another implication: In most cases, if the system is going get changed, the job falls to the serious performance consultant.

Figure 2-10. Troubleshooting the human performance system.

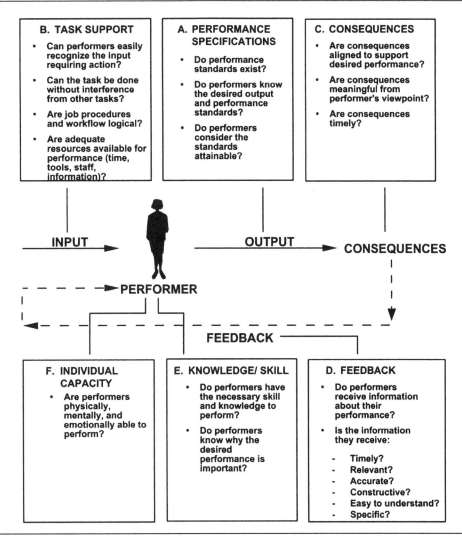

Reprinted with permission of Geary A. Rummler, Performance Design Lab, 2004.

HPS deficiencies may ultimately be traced to other factors in the organization, but the trail *starts* with the individual HPS.

Bert also needs to learn if the HPSs of individuals in a functional hierarchy are vertically aligned to support desired process or function performance. Why? Refer to the hierarchy of performers in figure 2-11a. If, for example, you are concerned with field sales reps turning in accurate and timely sales orders, it will be necessary for the performance expectations, measures, consequences, and feedback to be consistent for the sales reps and their superiors. If the field sales rep is expected to deliver consistent, sustainable performance, it will be necessary to ensure that the HPSs of all managers in the hierarchy are aligned. In contrast, if what is desired is accurate and timely sales orders from sales reps, but the district sales managers are held accountable (feedback and consequences) only for the *number* of orders, the organization is not going to get the desired performance from the sales reps on a consistent basis. Bert is hypothesizing that similar misalignments of the HPSs exist in NuPlant departments.

In addition to investigating whether the HPSs are aligned vertically, Bert must check to see if they are aligned horizontally across functions that must work together to perform or support a

Figure 2-11. Aligning human performance systems.

The human performance system must be aligned . . .

a. . . . vertically . . .

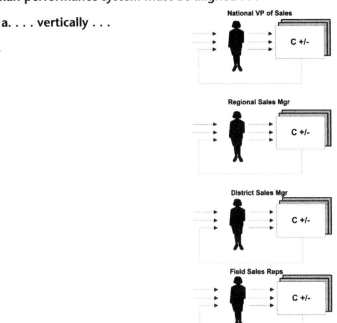

b. . . . and horizontally for the organization to be effective.

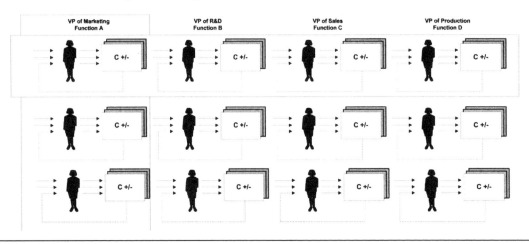

Reprinted with permission of Geary A. Rummler, Performance Design Lab, 2004.

critical cross-functional process (figure 2-11b). Why? If, for example, an organization is concerned with developing and introducing new products but it does not have the expectations, measures, consequences, and feedback aligned for the vice presidents (VPs) of marketing, research and development (R&D), sales, and production, the organization will never get the desired output from their new product development and introduction process. If the HPS of the marketing VP emphasizes staff budget, the HPS of

the R&D VP emphasizes time to market, the HPS of the sales VP drives total revenue without regard to product mix, and the HPS of the production VP focuses on unit cost, you can almost guarantee that new products will be late to market, over budget, incapable of meeting customer requirements, and short of revenue goals after launch.

If you expect consistent, sustainable performance from primary processes, it is necessary that the HPSs of all executives whose functions impact the primary processes are aligned horizontally (and then aligned vertically in every relevant department). Again, Bert is hypothesizing that such horizontal misalignments exist at NuPlant.

AOP Key Point 6:
Management Must Keep the Organization System Aligned

What Bert Knows. Bert understands that management is essential to an organization adapting successfully to its super-system and keeping its internal processing system meeting customer expectations and organization goals. The failure of an organization to be aligned at any point in the AOP framework is a failure of management. Furthermore, Bert knows that three elements make up effective management:

1. the management system or infrastructure made up of processes and procedures
2. management skills, as exemplified by the ability to work effectively within the management system to deliver desired results
3. leadership, consisting primarily of setting appropriate direction and enrolling the organization in following that direction

The focus in the NuPlant case study is on the management system. A subsequent chapter, however, addresses the relationship between management systems and leadership.

Bert has a framework for reviewing the management system of an organization. Bert knows that desired performance or results is a function of the three components shown in figure 2-12:

- *Performance planned:* Goals and plans (including necessary resources and processes to achieve the goals) are set and communicated to the performer, which may be an individual, a process, a company division, plant, or some other organizational entity. Performance planned equals "plan."
- *Performance executed:* The performer delivers the desired performance or results prescribed in the goals and plans. Performance executed equals "actual."
- *Performance managed:* Actual performance is monitored against the goals and plans, and, if a negative deviation is detected, a change signal may be sent. Performance managed equals an action to close the gap between "plan" and "actual."

Performance executed (PE) for the individual, process, or entity that performs the work is always a very visible component of this fundamental performance system. On the other hand, the performance planned (PP) and performance managed (PM) components, which constitute the brains of the performance system, tend to be invisible and flawed.

Figure 2-12. Components of the performance planned and performance managed system.

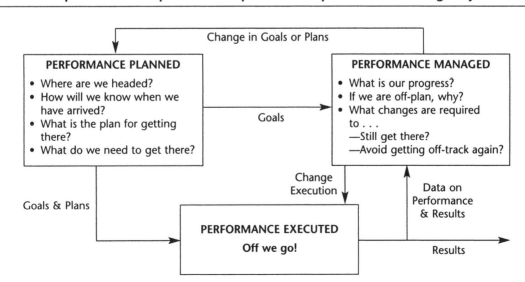

Reprinted with permission of Geary A. Rummler, Performance Design Lab, 2004.

Performance managed requires the performer to change PE in some way (e.g., better scheduling of staff). Or, PM may require that the PP component alter the goals, modify the strategy for achieving the goals, modify the operating plan and budget to better support the strategy, or implement some combination of these actions. This PP/PM combination constitutes the performance planned and managed system (PPMS) depicted in figure 2-13.

The PPMS is what makes it possible for the performance system to adapt to external changes and react to execution failures. It is the mechanism whereby the organization performance system is both an effective processing system and an adaptive system. In this regard, Bert knows that changes or solutions applied to PE will have only a temporary effect unless the PP/PM components are in place to ensure adoption as well as adaptation to changing business requirements.

Figure 2-13 provides you more detail about the functioning of PP and PM components. You might think of the PPMS as a sophisticated guidance-control mechanism—a management chip, if you will—the goal of which is to optimize the PE component and produce the desired results. A management system for an organization is a collection

of these management chips inserted at key junctures in the organization and linked together as shown in figure 2-14.

Figure 2-15, a variation of figure 2-14, is a powerful template for either troubleshooting an existing management system or designing a new management system.

Referring to figure 2-15, Bert knows that these are the common failures of management systems (identified with letters on the figure):

a. Components of PP, PM, or both are missing or badly performed at any level.

b. There is no link between PP and PM. Goals and plans are set, but there is no monitoring of "actual," nor is there a systematic attempt to close gaps between "plan" and "actual." When goals and plans are developed for the next period, there is no systematic look back at what the "actual" was for the past period.

c. Planning is not systematically linked downward through the organization.

d. Goals are not set for processes before they are set for functions, leading to suboptimization of critical processes that deliver value.

e. Performance data are not systematically linked upward through the organization. No

Figure 2-13. Detail of a performance planned and performance managed system (PPMS).

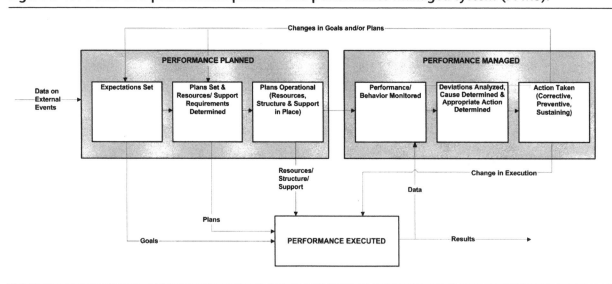

Reprinted with permission of Geary A. Rummler, Performance Design Lab, 2004.

Figure 2-14. The performance planned and performance managed system and the organizational hierarchy.

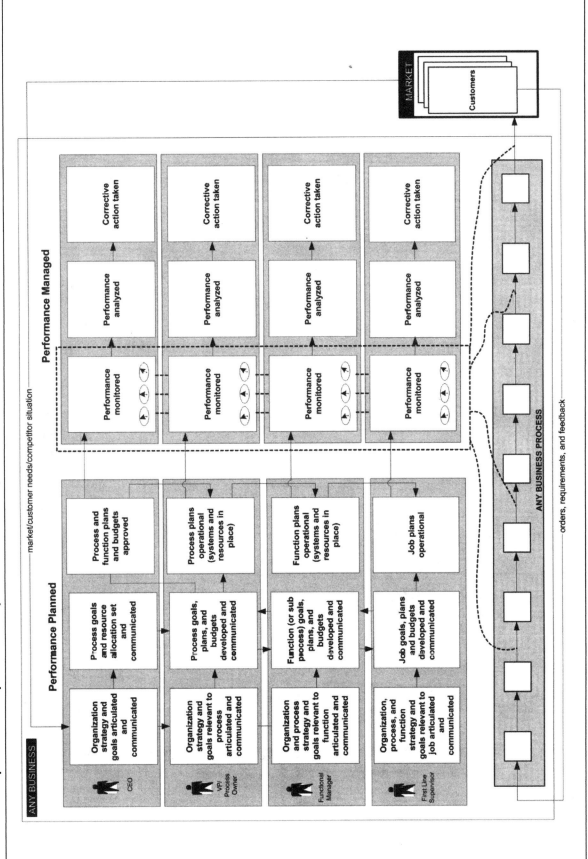

Reprinted with permission of Geary A. Rummler, Performance Design Lab, 2004.

Figure 2-15. The performance planned and performance managed system and common failures.

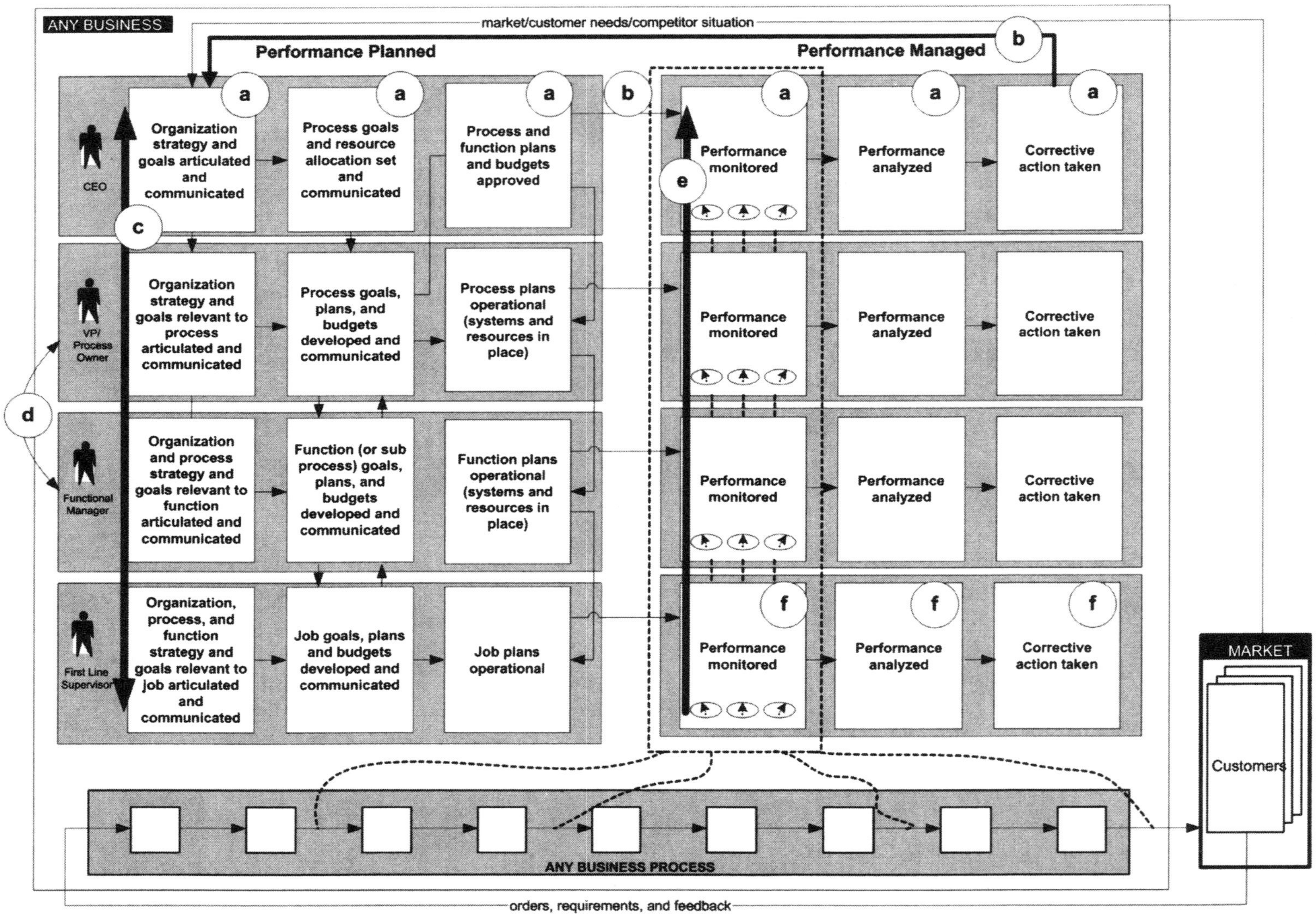

Reprinted with permission of Geary A. Rummler, Performance Design Lab, 2004.

attempt has been made to discern what data or information is critical to the unique value-add planning and managing decisions of each level of management.

f.   It is not clear at any level who does what or when in terms of monitoring performance data, diagnosing deviation in performance, and taking necessary action.

What Bert Is Looking for and Why. Bert will be examining the management system (i.e., the PPMS) for NuPlant and for its key processes, functions, and jobs. Using the template in figure 2-15, he will identify any disconnects in the management systems.

Why? He will do so to determine how the management systems need to be enhanced to keep NuPlant performing as desired in the future.

AOP Key Point 7: The Results Chain Must Link to a Critical Business Issue

What Bert Knows. Already Bert knows several things on this point. First, he knows that within the AOP framework of any organization, including NuPlant, a usually invisible results chain links these three primary levels of performance or results:

1.   organization-level performance or results, having to do with the expectations of financial stakeholders and customers—the two primary receivers of organization outputs
2.   process-level performance or results, which are necessary for the organization to produce its outputs and meet the expectations of customers and financial stakeholders
3.   job-level performance or results, which are necessary for primary and support processes to achieve their goals

Second, as a serious performance consultant, Bert is all about delivering results—organization results. He knows he must establish a results link or chain connecting organization, process, and job results.

A quick way to identify an organization results area is to discern what the critical business issue (CBI) is for the organization in question. The CBI becomes the anchor point for doing performance

consulting or performance analysis work; the performance consultant now has a results target and a project objective. If you look at the output side of the AOP diagram in figure 2-16, you can see that there are generally two primary sources for CBIs: impact on the customer and impact on financial stakeholders.

CBIs can be either problems or opportunities. In either case, they represent a gap in results between the current and the desired states. Examples of CBIs regarding the customer are

- a desire for greater market share
- increased customer complaints
- desire to increase the customer retention rate
- a rise in product returns

Examples of CBIs related to financial stakeholders are

- declining earnings, indicating another level of CBIs having to do with flat or declining revenues or increased processing or resource costs
- increasing earnings, indicating another level of CBIs having to do with growth in revenues or reduced processing or resource costs

Bert knows it is absolutely imperative that a performance consultant establish the CBI for any performance improvement initiative undertaken. If the consultant is working on an issue that is truly critical to the business, he or she is working on something that has priority over the multitude of less critical initiatives, will make a measurable difference, and has a high probability of having the necessary management support when it comes time to implement changes.

Because all CBIs are affected by the organization's primary and support processes, Bert knows it is also possible to identify related critical process issues (CPIs) and link those to CBIs. For example, if the CBI were loss of market share, a related CPI for the order fulfillment process might be time to get orders to customers.

Bert also knows that it is possible to link a CPI to a critical job issue (CJI). For example, if the CPI were time to get orders to customers, a related CJI

Figure 2-16. The anatomy of performance and potential critical business issues.

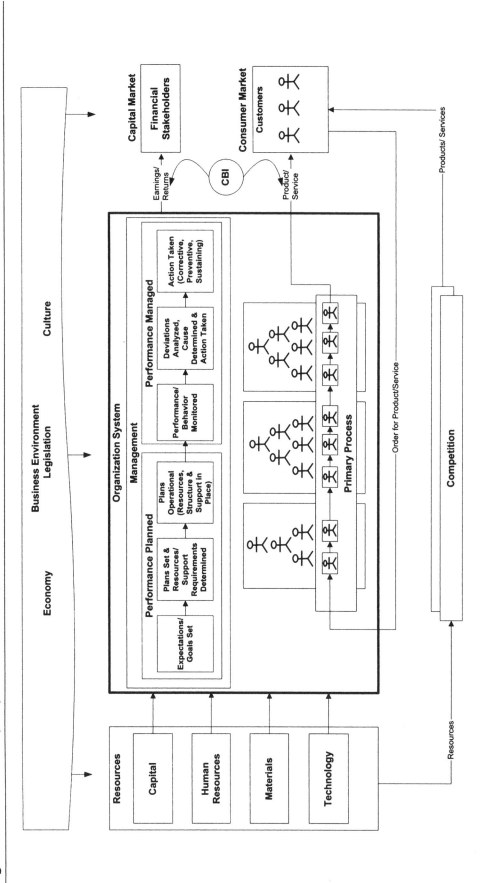

Reprinted with permission of Geary A. Rummler, Performance Design Lab, 2004.

for the sales rep job might be accuracy of sales orders. The idea is to establish a results chain like that shown on the AOP in figure 2-17.

The CJI, CPI, and the CBI constitute a results chain, which is largely invisible to most folks—managers and analysts alike. Nevertheless, it is a useful concept for Bert because he wants to show results. When he receives a request for help, he wants to define the relevant results chain(s) to see if the request can be linked to a CBI.

What Bert Is Looking for and Why. The NuPlant request starts right at the bottom of the results chain even though no results issue has been identified, just an "attitude problem" with a group of individuals and an assumption that "human relations training" will make a difference. In the context of the anatomy of performance, Bert must see if he can link production supervisor "attitudes" to some CJI and that issue to some NuPlant CPI, which, in turn, affects a NuPlant CBI.

Why? If Bert can't make that linkage, he is not going to pursue the NuPlant opportunity because he will most likely fail. He would not be able to demonstrate he has made a difference and, therefore, it would be unlikely that management would provide any support for making changes he might recommend. He would be accepting a major risk in responding to this request. Because he is an external consultant, Bert can walk away from a request that doesn't make sense. This option is not usually available to internal consultants. Tactics for how to deal with these situations are discussed in a subsequent chapter (ATR 2-5).

Making a Diagnosis

Earlier you read how physicians know what the "should," or healthy, human anatomy looks like and how diagnosis is basically about comparing the "should" model the doctors have in their heads or medical references to the "is" that they might see on an X-ray. Well, Bert has a similar "should" model for organization effectiveness provided by the AOP framework. Using the AOP diagram in figure 2-17 as a point of reference, Bert knows the following criteria, based on the AOP Key Points,

---

According to Rummler 2-5

I've invited you to have a look inside Bert's head to see his mental model—the anatomy of performance. You've seen what he knows about NuPlant before he's even set foot in the place, and you know what he will be looking for and why when he begins the project. The sequence in which I revealed the components of the AOP is not the sequence Bert (or any performance consultant) would follow to uncover the "is" AOP of NuPlant. That sequence will be discussed at the end of this chapter and demonstrated with the case study in the next chapter.

---

must be true for an organization to produce consistent, sustainable results:

1. Customer needs are *aligned* with shareholder needs.
2. Organization's goals are *aligned* with the reality of its super-system; i.e., adapt or die.
3. Primary processes are *aligned* to meet customer expectations and organization goals.
4. Support processes are *aligned* with primary process goals.
5. Functions, jobs, or roles are *aligned* to perform the required tasks of the processes.
6. Human performance system components are *aligned*—individually, vertically, and horizontally.
7. Management must do the *aligning*.

These AOP requirements constitute Bert's "should" template for organization effectiveness. It is all about having the components of the AOP aligned, from top to bottom. Points of misalignment are likely contributors to poor organizational results.

Bert will follow the same procedure as the physician, comparing his "should" model against the "is" reality. Conceptually, Bert will overlay the AOP comprising the seven "should" alignment criteria (listed above) on the NuPlant "is" and look for differences that appear likely to impact the gap in NuPlant results. In effect, he will ask of NuPlant:

1. Are the customer expectations of NuPlant consistent with the economic requirements of NuPlant?

Figure 2-17. The anatomy of performance and the results chain.

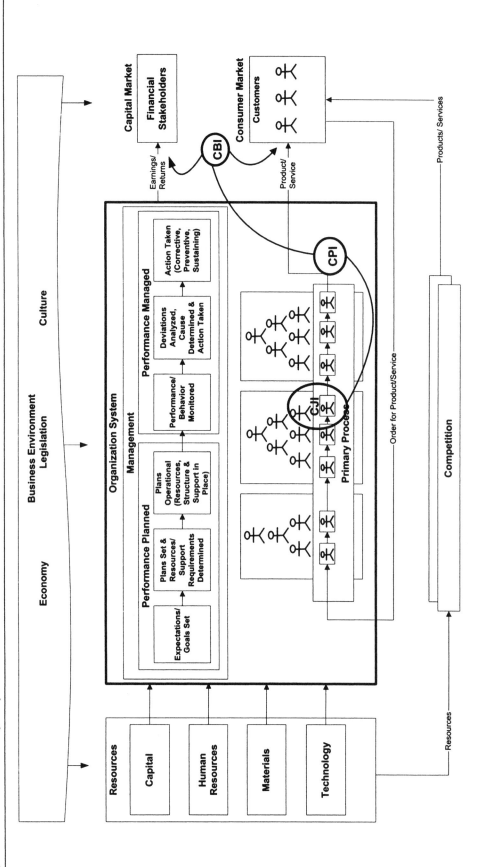

Reprinted with permission of Geary A. Rummler, Performance Design Lab, 2004.

2. Are the goals of NuPlant appropriate given the reality of its (and Big Auto's) super-system?

3. Are the goals of the primary processes aligned or consistent with the goals of NuPlant? Are the goals of each of the primary processes aligned with one another?

4. Do the support processes properly support the primary processes?

5. Are the jobs or functions aligned with the processes they are to support?

6. Are the HPSs of key performers aligned such that desired performance is likely? Are the HPSs aligned vertically in functions, ensuring consistent performance at all levels? Are the HPSs aligned horizontally across the organization, ensuring that cross-functional processes will deliver desired results?

7. Is management keeping the NuPlant organization system aligned? Are the necessary management systems in place? Is the necessary leadership in place?

It's clear that Bert's analysis is not an arbitrary fishing expedition ending with brainstormed recommendations. Rather, his analysis will involve systematic examination of NuPlant's "is" AOP compared to the "should" AOP template, identification of differences between "is" and "should," a determination of whether any differences are critical, and specification of changes to move "is" to "should."

Prescribing Changes

Physicians understand the human anatomy to be a system. Because all the components within that anatomic system are interdependent, physicians rarely prescribe a single action in response to a symptom. They are more likely to prescribe a solution set, consisting of a number of actions to address the fundamental health issue instead of a single medication to relieve certain symptoms. The doctor is likely to say something along the lines of "Here is a prescription to reduce your immediate physical discomfort, but here are the changes you need to make in your diet, exercise regimen, and work environment if you expect to return to good health and permanently rid yourself of the symptoms."

Assuming that the request from NuPlant leads to a CPI and CBI, as well as identification of specific gaps in results, Bert is unlikely to offer a simple, single solution. First, Bert's experience has taught him no silver bullet exists to get a complex system like NuPlant back on track. Second, and more important, he will not offer a single, simple solution because his systematic application of the AOP "should" template will identify a number of components out of alignment. The majority of misaligned components must be addressed if NuPlant is to ever reach its performance potential. Bert will probably prescribe a solution set—a comprehensive set of recommendations—to bring NuPlant into alignment.

The Analysis Process

Now it's time for Bert to get down to the nitty-gritty of the NuPlant project. He'll be following the results improvement process, or RIP, as described in the Introduction and pictured in figure 2-18. Bert is starting with the client's request: "We need human relations training for our production supervisors." Ideally, the project will unfold as described in the following sections.

Phase I

Bert's objective during phase I of the RIP is to see if he can establish a gap in results and define a project to close that gap. His plan will be first to visit NuPlant and see if a link exists between the concern about the production supervisors' "attitudes" and a CBI at the plant. He'll also learn what he can about the AOP of NuPlant (ATR 2-6).

If Bert succeeds in establishing a link to a CBI, he will next develop a project plan to close a gap in results, including selection of an engagement model (see figure I-2). Based on the project plan, he will submit a proposal to Big Auto to improve performance at NuPlant.

Phase II

During this phase of the RIP, Bert's objective is to identify the barriers to NuPlant achieving the desired results targeted as part of phase I and to

Figure 2-18. The results improvement process.

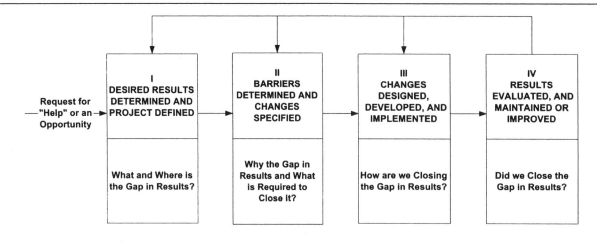

Reprinted with permission of Geary A. Rummler, Performance Design Lab, 2004.

specify the changes necessary to close any gap in results. In this phase Bert will endeavor to

- learn the NuPlant "is" AOP, including its role within the larger Big Auto system as well as the links among the production supervisors, production processes, and NuPlant productivity
- assess the NuPlant "is" AOP against the "should" AOP template

- find misalignments and evaluate their impact on the gap in results
- make recommendations to bring NuPlant into alignment and close the gaps in results

Phase III

Bert's objective in phase III is to guide the design, development, and implementation of the various changes recommended to close the gaps in results.

According to Rummler 2-6

Bert's objective during phase I of the RIP relates to that critical juncture in the life of a request for help. Can he establish a link between the request for help ("human relations training for production supervisors") and a CBI? If he is not able to establish such a link, he should bail out (i.e., graciously decline the opportunity to participate). The lack of a CBI is a big red flag warning about the failure looming ahead.

   Novice performance consultants need to be on the lookout for a couple of potential pitfalls. First, would-be performance consultants may be so flattered and so excited about being asked to help that they attempt to deliver the request with no link to a CBI. They will be sorely disappointed later if their intervention isn't implemented or if it is implemented and not supported. Their intervention will wither on the vine because no need was ever established upfront to offset the cost and aggravation of implementing or supporting it.

   Another pitfall may be encountered by performance consultants who plow ahead without establishing a link to a CBI but optimistically assume that one will emerge during the course of the analysis, development, and implementation. This is rarely the case, however. You will never have a better opportunity to prod management into articulating a CBI than before you commit to help.

   An internal consultant doesn't always have the latitude of an external consultant when it comes to avoiding a project with no CBI. In chapter 5, I address this reality and propose some tactics for dealing with requests that appear to have no link to a CBI.

Any more detail of what is required in this phase will have to await the specifics emerging from phase II.

Phase IV

In this, the final phase of the project, Bert will be working with NuPlant management to monitor and evaluate results data to determine what modifications to changes, if any, are required to close the targeted gap in results. Finally, along with NuPlant management, he will evaluate the value of the project.

The foundation for the evaluation done in phase IV is laid with the analysis conducted in phase I, where the CBI and a specific gap in results have been established (ATR 2-7).

According to Rummler 2-7

In this chapter, I described the ideal sequence of events for a performance analysis. In the next chapter, I'll reveal what Bert actually does—and why. In chapter 4 you'll have a chance to compare Bert's "actual" against the "ideal" process that was presented in this chapter.

CHAPTER 2 HIGHLIGHTS

1. The anatomy of performance is a framework that identifies the major factors or variables impacting individual performance and organization results. It applies to all organizations.

2. Key points inherent in the anatomy of performance include: (1) Organizations are systems; (2) Organizations are processing systems; (3) Organizations are adaptive systems; (4) Jobs or roles and functions exist to support the primary and support processes in an organization; (5) All performers are part of a human performance system; (6) Management must keep the organization system aligned; (7) The results chain links job results to process results to organization results.

3. There is an ideal or "should" anatomy of performance, in which:

- Customer needs are aligned with shareholder needs.
- Organization goals are aligned with the reality of its super-system.
- Primary processes are aligned to meet customer expectations and organization goals.
- Support processes are aligned with primary process goals.
- Function, jobs, or roles are aligned to perform the required tasks of the processes.
- The human performance system components are aligned—individually, vertically, and horizontally.
- Management is doing the aligning.

4. Performance analysis is about overlaying the "should" anatomy of performance template on an organization's "is" reality, identifying differences from the "should" elements, assessing the likely impact of the differences on the target gap in results, and specifying changes to close the gap in results.

5. The results improvement process has four phases:

- I. Desired results determined and project defined
- II. Barriers determined and changes specified
- III. Changes designed, developed, and implemented
- IV. Results evaluated and maintained or improved

The NuPlant Case Study

You'll now have a chance to watch over Bert's shoulder as he applies the RIP (results improvement process) to the NuPlant project. This chapter provides a high-level overview, emphasizing the project's general flow and chronology. You'll find detailed discussions of the project's key findings related to NuPlant in appendix A, and Bert's recommendations are included in appendix B (According to Rummler [ATR] 3-1).

The NuPlant case study covers only the first two phases of the RIP, which were described in the Introduction and depicted in figure 2-2. Bert was not involved in phases III and IV. Figure 3-1 shows the milestones in the chronology of project phases I and II. The organization of this chapter follows this chronology; each section has an updated milestone chart to show you just where Bert is in the results improvement process.

Phase I: Desired Results Determined and Project Defined

To address phase I of the RIP, Bert conducted an initial plant visit, designed a project for NuPlant, and prepared a proposal for phase II.

Initial Plant Visit

Bert visited NuPlant, along with the corporate training director and a representative of the stamping division training department (figure 3-2). Bert took a plant tour, and the visitors spent two hours talking with the plant HR manager.

When Bert left the plant site later in the day, he had learned that Big Auto had six stamping plants in its stamping division. The oldest plant among them (Old Plant) had been in operation for more than 35 years. The newest plant (NuPlant) was built five years ago. Not only was NuPlant the newest stamping plant in the industry—indeed, in the United States—but also it was the most highly automated stamping plant in the world. It covered a sizeable piece of real estate (figure 3-3) and employed approximately 3,000 people.

Despite its sophisticated automation and modern physical plant, NuPlant had never lived up to its production expectations and was currently

Figure 3-1. The first two phases of the results improvement process (RIP) as undertaken by Bert for the NuPlant project.

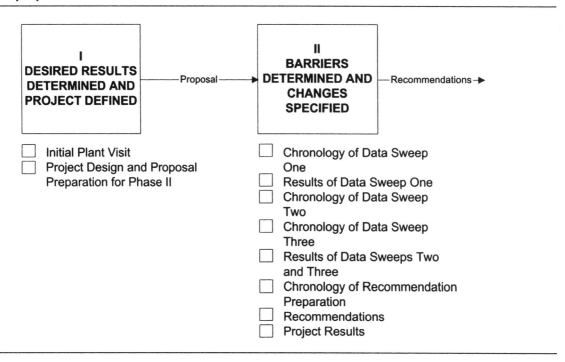

ranked at the bottom in division productivity, labor cost, yield, and scrap. In addition, NuPlant was experiencing difficulties in reaching a contract agreement with employee unions. Unpleasant incidents involving production employees and supervisors appeared to be contributing to a deteriorating union-management relationship. There was growing concern about the attitudes of first-line production supervisors toward their subordinates, and it was widely believed that the tension stemming from their attitudes was having an impact on

plant productivity and labor union relations (ATR 3-2).

> ## According to Rummler 3-2
>
> **M**any incidents pointed to growing problems between the hourly production workers and their supervisors, but the most memorable was the one I alluded to earlier in which some unknown hourly worker had placed a dead rat in a supervisor's lunchbox. That act was presumed to be retaliation for the supervisors' bad attitudes toward their subordinates.

Bert also learned that the original plant manager had been replaced three months earlier, a direct result of poor plant productivity and the still unsigned contract between the local union and management.

In an effort to make a positive contribution to improving the situation at NuPlant, the plant's HR manager had requested "human relations training for first-line production supervisors" from the division's training organization (ATR 3-3).

When Bert left NuPlant, he was beginning to form some hypotheses as to the cause of the problem ("poor supervisory attitudes") as initially

Figure 3-2. NuPlant project milestones.

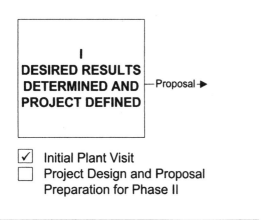

Figure 3-3. Aerial photograph of NuPlant.

formulated by the HR manager. Bert told the corporate training director that he was interested in looking closer at the NuPlant situation and would put together a proposal for conducting some sort of study (ATR 3-4).

Project Design and Proposal Preparation for Phase II

When Bert returned to his office, he met with several associates, and they began outlining an approach to analyzing the performance issues at NuPlant (figure 3-4).

To begin the proposal preparation and design of phase II, Bert first decided that the project goal was to determine what must be done to improve

---

According to Rummler 3-3

This situation is pretty typical. Well-meaning managers are frustrated and concerned with the deteriorating situation and want to do something—anything—to help, make a difference, or at least stop the pain. Without benefit of a holistic framework such as the AOP (anatomy of performance), implementing the common problem or solution default of training is unlikely to address the root cause of the results gap. It becomes the task of the serious performance consultant to go beyond the initial labeling of the problem or solution, to adroitly (and diplomatically) push back on the initial request, and investigate the symptom to see what's really going on and why.

According to Rummler 3-4

Kudos to Bert! A combination of understanding and faith in the AOP gave Bert confidence that he is going to be able to provide value to Big Auto by uncovering the real factors behind NuPlant's abysmal production output and poor supervisory performance.

Figure 3-4. NuPlant project milestones.

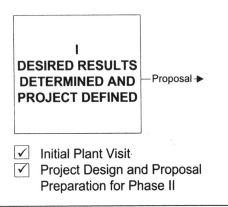

I
DESIRED RESULTS DETERMINED AND PROJECT DEFINED —Proposal➤

☑ Initial Plant Visit
☑ Project Design and Proposal Preparation for Phase II

the performance of NuPlant *and* the production supervisors (ATR 3-5).

The CBI was identified as plant productivity as measured by units produced, labor costs, yield, and scrap. Specific gaps in results in these parameters would be determined as part of phase II of the RIP.

Identifying the CBI and the gap in results are critical components of phase I of the RIP that Bert followed. These activities formed the basis for

According to Rummler 3-5

When Bert decided that the project goal was to improve the performance of NuPlant and production supervisors, it was a signal that he was moving the issue up the results chain from a critical job issue (CJI) to a critical business issue (CBI). There is an implicit assumption that a critical process issue (CPI) links the CJI and the CBI. The only way a job can affect an organization or a CBI is through an intervening process (chapter 2). The CPI would be established in phase II of the project.

defining the NuPlant project and preparing a proposal by answering these questions:

- What is Bert going to accomplish on this project?
- Why is he going to accomplish it?
- Where does Bert need to look to accomplish it (ATR 3-6)?

According to Rummler 3-6

On this project, the CBI and general results areas were identified in phase I. However, specific gaps (hard numbers) in results aren't going to be identified until Bert gets into phase II and learns more about NuPlant and the performance metrics used to manage NuPlant. From my experience, this order of things is not unusual, but these numbers do need to be determined before phase II is completed.

Based on his visit to NuPlant and his AOP mental model, Bert had now formed several hypotheses about what was happening in the plant and what factors were impacting NuPlant and supervisory performance. These hypotheses, summarized in table 3-1, are based on some of the AOP key points covered in chapter 2. The hypotheses have implications for what must be accomplished in phase II of the project (ATR 3-7).

Bert's initial discussions with the corporate training director had centered on a proposal to

According to Rummler 3-7

Fast, effective, and efficient performance analysis depends on the use of hypotheses—their generation and testing. This is the scientific method in action. The AOP is a powerful framework for making sound hypotheses. The idea is to generate a hypothesis about the client situation, which is reflected in the project design, and then through data gathering and analysis determine if the hypothesis is on target or not. If it is not on target, then additional hypotheses should be generated and tested. I recommend keeping a project journal to record your hypotheses and check periodically to see how they turned out over the course of the project.

Table 3-1. Dissecting Bert's hypotheses for the NuPlant project.

	Observation	Hypothesis	AOP Key Point Serving as Basis for Hypothesis	Phase II Implications
a.	NuPlant has under-performed for five years.	Something is fundamentally wrong with the production process, the management process, or both at NuPlant.	• AOP Key Point #2: Organizations are processing systems. • AOP Key Point #6: Management must keep the organization system aligned.	Must understand the production process and management system and their effects on plant productivity
		Production supervisors have little direct impact on the production process and, consequently, on the CBI of NuPlant's productivity. If production supervisors could make a significant impact on production performance, they certainly would have done so by now.	• AOP Key Point #4: Jobs/roles and functions exist to support the processes of the organization.	Must understand the relationship of the production supervisors to the production process
b.	Current production supervisor behavior toward direct reports is unacceptable.	The label "attitude" is misleading. The issue is supervisory *behavior*—what they do and don't do. An attitude is something observers infer about individuals, based on the behavior they observe. The performance consultant's focus must be on changing behavior.	• AOP #5: All performers are part of a human performance system (HPS).	Must understand the HPS of production supervisors and identify desired *behavior.*
		The current behavior of production supervisors toward their direct reports is a function of the supervisors' HPS. Most likely, the current pressure on production supervisors to increase NuPlant productivity, coupled with the fact they are unable to directly impact productivity (per the hypothesis above) has developed into expectations, consequences, and feedback that drive the current unacceptable behavior of production supervisors.	• AOP #5: All performers are part of an HPS.	
		Training in human relations, even if merited and effective, would have little impact on the CBI as long as the other factors in the NuPlant AOP were not addressed.	• AOP #5: All performers are part of an HPS.	Must align all components of the HPS to consistently achieve the desired behavior.

conduct a training needs analysis of the supervisor position to allow a fairly broad look at the supervisor role without committing to human relations training. However, in light of Bert's decision to use the CBI of plant productivity and test various hypotheses, he proposed to expand the definition of the project to "A Study of the Effectiveness of Production Supervision." This redefinition of the project would allow for a shift in focus from supervisor to plant performance and would make it possible to test all his hypotheses. The corporate training director subsequently agreed with the redefinition and committed to funding the project. (It turned out there was a general concern at corporate headquarters about the effectiveness of production supervisors throughout manufacturing, and it was thought that the results of this study might shed some light on that issue (ATR 3-8).)

To achieve the project goal, Bert was going to have to identify and assess all the factors at NuPlant that impacted supervisory and plant performance. In other words, he had to identify and analyze the relevant NuPlant "is" AOP. Bert's analysis strategy included contrasting the relevant processes and systems of NuPlant (which are failing) with those of the highly successful Old Plant. This technique (often referred to as analysis of exemplary performance) usually provides a quick test of the hypotheses developed by the performance consultant (ATR 3-9).

Bert planned to accomplish phase II of the RIP through a series of data sweeps that drilled down from a total system view of the organization to a

According to Rummler 3-9

Exemplary performance should not be confused with best practices. It is not exactly clear to me how things get identified these days as best practices. An exemplar (individual or organization unit) is identified based on measurable results. Then the analyst looks for the explanation or root cause behind the superior results. This analysis might uncover a set of behaviors, a particular HPS configuration, process, policy, or system that might subsequently be labeled a best practice. But, the starting point is always superior, measurable results.

closer examination of relevant processes and then to a closer look at relevant jobs. Bert knew that multiple, short data sweeps are more efficient and effective than trying to do everything at once. Gathering some information and then drilling down to get specific information ensures completeness and avoids unnecessary data gathering. A side benefit is that a series of data sweeps enables the client to see and understand what Bert was doing and avoids confusing the client by reporting data that may, in the end, turn out to be irrelevant.

The general project plan included the following activities:

1. Data Sweep One with a focus on identifying the relevant "is" AOP of NuPlant (departments and key processes and their relationships)
2. Data Sweep Two (influenced by the results of Data Sweep One) to examine in detail the

According to Rummler 3-8

Bert felt no need to call this project a "performance improvement" or "performance consulting" project—a common mistake of new or aspiring performance consultants. ("Wow, look at me! I'm doing something new and different. I am no longer just a trainer, I'm a performance consultant!)

Always remember that the ultimate goal is improved performance and results. The project goal is to find out what is required to achieve that ultimate goal. Bert is OK with calling the project anything that will help him achieve both the ultimate and the project goals. "Training Needs Analysis" is almost always a good cover. Everybody knows what training is; how threatening can it be? Where you might meet some resistance is when you begin to ask questions about budgets and finance. If you anticipate getting into that territory, you may need to broaden the project's label and provide a sound explanation to the people who might balk at providing this necessary information. The label "Effectiveness of Production Supervisors" is broader than "Training Needs Analysis" and also provides good cover. After all, everybody agrees that supervisory effectiveness can always be improved!

production system, management system, and supervisory roles at both NuPlant and Old Plant

3. Data Sweep Three to dig deeper in selected areas in NuPlant as needed

4. Summary of findings and development of recommendations to improve the performance of supervisors and NuPlant

The project plan outlined by Bert describes what must be accomplished in phase II of the RIP (Barriers Determined and Changes Specified). The output of phase II would be the specification of changes to improve the performance of supervisors and the plant. If the study recommendations were accepted, solutions would be designed and implemented per phase III of the RIP. The need for getting some recommendations as soon as possible and the lack of available internal resources at NuPlant to assist in the analysis led to Bert and the client agreeing to a project engagement model that would rely on Bert's team doing the analysis with input from NuPlant and other Big Auto staff. NuPlant and Big Auto would then undertake phases III and IV of the RIP without the help of Bert's team.

A proposal was developed and subsequently accepted by the corporate training director. Bert estimated that phase II of the project would take approximately 12 weeks to complete. Bert identified two associates to work with him; one associate joined Bert in the data gathering and analysis, and the other associate played the role of technical specialist. In all, Bert was involved in the project about three-fourths time, his data-gathering associate close to full time, and the specialist about one-eighth time.

Phase II: Barriers Determined and Changes Specified

Table 3-2 presents the overall project chronology of phase II of the NuPlant project (ATR 3-10).

Chronology of Data Sweep One

Using figure 3-5, you can track Bert's progress in the RIP.

Figure 3-5. NuPlant project milestones.

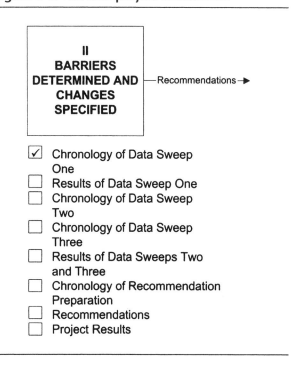

Weeks One and Two. Bert and his two associates arrived at NuPlant and met with the HR manager to outline their data-gathering plans for the first week. The goal for the week was to understand

Table 3-2. Chronology for phase II of the NuPlant project.

Week	Project Activity	Location	Activity
1	Data Sweep One	NuPlant	Data gathering and analysis
2	Data Sweep One	NuPlant	Data gathering and analysis
3	Data Sweep One	Office	Data analysis and planning next data sweep
4	Data Sweep Two	Old Plant	Data gathering and analysis
5	Data Sweep Two	NuPlant	Data gathering and analysis
6	Data Sweep Two	NuPlant	Data gathering and analysis
7	Data Sweep Two	Office	Data analysis and planning next data sweep
8	Data Sweep Three	NuPlant	Data gathering, testing likely recommendations, and analysis
9	Recommendations	Office	Data analysis and finalization of recommendations
10	Recommendations	Office	Preparation of final report and presentation
11	Recommendations	NuPlant	Presentation of final report and recommendations to NuPlant
12	Recommendations	Big Auto Headquarters	Presentation of final report and recommendations to Big Auto headquarters

- the total production system and the role supervisors played in that system
- what various managers (plant and division) thought were the causes of current performance at NuPlant
- how performance of supervisors and the plant were measured
- the economics of the plant
- the role of the plant in division and corporate performance

Bert's team had a thorough tour of NuPlant and met with the plant manager and his staff to review the project goals and process (ATR 3-11).

Bert's performance consulting team asked senior production management to identify the "best" and "poorest" managers and supervisors using whatever hard data were available. The team then began data gathering and analysis by

- interviewing all managers associated with production
- interviewing and observing the "best" and not-so-good first-line supervisors from the two shifts

According to Rummler 3-11

Always try to get a look at the work environment of the performers in question. Arrange for a tour of the store, office, call center, sales floor, or warehouse. If the project involves sales reps who are on the road, travel with them for a day or more.

- interviewing and observing a number of general supervisors to whom the supervisors reported from both shifts
- interviewing a sample of hourly employees from each shift

Bert's performance consulting team members shared and summarized the results of their interviews and observations each day and recorded preliminary findings (ATR 3-12).

According to Rummler 3-12

Ideally, the data gathering team is given access to an office or conference room at the site that can function as a project room. This area should provide enough wall space to post pictures or maps that summarize what the team is learning. If the performance consultant is unable to commandeer such space, he or she probably will have to deal with the limitations of a hotel room.

Week Three. Bert and the team retreated to their company office and the project room to analyze the data they had gathered thus far and to document their understanding of the production system, supervisory roles, and the management system.

The team also planned the data-gathering strategy for Data Sweep Two, which included a visit to Old Plant (the exemplary performer) as well as a return to NuPlant.

Results of Data Sweep One

As you can see in figure 3-6, Bert and the performance consulting team are making some progress in phase II of the RIP.

NuPlant's Organizational Structure. During his first visit to NuPlant, Bert obtained a copy of the plant organization chart (figure 3-7), which he posted on the wall of the room he was able to commandeer at NuPlant.

Probably the single most important document for the performance consultant is the organization chart for the entity being analyzed. On a single page it shows the major functions involved in making the organization work and the relationships that exist

Figure 3-6. NuPlant project milestones.

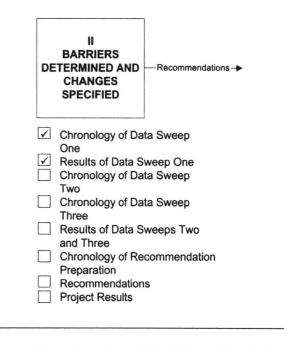

among those functions. This information is the beginning of understanding the organization as a system and the relevant AOP. The organizational structure can spark some early hypotheses about where the system might be broken (ATR 3-13).

Surveying the Managers. As part of the data gathering in Data Sweep One, the performance

---

According to Rummler 3-13

Take a closer look at figure 3-7. Each box on the chart represents a department or function. Everywhere that such a box exists is the potential for what are called functional or departmental silos, in which the interests of the box are likely to be paramount to the staff and managers therein, taking priority over the needs of the total organization; that is, NuPlant. In NuPlant's organizational chart, it appears that the production manager is probably the only manager at that level who truly is directly accountable for NuPlant production. All the other managers are going to be accountable for their individual departments or silos. I would be willing to hypothesize that these other managers are all going to be focused primarily on their department goals and secondarily on meeting the goals of the production manager, which are the production goals of NuPlant.

Figure 3-7. NuPlant's organizational chart.

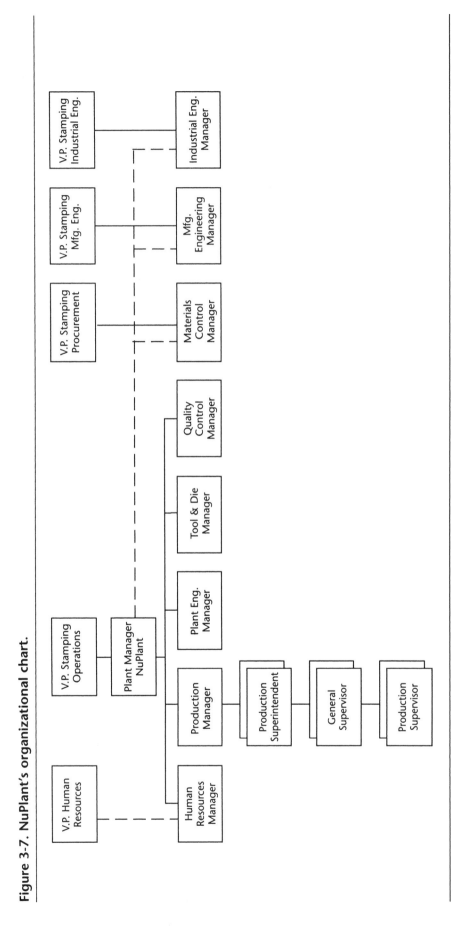

consulting team asked all NuPlant function managers, "What do you think contributes to NuPlant's poor performance?" A representative sampling of manager responses appears in table 3-3 (ATR 3-14).

NuPlant's "Is" AOP. By the end of the first day of their visit to NuPlant, Bert and his team began to develop the picture shown in figure 3-8 and continued to add to it until they could show all the components that appear to impact the production process and plant performance. This picture summarizes the performance context of a NuPlant production supervisor. It is a summary of the relevant "is" AOP of NuPlant. Most all the potential factors impacting the gaps in results are captured on this single page, which Bert and the team posted on the wall of their workspace along with NuPlant's organizational chart. Pictures or maps like this are great tools for capturing, displaying, and communicating findings (ATR 3-15).

It is always interesting to contrast the typical view of a plant like that shown in the aerial photograph in figure 3-3 and the skeletal view of the plant's AOP in figure 3-8. This "X-ray" view of the essentials of performance for NuPlant is the starting point for Bert and his team. What Bert has done is convert the generic AOP diagram shown in figure 2-3 to the specific NuPlant relevant "is" AOP. This diagram also makes it possible to envision how a results chain can be established to link the production supervisor, the production process, and NuPlant productivity.

If you take a moment to look at figure 3-8, you will see that the performance of NuPlant—as measured by units produced, labor cost, yield, and scrap rate—is a function of the following items, which correspond to the letters in figure 3-8:

A. *The production/press line:* The press line is approximately 50–75 yards long and contains anywhere from six to 12 individual presses—many of which are five stories tall—and several welding machines. Steel is fed in one end of the line, goes through a series of these presses, and emerges from the other end of the press line minutes later as an automobile hood, door, quarter panel, or some other automotive component. This is the primary production process around which everything revolves at NuPlant. There are approximately 30 such press lines in NuPlant, occupying a substantial amount of real estate.

B. *Production scheduling:* This organization schedules how many of which parts are to be run on each press line. Press runs last a minimum of one shift and up to several days each.

C. *Human resources:* This organization provides the necessary labor to staff the press line. An average of 22 workers work on each press line.

According to Rummler 3-15

Please take a moment to understand the diagram in figure 3-8. It is important for a couple of reasons. First, it is basic to understanding the rest of the discussion of NuPlant. Later I will relate all the project findings and subsequent recommendations to this diagram. Second, it is an example of the application of a fundamental tool for analyzing and improving results, and you should become comfortable with it. Understanding the performance context of every request for help (which is what this type of diagram does better than anything else) is absolutely essential for a performance consultant who endeavors to make a difference.

According to Rummler 3-14

Asking all managers about their perceptions of the problems that prevent NuPlant from achieving its desired results is a useful tactic. It immediately gets all the managers involved in the project and provides some baseline data on perceptions about the "problem." As you can see from table 3-3, there was little consensus on the part of the managers and scant helpful insight. But, it was useful to understand how confused and overwhelmed the managers were at this point. They were, in fact, clueless about what was causing poor plant performance and what to do about it. These findings also illustrate the challenges (and limitations) one faces when relying heavily on client personnel to identify accurately the cause of performance problems and to generate effective corrective action.

Table 3-3. Function managers' responses to the question, "What do you think contributes to NuPlant's poor performance?"

Manager	Response
Plant Engineering Manager	• Screwing from hourly people. • Weak supervision. • Superintendent and general supervisors are OK; supervision below is the real problem. • Need training.
Industrial Engineering Manager	• Baling wire fixes. • Low morale—too much management interference. • Attitude of "let management do it." • First and second shifts are like two different plants. One shift changes what the other shift tried to do. • Need human relations courses.
Materials Control Manager	• Lack of pride in work. • Lack of cooperation among subordinates. • Lack of respect for management.
Manufacturing Engineering Manager	• Training session needed badly. • Plant is over-sourced. • Quick fixes rather than long-range solutions. • Standards are higher than other plants. • Quality of engineering not too good.
Tool and Die Manager	• Attitude—supervision and hourly. • Bad habits. • Don't meet promise dates. • Inconsistent quality control. • Labor relations not backing us. • People playing cards when line is down.
Production Superintendent (second shift)	• Overloaded plant. • Receive people here who couldn't make it elsewhere. • New generation workforce.
Production Manager	• Supervision attitude in Tool and Die. • Battle between die room and press room. • Plant is not set up to run at volume. • Lack of cooperation among departments. • Lack of communication.

D. *Maintenance:* This operation is responsible for keeping the highly automated lines operating. They carry out preventive maintenance and carry out electrical and mechanical repairs on the lines.

E. *Die set:* This operation changes the stamping dies every time a line is converted from making one part to another (e.g., from doors for Model *X* to hoods for Model *Y.*) These changes involve the use of large overhead cranes to hoist 10-ton stamping dies into and out of position. On average it takes six hours to convert a line, during which time the entire line is shut down. Most of this work is done on the third, or maintenance, shift.

F. *Die repair:* Frequently the stamping dies develop cracks or are otherwise damaged during use and must be removed to this operation for repair. It is the job of the maintenance and die set functions to identify dies that need repair.

Figure 3-8. Major components of the NuPlant production system—the "is" AOP.

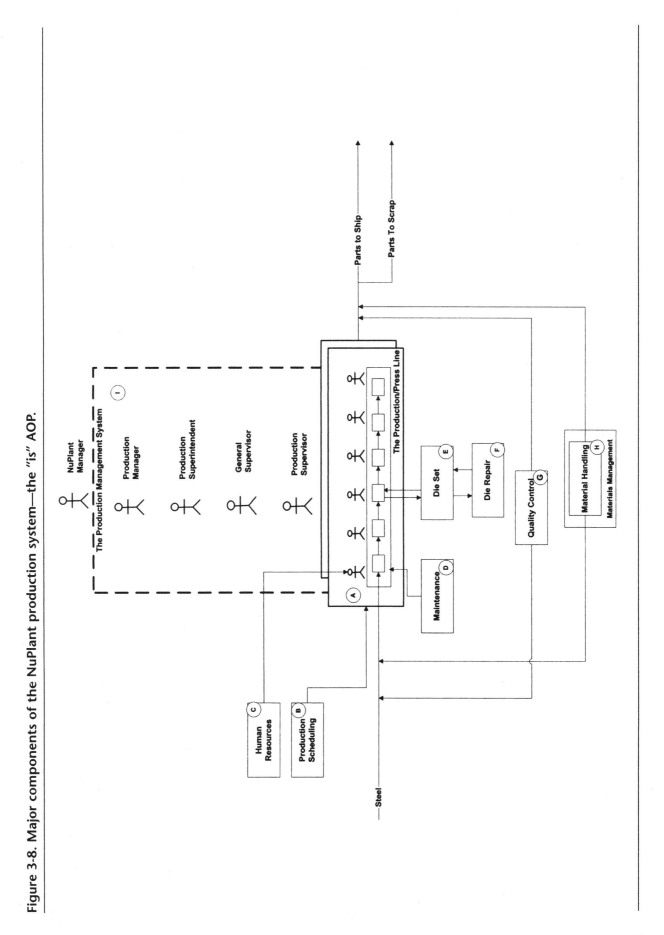

G. *Quality control:* This organization inspects incoming steel and outgoing finished parts as they come off the press line.

H. *Material handling:* This operation is responsible for moving all material throughout the plant. In particular, it moves the incoming steel to the press line and finished parts to either shipping (by railcar) or to scrap for recycling.

I. *Production management system:* This function includes (1) the production supervisor who is generally responsible for supervising two of the 30 press lines during an eight-hour shift; (2) the general supervisor, who is responsible for supervising five production supervisors each shift; (3) the two production superintendents, each of whom is responsible for the production of one shift; and (4) the production manager, who is responsible for all production for NuPlant (ATR 3-16).

According to Rummler 3-16

Now it's time for you to do some work. Take a pencil or pen, and highlight the production supervisor in figure 3-8 because this position is the alleged source of the "bad attitude" that is causing all the productivity problems at NuPlant. Given this picture of the relevant "is" AOP of NuPlant, do you think that is a sound hypothesis? Probably not.

Are there some other possible causes of poor performance? I think so. In fact, my hypothesis (and Bert's as well) is that the production supervisors have hardly any direct impact on plant productivity even though they are held accountable for press line productivity. No wonder they have bad attitudes! See how useful this system diagram can be in constructing hypotheses for poor performance? You can't beat it! Well, let's move on and see what we shall see.

Analyzing NuPlant's Processes. As part of Data Sweep One, Bert and his team had to really dig into NuPlant operations to conceive how the production system was supposed to work and understand the role of the production supervisor. Figure 3-9 provides a graphical context for their findings.

Briefly, as you can see on figure 3-9, the production system works like this: The production

scheduling organization (A) schedules a part (e.g., automobile hood, part #999) to be stamped on press line #10. For example, production scheduling might plan a run of 7,500 parts to be made on this line. Given the standard operating assumption that this line should be able to produce 200 parts an hour, five eight-hour shifts should produce 8,000 parts. Allowing for a scrap rate of 5% (400 parts), that should provide a net of 7,600 good parts for the five shifts. In preparation for this run, the necessary dies (B) are set on the line, a process that takes about six hours. Given that it takes so long to set a line for a particular part, scheduling has guidelines as to the minimum and optimal run length for each part. It is highly uneconomical to set a line with the necessary dies, run only 500 parts, and then reset the line for another part. Once the line is set for part #999, the appropriate number and size of steel sheets called blanks (C) are moved to the head of the stamping line by material handling (D).

The steel blanks go through a series of stamping operations (E) and eventually emerge at the end of the stamping line as automobile hood part #999 (F). A computer automatically records the number of impressions (hits) made by the last press on the line (G), providing production scheduling with a continuous record of the apparent number of parts produced by the line. The finished parts are then loaded onto a rack as they come off the end of the line. When the rack is full (it holds 30 finished car hoods), it is moved by materials handling (H) to an inspection station (I), where quality control checks the parts to see if they meet various standards (ATR 3-17).

Parts that meet quality control standards are loaded onto another rack and moved by material handling to the shipping dock, for shipment (J) by

---

According to Rummler 3-17

A basic principle of Total Quality Management (TQM) is that you don't "inspect-in" quality for a product; you "build-in" quality. The quality control process at NuPlant appears to be a clear violation of that principle.

Figure 3-9. How it works.

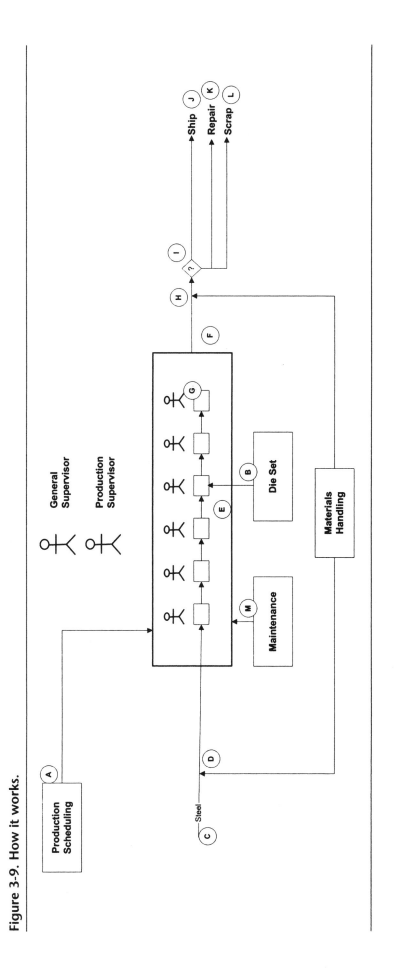

The NuPlant Case Study

53

rail to the appropriate assembly plant. Parts that do not meet the standard are either put on a rack destined for repair (K) or on a rack designated as scrap (L). The parts on the scrap rack eventually are chopped, baled, and sent to a vendor for recycling. Material handling is not supposed to move any of these racks after inspection without official tags on the racks that designate whether they are "ship," "repair," or "scrap." Quality control manages these tags and carefully records the number of ship, repair, and scrap parts and forwards these numbers to production scheduling at the end of each shift. Production scheduling then subtracts the number of scrapped and repaired parts from the number of impressions recorded for that line to arrive at a net production figure for that shift on that line.

The major measure of stamping line productivity is off-standard direct labor cost. It is calculated thus: Line #10 is scheduled to produce 200 impressions (hits) of part #999 an hour, for a total of 1,600 for the shift. There are 20 workers assigned to the line for this part. That means that the standard is 20 hours of labor to produce 200 hits per hour, or 160 hours of labor per shift to produce 1,600 hits per shift. (For ease of calculation, Bert is not taking into account work breaks, which would mean a net of less than eight hours per shift.) The direct labor standard for part #999 therefore is 0.10 hours per part (20 divided by 200). If the stamping line produces 200 or more #999 parts per hour, the line will have a positive direct labor cost variance and will be in the black. Conversely, if the line produces fewer than 200 in an hour (say, 150), the ratio of parts to labor increases to 0.133 hours per part, which is a negative variance, and the line is considered to be in the red for the hour.

The Production Supervisors: Trapped in the Red. There is a great deal of pressure on the first-line production supervisor to see that the line does not end up in the red for the shift. Being in the red is not a good thing for the career of the supervisor. An issue is that the measure of parts produced per hour is based on the hits recorded by the last press on the line, not the number of "ship" parts that pass quality control inspection each shift. Therefore, production scheduling is operating most of the time with flawed or incomplete data. The computer tells production scheduling that line #10 had 1,600 hits during the first shift, equal to the volume that was planned. However, quality control may scrap 100 of those parts for some defect and send another 75 off for repair, leaving an actual figure of 1,425 for the shift.

The data on defective parts don't reach production scheduling for several hours after the end of the shift. In the meantime, the supervisor on the first shift of line #10 is in the black regarding direct labor because the line recorded the necessary 1,600 hits. One of the troublesome aspects of this measure is that it encourages a supervisor to keep a line running at all costs (to keep the hits on target) rather than stop the line because some problem is generating bad parts. Likewise, if a line goes down due to some mechanical problem, the supervisor will do everything in his or her power to get the line running again, so that the number of hits is close to standard by the end of the shift (ATR 3-18).

According to Rummler 3-18

Bert and his performance consulting team have done a great job of describing the production process and the relationships among the various functions at NuPlant. This description is a good illustration of the level of detail that a serious performance consultant must understand.

You need to put yourself in the position of the performer in question (in this case, the production supervisor) and understand the nitty-gritty of the job and the HPS. As you are learning about the job, ask yourself, "Could I do this job?" "Are the expectations clear?" "Do these expectations make sense?" "Do these measures of the job make sense?" "Are the apparent consequences for performance balanced to get the desired performance?" "What has to be changed in order for me to be successful at this job?"

After you have a thorough understanding of a job and the HPS, you should be in a position to start hypothesizing some causes of poor performance and identify plausible corrective actions.

Now here's where it starts to get interesting. NuPlant is under increasing pressure and scrutiny because it has fallen to the bottom of the stamping division in volume (actual units shipped versus planned), amount of scrap, and off-standard direct labor. Regarding the latter measure, the overall *plant* is in the red. Division is so concerned about this labor cost measure that it now is asking NuPlant to report twice per shift on the status of direct labor cost. This means that the general supervisors check the labor productivity of each press line/production supervisor at the end of the first four hours of the shift and at the end of the shift. These numbers are summarized and forwarded to NuPlant management and then to the division. There is immense pressure on supervisors to be in the black at the end of each shift.

The most critical time in the plant is the start of the first shift each day. Any new part runs have been set overnight (on the third shift) and are now going to run for the first time. Productivity for the first hour or two is going to be below standard as the workers adjust to the altered tasks, the press pressures are fine-tuned, the reset (and perhaps repaired) dies are tested for the first time, and material handling struggles to get the required steel blanks to each line. So on the first shift of any given day, 10–20 of the 30 press lines may be starting a new part. Given that the production supervisors are supervising two lines each, they may be overseeing the start-up of two new part runs. At the beginning of any shift, the supervisor has the staff of two lines assigned, or being charged, to them. If they are having trouble getting a line started, they are being charged those direct labor costs until such time that the line is officially deemed inoperable by maintenance. At that point, the staff is put back into a pool for assignment to other lines and the supervisor is off the hook for labor costs on that line, that day.

A general rule of thumb among production supervisors is that if a supervisor can't get a line started producing hits in the first 45 minutes of a shift, there is no way they will be able to generate enough hits in the remaining seven hours and 15 minutes of the shift to get back into the black for the shift. This "point of no return" produces some

interesting behavior on the part of production supervision (ATR 3-19).

According to Rummler 3-19

Here's an example of the seemingly bizarre (but predictable, if you think about it) behavior of the production supervisors. They would point out to the maintenance people working on a down line that if they can't get a line back up in the first 45 minutes of the shift, it sure would be helpful if they could declare the line down for the remainder of the shift. If this happens, the labor charges for that line are shifted elsewhere, and the production supervisor is off the hook for that line.

There was no end of resourcefulness on the part of production supervisors when it came to finding ways of escaping from the box that the system had placed them in. Remember my earlier words, "Put a good performer in a bad system, and the system will win every time"? These production supervisors were trapped in a bad system. If they couldn't escape the system, they did what they could to beat it.

A Look at the Big Picture. Having learned how NuPlant's production system works and the role of the production supervisor, Bert and his team took a look at the larger system within which NuPlant operates. NuPlant is part of the stamping division, which, in turn is part of North American Vehicle Operations, which is a major component of Big Auto (figure 3-10). It is predictable that there are factors in the larger system that affect NuPlant's performance and vice versa. Bert needs to understand the system performance context of NuPlant early on.

Chronology of Data Sweep Two

Figure 3-11 will refresh your memory about where Bert and his team are in the RIP.

Week Four. Bert and his data-gathering colleague arrived at Old Plant, met with the HR manager to outline their data gathering plans for a three-day visit, and had a brief plant tour (ATR 3-20).

Figure 3-10. NuPlant and its larger system.

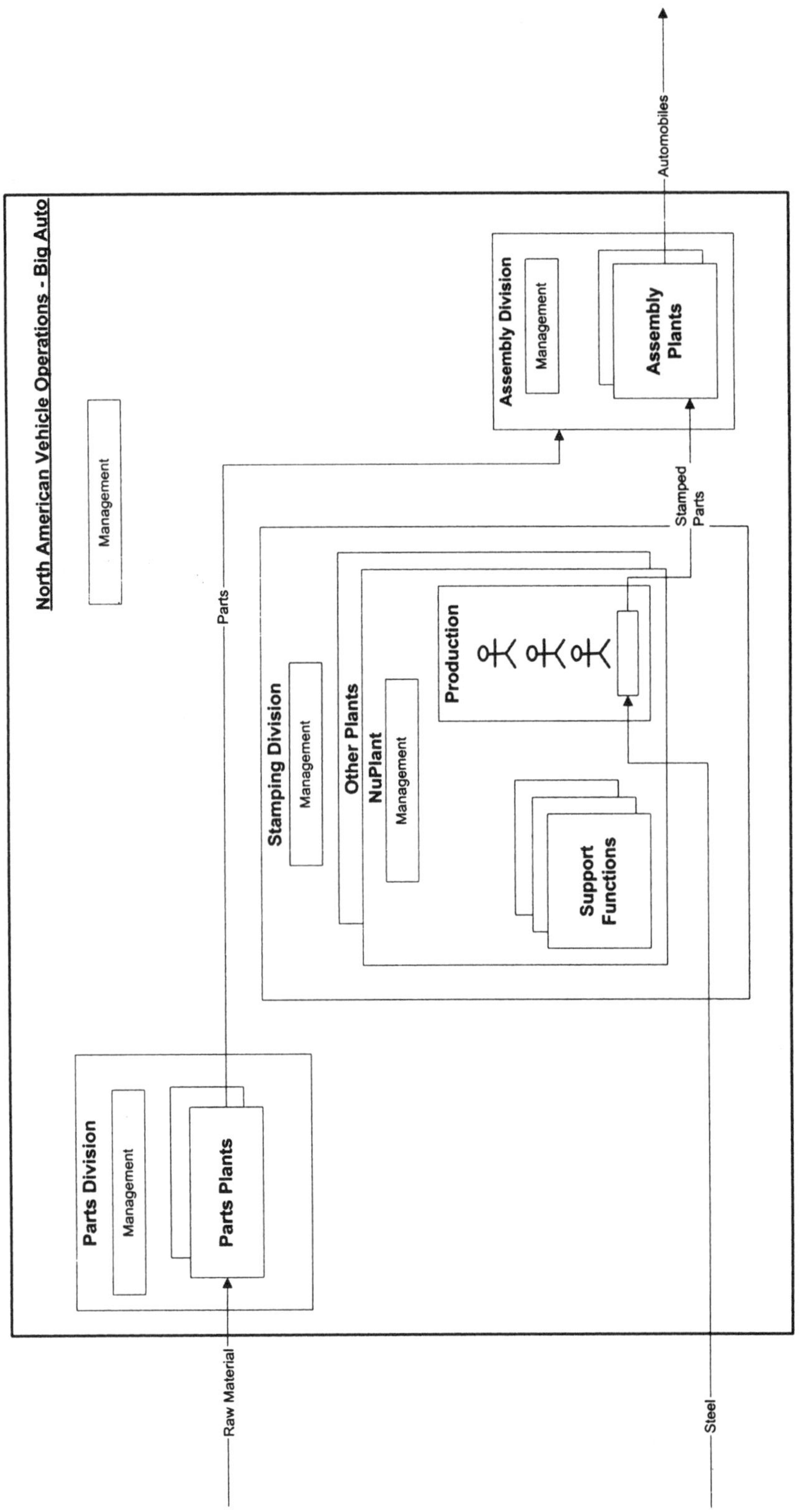

Figure 3-11. NuPlant project milestones.

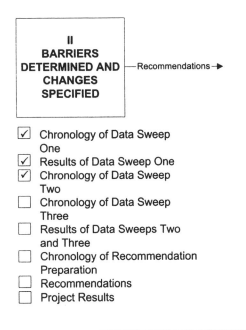

- ☑ Chronology of Data Sweep One
- ☑ Results of Data Sweep One
- ☑ Chronology of Data Sweep Two
- ☐ Chronology of Data Sweep Three
- ☐ Results of Data Sweeps Two and Three
- ☐ Chronology of Recommendation Preparation
- ☐ Recommendations
- ☐ Project Results

According to Rummler 3-20

As mentioned earlier, Old Plant was an exemplary performer, as far as stamping plants went at Big Auto, whereas NuPlant was at the bottom of the pile. It's hard to reconcile these differences in performance because Old Plant was the oldest, least automated plant in the stamping division, and NuPlant was the newest and most automated plant.

Bert wanted to look at Old Plant so he could begin to understand what contributed to its exemplary performance. Incidentally, management at NuPlant and the stamping division hypothesized that what made the difference at Old Plant were the "skilled European craftsmen" that Old Plant employed, in contrast to the new generation workforce that NuPlant was forced to employ as a function of the local job market. You'll read more about this interesting theory later.

The data gathering goals for the visit to Old Plant were to

- understand the Old Plant production system, measures, management system, and supervisory roles so they could be compared to those of NuPlant.

- gather historic production data for a 16-week period for further analysis of the off-standard direct labor measure. (These data were not available at NuPlant.)

Not much time was required to gather these data at Old Plant because Bert's team now had a good AOP template of a stamping plant and sound hypotheses about what to look for. For example, the team already knew in general how the production system worked.

Bert and his team spent the last two days of the week in their office processing the data from Old Plant and refining the data-gathering requirements for the next trip to NuPlant.

Weeks Five and Six. Bert and his data-gathering colleague arrived at NuPlant, checked in with the HR manager, and reviewed the data-gathering plan for these two weeks (ATR 3-21).

According to Rummler 3-21

Up to this point, Bert has been trying to understand the "is" AOP of NuPlant. Although he has been casually comparing the "is" he is seeing to the "should" AOP principles he has in his head (per the discussion in chapter 2), he will now begin to compare "is" to "should" with more rigor. The visit to Old Plant confirmed his AOP "should" principles in a stamping plant setting, as he saw many of them at play and contributing to the difference in results of the two plants.

During this two-week period, Bert and the team undertook a critical review of all the relevant production and management systems in search of disconnects and their underlying causes. This task would require more focused interviews with key individuals and more observations of critical interactions and transactions in the plant (ATR 3-22).

Bert further conceptualized NuPlant's "should" AOP in terms of the production system, management system, and supervisory roles. He also started to formulate some preliminary recommendations for ways to improve the productivity of NuPlant and

Figure 3-12. NuPlant project milestones.

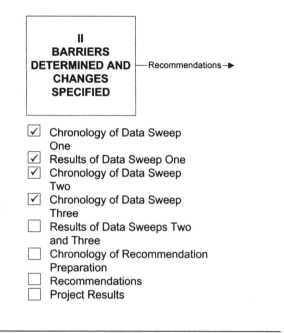

the performance of the production supervisors. He and his data-gathering colleague collected the necessary information, which they shared and summarized each day.

Week Seven. Bert and his team shifted their work back to their company offices. At this point, the team began to compare systematically NuPlant's "is" AOP to the "should" of an effective AOP, identifying discrepancies between the two and developing recommendations to close the gaps.

The team members found that there were still some holes in their knowledge of NuPlant and developed a data-gathering plan for Data Sweep Three to fill those holes.

Chronology of Data Sweep Three

As you can see from figure 3-12, Bert is making serious inroads into phase II of the RIP.

Week Eight. Once again, Bert and his colleague arrived at NuPlant and checked in with the HR manager to review their plan. This sweep was to include another two- or three-day visit to NuPlant and several telephone interviews with managers at Old Plant. Also, as part of the visit at NuPlant, Bert planned to begin testing some of the performance consulting team's tentative recommendations on various managers and supervisors to assess the recommendations' feasibility and likely level of acceptance and support (ATR 3-23).

Results of Data Sweeps Two and Three

Figure 3-13 provides you with another check on the NuPlant project milestones.

It's time to get out your Post-it notes so that you can mark your place as you flip among several sections in this book. A high-level summary of the findings from Data Sweeps Two and Three follows. The findings that are labeled with the letter *A* pertain to the production supervisors' performance at NuPlant. The findings labeled with the letter *B* pertain to plant performance at NuPlant and Old Plant. The letter *C* denotes important findings related to the entire stamping division.

The locations of the project findings in the NuPlant AOP are shown in figure 3-14. The findings for the stamping division are highlighted on figure 3-15, a few pages hence. You can use the labeling

Figure 3-13. NuPlant project milestones.

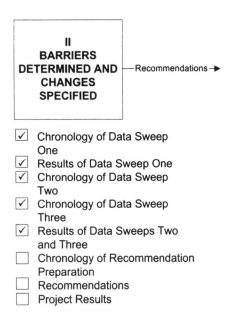

- ☑ Chronology of Data Sweep One
- ☑ Results of Data Sweep One
- ☑ Chronology of Data Sweep Two
- ☑ Chronology of Data Sweep Three
- ☑ Results of Data Sweeps Two and Three
- ☐ Chronology of Recommendation Preparation
- ☐ Recommendations
- ☐ Project Results

system for the findings (for example, A1 or B2) to locate the pertinent general discussion here in this chapter or the corresponding details in appendix A, which contains the detailed findings and the rationale behind them, or you can cross-reference the associated recommendation in appendix B. The findings have been organized this way so you can get an overview of the findings in this chapter and then drill down in appendix A as your curiosity or desire to master the report dictates. The findings in appendix A are excerpted from the actual project final report (ATR 3-24).

 Summary of Bert's Findings

A1. Production supervisors have little control over the factors critical to plant productivity.

A2. Production supervisors receive little objective performance feedback on a daily basis.

A3. The productivity of NuPlant will not be significantly affected by training production supervisors. The supervisors' failure to perform has limited impact on plant productivity and is seldom attributable to lack of knowledge of what to do.

B1. The production system currently measures and emphasizes an inappropriate performance variable—direct labor cost.

B2. There is no data storage that can function as a "memory" for the production system.

B3. There is little or no feedback to production supervision on the consequences to the system of its poor performance.

B4. The NuPlant scheduling system (in contrast to Old Plant) does not have the data necessary to realistically and effectively schedule production.

B5. The NuPlant production scheduling work environment is a contributor to lack of scheduling effectiveness.

B6. The first hour line start-up is ineffective and costly.

B7. Lines frequently run when it is more cost effective to shut them down.

B8. The indirect budgeting system tends to be counterproductive in times of stress.

B9. The organization of responsibilities of the three lower levels of production management is inadequate for coping with the current production problems.

B10. Several knowledge deficiencies exist in production supervision and management.

B11. The introduction of new production workers into the production crews during the first hour line start-up every day is extremely inefficient and counterproductive.

B12. Old Plant has an early-quit policy that provides a significant incentive to production workers for high productivity and yield. There is no such system at NuPlant.

Figure 3-14. Major components of NuPlant's production system and location of findings from Data Sweeps One and Two.

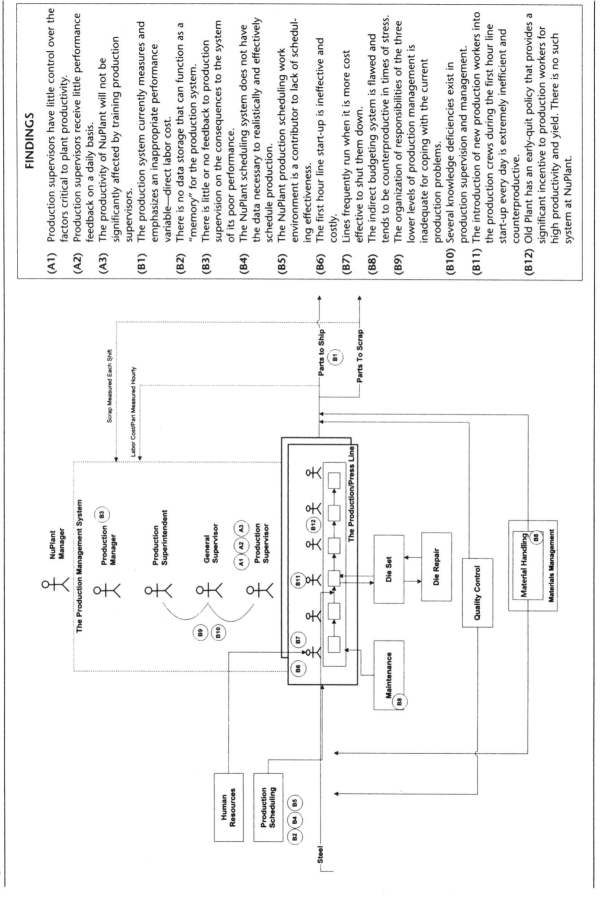

FINDINGS

(A1) Production supervisors have little control over the factors critical to plant productivity.

(A2) Production supervisors receive little performance feedback on a daily basis.

(A3) The productivity of NuPlant will not be significantly affected by training production supervisors.

(B1) The production system currently measures and emphasizes an inappropriate performance variable—direct labor cost.

(B2) There is no data storage that can function as a "memory" for the production system.

(B3) There is little or no feedback to production supervision on the consequences to the system of its poor performance.

(B4) The NuPlant scheduling system does not have the data necessary to realistically and effectively schedule production.

(B5) The NuPlant production scheduling work environment is a contributor to lack of schedul-ing effectiveness.

(B6) The first hour line start-up is ineffective and costly.

(B7) Lines frequently run when it is more cost effective to shut them down.

(B8) The indirect budgeting system is flawed and tends to be counterproductive in times of stress.

(B9) The organization of responsibilities of the three lower levels of production management is inadequate for coping with the current production problems.

(B10) Several knowledge deficiencies exist in production supervision and management.

(B11) The introduction of new production workers into the production crews during the first hour line start-up every day is extremely inefficient and counterproductive.

(B12) Old Plant has an early-quit policy that provides a significant incentive to production workers for high productivity and yield. There is no such system at NuPlant.

C1. Stamping division emphasis on plant labor costs results in a more costly reduction in material yield.

C2. NuPlant's failure to deliver per the set production schedule is impacting the larger system and further stressing the NuPlant system.

Finding A1. Production supervisors have little control over the factors critical to plant productivity (ATR 3-25). (For more detail on this finding, see appendix A.)

Finding A2. Production supervisors receive little objective performance feedback on a daily basis. They see no data on their performance over time and, therefore, have no objective evaluation of their effectiveness (ATR 3-26). (For more detail on this finding, see appendix A.)

Finding A3. The productivity of NuPlant will not be significantly affected by training production supervisors (ATR 3-27). (For more detail on this finding, see appendix A.)

Finding B1. The production system currently measures and emphasizes an inappropriate performance variable—direct labor cost (ATR 3-28). (For more detail on this finding, see appendix A.)

According to Rummler 3-25

The insight behind this finding runs counter to the prevailing myth at NuPlant and the stamping division that performance problems were attributable to the supervisors' "bad attitudes." The performance consulting team offered two views to support its findings regarding production supervisor performance. First, a process view presented in figure A-1 (appendix A) shows the total production process that generates the desired plant results and the control production supervisors have over that process. Second, table A-1 summarizes a number of important factors regarding the production process and the role of supervisors. Probably many supervisors intuitively understood what the consulting team discovered, but this was the first time a case had been made in an objective, unbiased way.

According to Rummler 3-26

The project report offers a thorough and detailed description of this finding and its consequences: "The supervisors have no objective means of determining what their overall performance is over time; they can't compare today's performance against their normal performance (indeed they may not know what normal is); they can't tell whether the changes they are making regarding a particular part are having any effect on performance. In short, they can't evaluate whether they are having any affect at all on performance. Without this kind of information, the supervisor has to be ineffective and highly frustrated." A description such as this preempts a question often heard from clients, "What do you mean by that?"

According to Rummler 3-27

Please take the time to read the detailed finding in appendix A. I think that three aspects of this finding are of particular interest:

1. This finding quickly addresses the underlying assumption of the original request ("We need human relations training for supervisors"). First, supervisors have little impact on plant productivity, and, second, the supervisors' failure to perform is seldom attributable to lack of knowledge of what to do. Therefore, training isn't going to solve the problem.

2. Second, finding A3 educates the client about the human performance system (without calling it that) and illustrates the concept with immediate application to the supervisor's job.

3. Additionally, this finding provides an example of how to present a great deal of relevant detail to support a conclusion. In the final report, each major production outcome/output is analyzed in detail as to why the production supervisor is not likely to perform as required. Again, this finding does not rely on weak generalizations about supervisory performance, but rather a detailed analysis using a powerful model or framework—the human performance system.

Finding B2. There is no data storage that can function as a "memory" for the production system. (For more detail on this finding, see appendix A.)

There is no relevant history of performance at NuPlant. No records are maintained to show how a line has performed over time or how a part has performed over time (e.g., actual production vs. scheduled, actual cost vs. budgeted or allowed costs). Performance data are seldom retained beyond a week and generally are not available below the superintendent level. And, data that are collected are not broken out by shift and line.

As a result, there is no cumulative record ("memory") of past performance so that trends could be noted, problems diagnosed, and results evaluated. Individuals (supervisors and general supervisors) and departments (quality control, material handling, plant engineering) remember problem parts and try to correct or compensate, often to the disadvantage of another department and the detriment of the plant (ATR 3-29).

Finding B3. There is little or no feedback to production supervision on the consequences to the system of its poor performance. (For more detail on this finding, see appendix A.)

The production supervisors (and often the general supervisors) are ignorant of the effects of their actions and are not accountable for the results. This would cease to be a problem if a memory system were installed as per finding B2.

Finding B4. The NuPlant scheduling system (in contrast to Old Plant) does not have the data necessary to realistically and effectively schedule production. Figure A-2 (in appendix A) is a good example of how a visual image can be used to

- help the analyst understand a complex system and its possible deficiencies
- communicate a complex topic and detailed findings and recommendations
- set up logical recommendations by comparing the "is" system in figure A-2 to the "should" system in figure B-5 (appendix B) (ATR 3-30)

Finding B5. The NuPlant production scheduling work environment is a contributor to lack of scheduling effectiveness (ATR 3-31). (For more detail on this finding, see appendix A.)

Finding B6. The first hour line start-up is ineffective and costly. (For more detail on this finding, see appendix A.) First hour production is, by and large, outside the control of the production supervisor and general supervisor, even though they frequently get burned for it. Although Bert and his team did not identify a specific cause, the continuing problem is most likely a manifestation of lack of data on actual die-set time and realistic net (production) predictions for a run. The result is that unrealistic schedules are set (and subsequently not met) and the real problems never get corrected.

Finding B7. Lines frequently run when it is more cost effective to shut them down. (For more detail

According to Rummler 3-30

As a basis for this finding, Bert has used his "should" AOP template to good effect. Old Plant clearly had superior productivity. But why? One of Bert's AOP "should" principles centers on what an effective "plan" and "manage" system must have (chapter 2). So, when Bert looked at Old Plant, one of the critical areas he and the team examined was the scheduling system—clearly the brain of the operation. His examination of this function in Old Plant convinced him that its scheduling system was a major contributor to exemplary productivity and seemed to constitute an exemplary approach to production scheduling. Bert and his team were able to see clear differences between the two plants in regard to the operation of the scheduling function, which explained the effectiveness of one system and the ineffectiveness of the other. This finding suggested a "should" system for NuPlant.

According to Rummler 3-31

A couple of points: First, this finding is another example of the value of having an exemplar to highlight issues with the "is" AOP and to help generate ideas for a "should" AOP. Second, Bert and the team made excellent use of observational data to compare performance at the two plants (table A-3). Developing this matrix helped Bert and his team sort through and categorize their observations of the two systems. The resulting matrix also served to efficiently communicate much important information to the client. The data in the matrix are fairly subjective and based on limited observations, but, for the client, the observations rang true.

on this finding, see appendix A.) The various factors encouraging a supervisor to run marginal and scrap pieces have been discussed earlier. It is also apparent that in many cases supervisors and general supervisors *don't* know when it is most cost beneficial to shut down the line.

Finding B8. The indirect budgeting system is flawed and tends to be counterproductive in times of stress. (For more detail on this finding, see appendix A.)

This finding is a great example of how traditional wisdom in an organization can be imperfect and, consequently, be at the root of a pervasive and significant problem. For years, in conventional stamping plants, determining indirect labor budgets (for such things as equipment maintenance) as a percentage of direct labor made sense. That is, if there were 500 people assigned to stamping lines on a given shift, then the indirect labor assigned to perform the maintenance on those lines during that shift would be 40, or 8% of the direct labor.

But, along comes NuPlant, which had 10 times the automation of the conventional plants (which translates into roughly 10 times the number of machines potentially requiring maintenance) *and*, because of the automation, required only 60% of the direct labor (300 people) necessary in a conventional plant. Given all this and the standard indirect labor percentage of 8% used for all other plants, the indirect labor available to maintain the heavily automated stamping lines at NuPlant was 24 people (8% of the 300 direct labor "heads" on the shift). There was no way this stamping division "standard" could work at NuPlant! Consequently, the automation was in serious disrepair, subject to more breakdowns and lost productivity (ATR 3-32).

Finding B9. The organization of responsibilities of the three lower levels of production management is inadequate for coping with the current production problems (ATR 3-33). (For more detail on this finding, see appendix A.)

Finding B10. Several knowledge deficiencies exist in production supervision and management. (For

According to Rummler 3-32

Many managers on the line knew this model for determining indirect labor was flawed, but comments on the situation were viewed as whining. After all, the macho-manufacturing credo is, "When the going gets tough, the tough get going!" Plus, this was the way it had always been done in the division. It took an outsider like Bert to point out that "the emperor had no clothes on" and to justify a reexamination of this flawed formula.

According to Rummler 3-33

I'd like to point out several things regarding this finding: First, this was an important observation because the issue was a major contributor to poor plant productivity. Second, it is an example of looking at an entire hierarchy of managers and their relation regarding performance. Third, this is yet another application of the HPS and the critical starting point of setting the right expectations. In this case, NuPlant had three levels of supervision all doing virtually the same thing and not particularly well, either. (You might sneak a peek at recommendation #4 in appendix B to see where this finding is headed.)

---

more detail on this finding, see appendix A.) The knowledge deficiencies are

- understanding of job responsibilities
- ability to effectively diagnose the operational system
- provision of adequate feedback to workers on quality and performance
- necessity of providing reinforcement to workers for making constructive comments

Finding B11. The introduction of new production workers into the production crews during the first hour line start-up every day is extremely inefficient and counterproductive. (For more detail on this finding, see appendix A.)

Finding B12. Old Plant has an early-quit policy that provides a significant incentive to production workers for high productivity and yield. There is no such system in NuPlant. (For more detail on this finding, see appendix A.)

This finding carries some interesting implications. First, some background: It was believed at NuPlant and at the division level that at least some of the productivity differences between NuPlant and Old Plant could be attributed to the characteristics of the two different workforces employed at the plants. Old Plant was staffed with mature "skilled European craftsmen," whereas NuPlant had to make do with a workforce that was mostly young men with long hair, tattered jeans, and plen-

ty of attitude but little company loyalty. They would leave in a flash for a job that had less hassle (forget pay) than what they were subjected to at NuPlant. Nevertheless, the workers at NuPlant were certainly smart enough to do their jobs properly if given a chance.

Old Plant was built in 1948 on the U.S. East Coast, at the end of World War II. At precisely the time the plant was ready for staffing, the first displaced persons (refugees) from Western Europe were arriving. Big Auto sponsored these families, transported vast numbers of them to the community in which Old Plant was to operate, and employed them even to the time of this project. Needless to say, these employees were loyal, but Bert could find no evidence that Old Plant performance was in any way a function of any "skilled European craftsmanship" because for the most part these workers were simply operating mammoth stamping presses, not building or repairing things. Granted, Old Plant had somewhat superior operating systems (e.g., the scheduling function), but what could explain the difference in productivity (ATR 3-34)?

The early-quit system introduced an interesting dynamic that shed more light on why Old Plant was an exemplary performer. The chance to get off the line early was a major incentive to achieve the line's production goals as soon as possible. This, of course, was a goal shared by most every one of the

---

According to Rummler 3-34

You're not going to believe this! Bert's team observed that at Old Plant some stamping lines were idle 30–60 minutes before the end of the shift. When they started to ask questions, they discovered a procedure called an early-quit system. Here's the deal: When a production line met its production and scrap goals for the shift, the line shut down, and the hourly workers were allowed to leave the line and go to the cafeteria, where many played cards until the end of the shift. This procedure existed only at Old Plant and was such an anomaly in Big Auto's labor contracts that initially no one at NuPlant or the division volunteered any information about it with Bert's team.

---

22 to 25 individuals on the line. As a result, all the line workers functioned as a team, helping each other when necessary. New employees assigned to the line got plenty of help from experienced employees. If there was a potential problem with equipment or support for the line, employees would alert the production supervisor to the situation and exert pressure to see that the *potential* problem was fixed long *before* it became a problem. As a result, Old Plant had one of the best records in the stamping division in terms of line downtime.

Needless to say, the picture was quite different at NuPlant where the only relief from working the line was for the line to stop for one reason or another. There was no incentive for NuPlant hourly workers to look for ways to improve the productivity of their lines (ATR 3-35).

According to Rummler 3-35

The early-quit phenomenon was interesting for two reasons: First, it was a policy, procedure, or practice that appeared quite insignificant in the grand scheme of things, but it had a huge impact on results. Second, intriguing though this seemingly exemplary practice was, it ran counter to the prevailing policy of the company.

Such situations are not unique. Sometimes a job practice that contributes significantly to exemplary performance is for some reason deemed verboten *by current management policy. When this is the case, the performance consultant can try a couple of things:*

- *Look to see what is fundamentally sound about the practice and see if it can be approximated in some way that would be acceptable under the current policy or a minor modification of the policy.*
- *Recommend that the policy be changed. You might want to test the waters to see how radical a change is required. Sometimes policies have been on the books for years for reasons nobody can remember, and they can be altered or dropped with a little visibility and persistence.*

So, it turned out that "skilled European craftsmen" had nothing to do with Old Plant's superior productivity.

Finding C1. Stamping division emphasis on plant labor costs results in a more costly reduction in material yield (figure 3-15) (ATR 3-36).

According to Rummler 3-36

Findings C1 and C2, which are discussed in the sections that follow, underscore the importance of performance context. Some problems can never be solved at the level the performance consultant is operating in because he or she never understands the larger picture. NuPlant operates within a system that includes the entire stamping division, North American Vehicle Operations, and Big Auto. NuPlant both impacts and is impacted by what goes on in those components of its super-system.

Within the stamping division, division materials (A) is accountable for the cost of materials, a large part of which is steel. At the same time, plant production management (B) is accountable for labor cost. Division (C) pressure on plants to meet labor cost goals translates into pressure on production supervisors and general supervisors to meet *hourly* labor cost goals. In an effort to meet these hourly labor cost goals (which is difficult given the factors that can shut down a press line), production supervisors make decisions that cause high scrap rates and lower yields on steel. However, nobody at the plant level is accountable for yield or the amount of good parts "out" given the tons of steel put "in" (ATR 3-37).

Finding C2. NuPlant's failure to deliver per the set production schedule is impacting the larger system and further stressing the NuPlant system. Both stamping and assembly plants are producing to an ideal schedule set by North American Vehicle Operations scheduling (D), (E), and (F). In the event that NuPlant ships less than the scheduled amount of acceptable parts to an assembly plant, thereby jeopardizing the ability of the assembly plant to meet its schedule, an urgent short order (G) is sent to NuPlant.

Figure 3-15. Overview of stamping division operations.

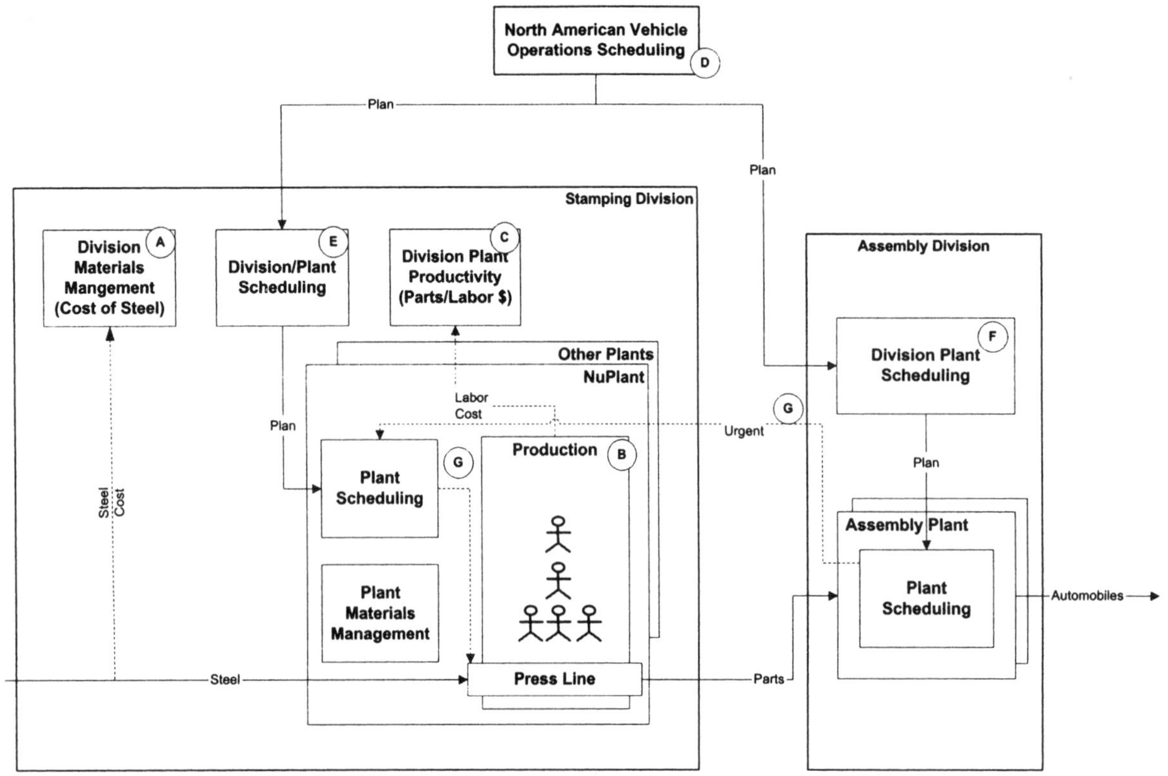

According to Rummler 3-37

This observation is a good example of why a performance consultant needs to understand the larger system in which the target system (NuPlant) operates. The way the stamping division has seen fit to manage the two variables of raw materials (steel) and labor leads to the suboptimization of the plant and the entire division's system of production. Nevertheless, this suboptimization of the plant is not something that can be solved at the plant level—it is clearly a division-level problem. The argument for what must be changed is presented in recommendation #1.

In order to avoid being responsible for shutting down an assembly line (a serious no-no), NuPlant must reset the press line (a five- to eight-hour operation), run the short part on an emergency basis (potentially requiring overtime pay), and ship the finished parts to the assembly plant by air freight. The emergency response has significant negative impact on the overall productivity of NuPlant.

This observation illustrates the consequences to the North American Vehicle Operations system (and back to NuPlant) of NuPlant failing to deliver as promised. Failing to get it right the first time leads to having to do it again, disrupting scheduled production, and putting the plant even further behind. It is a downward spiral of increased inefficiency and lowered productivity. And, all the findings discussed previously conspire to force the situation more out of control (ATR 3-38).

Chronology of Recommendation Preparation

Bert and the performance consulting team are coming down the home stretch, as you can see from the project milestones shown in figure 3-16.

Weeks Nine and Ten. Bert and his team finalized and prioritized their recommendations. They have compared the NuPlant "is" AOP with their "should" template and, as you can imagine, had a number of

Figure 3-16. NuPlant project milestones.

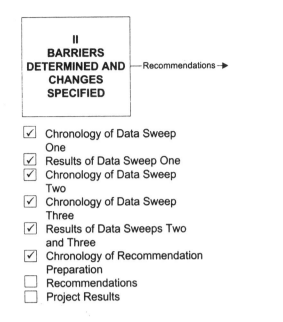

II
BARRIERS
DETERMINED AND —Recommendations→
CHANGES
SPECIFIED

- ✓ Chronology of Data Sweep One
- ✓ Results of Data Sweep One
- ✓ Chronology of Data Sweep Two
- ✓ Chronology of Data Sweep Three
- ✓ Results of Data Sweeps Two and Three
- ✓ Chronology of Recommendation Preparation
- ☐ Recommendations
- ☐ Project Results

According to Rummler 3-39

The basis for both sorting through the various insights and for organizing the final recommendations is the AOP framework built on the understanding that NuPlant is a system and that this system must be made whole. You will hear more about this as you look more closely at the recommendations.

According to Rummler 3-38

There is a saying that "It is hard to remember the objective was to drain the swamp when you are up to your waist in alligators." The tragedy at NuPlant is that everyone is so consumed by fighting the alligator of labor costs and their side effects that no one has the time, energy, or perspective to drain the swamp.

insights into the causes of NuPlant's various problems and a variety of thoughts on possible improvements. Now the team must sort through these insights and possible improvements to identify and organize those recommendations that will provide improvements in plant performance that are both immediate and sustainable over time (ATR 3-39).

During this two-week period, Bert and the team designed and wrote the final report describing their findings and outlining their recommendations. They also developed prototypes of key recommendations to illustrate what is intended by recommendations and thereby increasing the probability they will be accepted and implemented. Once they have developed the report, they

worked up an executive summary presentation and planned how they will present the final report to the client (ATR 3-40).

Week Eleven. Bert and his colleague once again visited NuPlant and this time presented the final report to the plant HR manager and the corporate training director. This group, in turn, presented the final report to the plant manager. The report was well received by the plant manager, who charged the HR manager with developing a plan for implementing those recommendations under the control of NuPlant.

According to Rummler 3-40

The output of the performance consulting team's work is not going to be your standard PowerPoint presentation. They have painstakingly prepared a blueprint for the effective performance of NuPlant—with nearly the same level of detail you might find in an architect's blueprint. This "blueprint" will ultimately be reviewed by a number of parties and must both make the case for change and (like the architect's blueprint) provide detailed guidance as to what must subsequently be built.

Week Twelve. Bert and his colleague visited Big Auto headquarters where they presented the final report to a meeting attended by the corporate training director and representatives of North American Vehicle Operations and the stamping division. The report stimulated considerable conversation and a commitment to look into changes that could be made at the division level.

At this point, the project is formally complete and the contract for a "Study of the Effectiveness of Production Supervision" is fulfilled. Bert and his team, as you will recall, were engaged to carry out the first two phases of the results improvement process (RIP). Phase III (Changes Designed, Developed, and Implemented) and phase IV (Results Evaluated and Maintained or Improved) were completed successfully by NuPlant and Big Auto without any assistance from Bert and his team (ATR 3-41).

According to Rummler 3-41

In the literature of performance consulting these days, much attention is paid to implementation and evaluation, the equivalents of phases III and IV of the RIP. Although phases III and IV are critical, my experience suggests that implementation and change management become less of an issue if the following are true:

- *A strong business case has been built around a CBI in phase I (as in the case of NuPlant where the subtext of the CBI was survival of the plant). And, the task of evaluation is much easier if you and the client have agreed upfront on the CBI and the specific gaps in results.*

- *The analysis in phase II has dug deep, past the predictable smokescreens (e.g., "human relations training for supervisors") to uncover the root causes that make trying to do a job a living hell.*

- *The proposed changes get at issues that are near and dear to individual performers. I have seen few cases where performers resist changes that involve removing barriers to their success in the workplace. My suspicion is that many times too big a deal is made out of anticipated resistance to change. All the change management artillery needed to overcome resistance to change may be the result of, or a cover for, phases I and II not being done well.*

Recommendations

Take another look at the project milestones to see how far Bert has come (figure 3-17).

The final recommendations of Bert and his team are summarized in table 3-4. They are shown in this table as brief recommendation "headlines,"

which are easy to manage for presentation (ATR 3-42). The full recommendations are given in appendix B.

According to Rummler 3-42

Anticipating that the client might pressure him to prioritize individual recommendations ("Well, if we were going to implement only two of your recommendations, which would you suggest?"), Bert has presented the client with two implementation scenarios—ideal and crash. His intent is to guide the client to choose between the two alternative scenarios to preclude the possibility that the client might try to pick and choose among the individual recommendations. As it turned out, this strategy worked well for Bert at NuPlant.

Moving from left to right across the table, you can see the 10 major recommendations that the team is making and then an indication of which four recommendations are deemed *critical* to effecting an immediate turnaround of NuPlant. Next, the table suggests the *ideal* sequence of implementation of the 10 recommendations. Where two recommendations have the same

Figure 3-17. NuPlant project milestones.

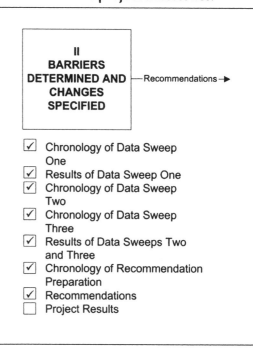

Table 3-4. Summary of recommendations and sequence of implementation.

	Recommendation	Critical to an Immediate Turnaround?	Ideal Implementation Sequence	Crash Implementation Sequence
1.	Measure performance by material yield and net productivity.	No	One	Five
2.	Install a data system that will provide a production system "memory" function.	Yes	Two	Two
3.	Provide feedback to all production supervision • frequently • in a cumulative format • on production, late shipping, plant chargebacks, and rework • in a way that can yield information to manage the production system	No	Three	Four
4.	Change production supervision responsibilities.	Yes	Four	Three
5.	Change the scheduling system.	Yes	One	One
6.	Alter the basis for determining certain indirect labor budgets.	No	Six	—
7.	Change current start-up procedures.	Yes	Two	Two
8.	Provide decision guides for supervisors and general supervisors on shutting down lines.	No	Five	—
9.	Train production supervision in new responsibilities.	No	Four	Three
10.	Train production supervisors and general supervisors in selected topics.	No	Seven	—

ranking, the intent is that they will be implemented simultaneously. Note that the numbers do not indicate priority but merely the recommended sequence of implementation, given that not all recommendations will be (nor should be) implemented simultaneously. Considering that following an ideal sequence is unlikely given the pressure on NuPlant, the rightmost column indicates a recommended *crash* implementation sequence. Again, the numbers indicate sequence, not priority. The crash sequence is based on the assumption that the client may run out of energy or resources as it tries to do the right thing, in which case the client should definitely do the items in the crash sequence and in that order. If the client follows the crash implementation sequence, it will address all those items critical to a turnaround (ATR 3-43).

Bert's set of recommendations demonstrates breadth and comprehensiveness. They range from a radically new measurement system for the division and NuPlant to a rethinking of production management roles to job aids and training for production supervisors. Truly, he is offering a solution set that adheres to the tenets of *serious* performance analysis and consulting.

The basic template that Bert uses on performance improvement projects like NuPlant is the anatomy of performance based on the premise that organizations are systems. Using the AOP template allows Bert to see where disconnects exist in the client organization system, preventing the organization from effectively and efficiently producing the desired results.

Bert's observations are never random or arbitrary, never brainstormed or just pulled out of a hat. They are all part of helping the client organization system produce the desired results. Therefore, for the organization to achieve its results goals (and for Bert to meet his goal of assisting the organization), the organization *must* implement the vast majority of his recommendations. And, they must be implemented as a whole or as a solution set, as mentioned earlier. Bert's presentation emphasizes that the recommendations constitute a whole, which needs to be implemented as a package to achieve the desired result. Figure 3-18 demonstrates where each recommendation impacts a critical component of the organization system or AOP (ATR 3-44).

More comments on the organization of the recommendations can be found in the introduction to appendix B.

The following sections address each of Bert's recommendations. You can find a detailed description of each recommendation, frequently with prototypes, in appendix B.

According to Rummler 3-43

How many recommendations can a client handle without being overwhelmed? Bert settled on a set of 10, which I think is a reasonable number. Using the NuPlant AOP framework makes it possible to present a relatively high number of recommendations in a logical way. But, among performance consultants it seems that there are at least two schools of thought about the number of recommendations you should present to the client.

One school seems to advocate feeding the client a few recommendations at a time, reflecting concern about change management issues and avoiding a situation in which the client feels overwhelmed. I belong to the school that favors presenting the entire set of recommendations at once.

Why? First, Bert was hired to help NuPlant obtain results critical to its survival, and I see his job as providing them with a comprehensive blueprint for doing just that. Presenting some subset of these recommendations makes no sense, because implementing them piecemeal will not accomplish the project goals. Second, the recommendations constitute an integrated, interdependent set of actions, designed to work together to address a complex system problem. To separate them compromises the solution set. No single solution in the set would make a dent in NuPlant's problems. Third, in many cases I like to use the recommendation list as a device to educate the client on what should be done, even though it is doubtful that all the recommendations will be implemented at once. In such cases, I'm taking the opportunity to expand their horizons as to what they could or should do to improve performance. If I am going to continue working with these folks, I have planted a seed about what needs to be done next.

Figure 3-18. Major components of NuPlant's production system and location of recommendations.

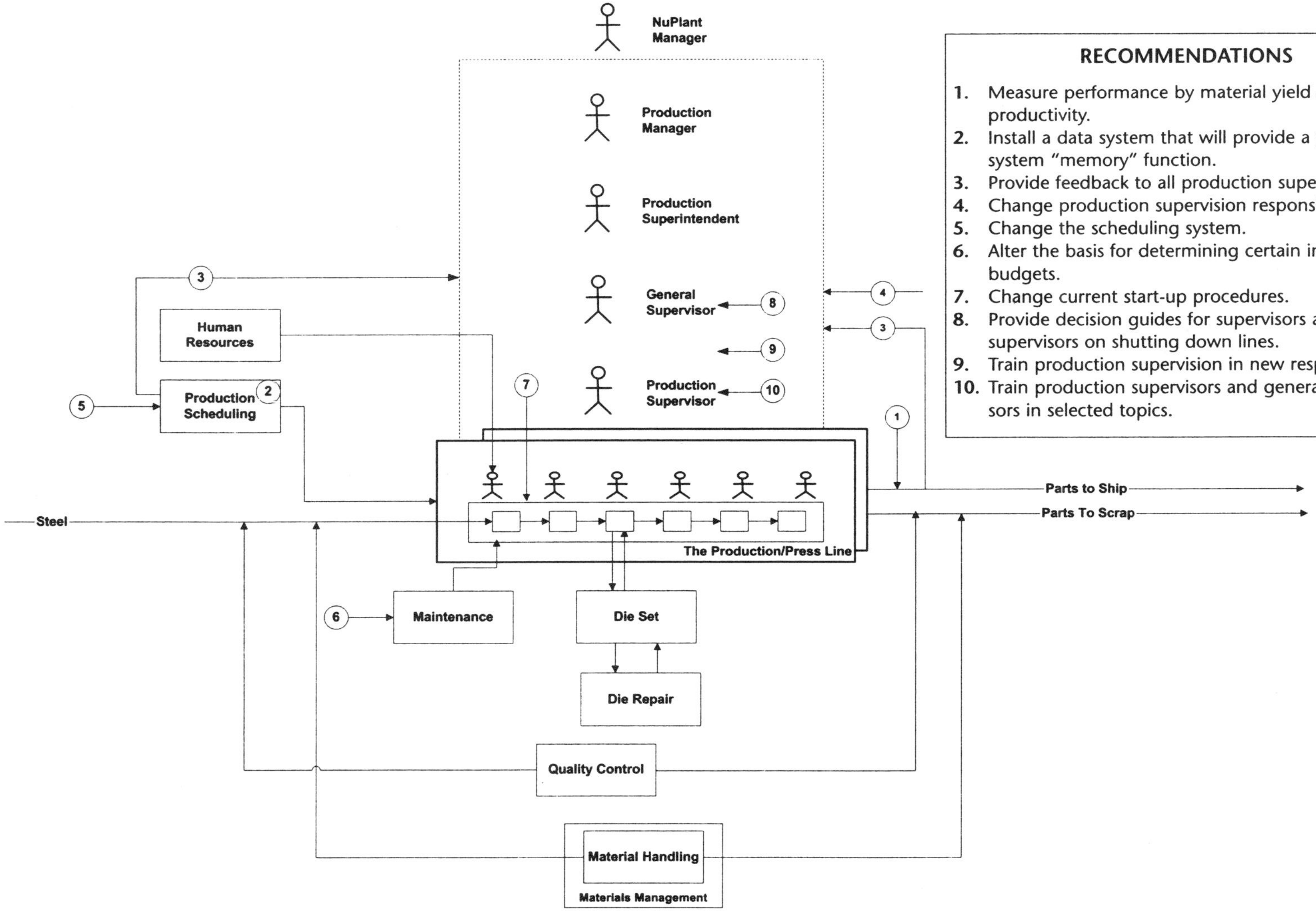

RECOMMENDATIONS

1. Measure performance by material yield and net productivity.
2. Install a data system that will provide a production system "memory" function.
3. Provide feedback to all production supervision.
4. Change production supervision responsibilities.
5. Change the scheduling system.
6. Alter the basis for determining certain indirect labor budgets.
7. Change current start-up procedures.
8. Provide decision guides for supervisors and general supervisors on shutting down lines.
9. Train production supervision in new responsibilities.
10. Train production supervisors and general supervisors in selected topics.

According to Rummler 3-44

If you have educated the client about the anatomy of performance, diagrams such as those in figures 3-14 and 3-18 can help you keep findings and recommendations in a system context and stress the point that implementation of two or three isolated recommendations will not deliver the desired results over the long haul. I've also found that clients can deal with a longer list of recommendations if they can see the logic of how all the recommendations fit together like pieces of a puzzle. The AOP framework provides that logic.

Recommendation #1. Measure performance by material yield and net productivity. (For more detail on this recommendation, see appendix B.) This recommendation appears as #1 in the ideal implementation sequence (table 3-4) (ATR 3-45).

According to Rummler 3-45

This recommendation cuts right to the heart of NuPlant's CBI and addresses a root cause of poor plant and supervisor performance. As you can see in figure B-1 (appendix B), Bert used an effective graphic presentation to support the argument. The recommendation includes specific measures to be adopted and relies on a strong supporting argument, which was aimed at the stamping division, as well as at NuPlant. Bert knew who the decision makers were at both levels and aimed this recommendation at them in the hope that this study might precipitate a badly needed change, which would have to come from the division level. (In fact, it did!)

Recommendation #2. Install a data system that will provide a production system "memory" function. (For more detail on this recommendation, see appendix B.) This recommendation was critical to an immediate plant turnaround and second in either implementation sequence (ATR 3-46).

Recommendation #3. Provide feedback to all production supervision

- frequently
- in a cumulative format
- on production, late shipping, plant charge-backs, and rework
- in a way that can yield information to manage the production system

According to Rummler 3-46

Here, Bert supports a critical recommendation with prototypes—one a data display (table B-2) and the other a tool or job aid (figure B-3). Prototypes like these leave no question as to what is intended by the recommendation and its value. The full recommendation as provided in appendix B also includes a good discussion of how these data should be used to manage productivity.

This recommendation (appendix B) is a mini-lesson in how to design a feedback system. First, it sets out the criteria for an effective feedback system. Then it presents a good example of a single feedback document that tracks direct labor/OS (off-standard), yield, delayed costs, downtime, and overtime. It prescribes where these data should be displayed and the time intervals for updating and reviewing. Finally, it describes how the form can be used to provide feedback on the performance of production supervisors, the line, and support functions.

Recommendation #4. Change production supervision responsibilities. (For more detail on this recommendation, see appendix B.) This recommendation illustrates several points. First, it clarifies the roles of three levels of management. It makes explicit the unique value-add of each level of management. Table B-4 spells out the measures of performance, timeframe, and resources for each level. Then table B-5 specifies the responsibilities of each level and how they should be measured. Finally, figure B-4 even proposes the information flow and emphasis for each level (ATR 3-47).

Recommendation #5. Change the scheduling system (ATR 3-48). (For more detail on this recommendation, see appendix B.)

Recommendation #6. Alter the basis for determining certain indirect labor budgets. (For more detail

> ### According to Rummler 3-47
>
> **W**ith this recommendation, Bert provides another example of how he goes beyond a general recommendation ("change production supervision responsibilities") to provide specific detail on exactly what the changes should be.

> ### According to Rummler 3-48
>
> **Y**ou may remember that I noted earlier that finding B4 included a schematic (figure A-2) of the "is" scheduling system at NuPlant. This recommendation is built around a similar schematic (figure B-5) of a proposed "should" scheduling system. A comparison of the two schematics makes it very clear where the critical differences lie.

on this recommendation, see appendix B.) Here Bert offers a detailed recommendation built on a solid understanding of the issue and what's required to address it. This recommendation has profound long-term significance for both NuPlant and the stamping division.

Recommendation #7. Change current start-up procedures (ATR 3-49). (For more detail on this recommendation, see appendix B.)

Recommendation #8. Provide decision guides for supervisors and general supervisors on shutting down lines. (For more detail on this recommendation, see appendix B.) Once again, Bert provides a

> ### According to Rummler 3-49
>
> "But, we've always done it this way!" Performance consultants hear this line all the time from their clients. Bert, with his "fresh eyes," could see where a relatively simple change in a personnel procedure, fully under the control of NuPlant, could provide immediate and significant relief from the pressure-cooker environment of the production supervisor. When Bert and his team pointed out that the existing startup procedure made no sense and was counterproductive, agreement and change were swift.

prototype job aid (figure B-6) that could make a big difference in controlling a costly problem.

Recommendation #9. Train production supervision in new responsibilities. (For more detail on this recommendation, see appendix B.) This recommendation calls for training the production supervisors on their new responsibilities as outlined in recommendation #4.

Recommendation #10. Train production supervisors and general supervisors in selected topics (ATR 3-50). (For more detail on this recommendation, see appendix B.)

> ### According to Rummler 3-50
>
> **T**his recommendation is important for a couple of reasons. First, it addresses some important opportunities. But, almost as important is the fact that this project started with a request for training for production supervisors. It would be prudent for Bert to recommend some training. This is not the training the plant had initially requested ("human relations"), but it is, nevertheless, relevant training for supervisors in support of Bert's other recommendations.

Project Results

As you can see from Bert's progress through the project milestones (figure 3-19), he's concluded phase II of the RIP.

In accordance with the recommendations of the performance consulting team, NuPlant immediately began to

- change production supervision responsibilities and provide necessary training in the new roles
- upgrade the production scheduling system and change the ground rules for production supervisors' interaction with scheduling staff
- provide recommended feedback to production supervision
- develop decision guides for production supervision on shutting down lines
- modify line start-up procedures

Figure 3-19. NuPlant project milestones.

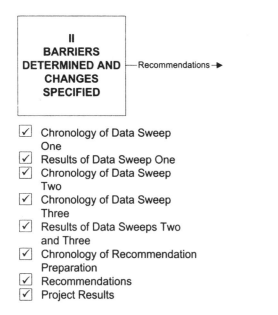

☑ Chronology of Data Sweep One
☑ Results of Data Sweep One
☑ Chronology of Data Sweep Two
☑ Chronology of Data Sweep Three
☑ Results of Data Sweeps Two and Three
☑ Chronology of Recommendation Preparation
☑ Recommendations
☑ Project Results

At the same time, the stamping division made an exception to the indirect labor standard for NuPlant, freeing up additional critical resources for maintenance and material handling. Within six months of implementing these changes, NuPlant was the number two plant in the stamping division (as measured by direct labor cost, scrap, and delivery to schedule), and the relationship between production supervisors and their direct reports was considered "normal."

Ultimately, the study prompted the stamping division to modify its indirect labor formula to take into account individual plant realities. Additionally, the division changed plant productivity metrics to capture yield. The study formed the basis of a fundamental redesign of the roles of the production supervisors and general supervisors within Big Auto worldwide (ATR 3-51).

Final Report Postscript

The following is an excerpt from the introduction to the project final report:

"Implicit in the request for the study was the assumption that the production supervisor was a key factor in, if not part of, the cause of these various problems. It was also implied

---

According to Rummler 3-51

This project was a rewarding one for Bert and his team. In addition to making a significant impact on the overall performance of NuPlant, the project liberated the production supervisors from a horrendous human performance system and "acquitted" them of charges that they had bad attitudes and were the cause of poor plant performance.

---

that the supervisors' behavior and attitude would most likely require changing through some form of training. These were reasonable assumptions, given the data available."

As you see, the final report (appendixes A and B) presents findings and recommendations that do not support NuPlant's initial assumption about the role of supervisory attitudes in poor plant productivity. But, because the question of supervisor attitude was so central to the initiation of the study, Bert and his associates felt it necessary to address this topic directly, but at the end of the final report (ATR 3-52).

According to Rummler 3-52

Many serious performance consultants—myself included—subscribe to a behavioral view of the world that says that attitude is an inference based on observed behavior. This behavior is usually (certainly, in the case of NuPlant production supervision) the result of a punishing human performance system. In the NuPlant case study, the punishing HPS emanated from the negative consequences experienced by production supervisors when their direct labor measure was in the red.

A reminder: The objective of this case study was to demonstrate what serious performance consultants do, not how they do it. I wanted to give the reader a feel for what is involved in a sizeable performance consulting project and a look at the types of findings and recommendations involved in *serious* performance improvement.

CHAPTER 3 HIGHLIGHTS

1. You watched over Bert's shoulder as he tackled the case of NuPlant, which was the poorest performing plant in the stamping division of Big Auto. The project started with an assumption that production supervisors' "attitudes" toward hourly employees was a significant factor in poor plant performance.

2. For his performance analysis, Bert relied upon the results improvement process (RIP). The case study covers the first two phases of the RIP:
   - I. Desired Results Determined and Project Defined
   - II. Barriers Determined and Changes Specified

3. During phase I, the project definition moved from "human relations training for first-line production supervisors" to "A Study of the Effectiveness of Production Supervision." The critical business issue for the project became plant productivity.

4. The engagement model used during the first two phases of the project was the consultant doing the work with input from the staff of NuPlant.

5. Phase II of the project took 12 weeks to complete and required three data sweeps.

6. The performance analysis of NuPlant productivity by Bert led to 17 findings, which are summarized in this chapter and fully explicated in appendix A.

7. The findings resulted in 10 recommendations to improve the supervisors' and plant performance. The recommendations are discussed in this chapter and fully explicated (along with prototypes of job aids and so forth) in appendix B.

8. Phase II (and the project) concluded with the submission of a detailed report to the NuPlant general manager and his staff (appendixes A and B).

9. Phases III and IV were implemented by the staff of NuPlant without Bert's assistance.

10. NuPlant adopted the majority of Bert's team's recommendations. Within six months of commencing implementation of the recommendations, NuPlant was the number two plant in the stamping division (as measured by direct labor cost, scrap, and delivery to schedule), and the relationship between production supervisors and their direct reports was considered "normal" for the division.

11. In addition to improvement in the performance of NuPlant, the study prompted changes in various stamping division management practices and became the basis of a fundamental redesign of the roles of the production supervisors and general supervisors within Big Auto worldwide.

4

Case Study Debrief

Now you've seen a pretty detailed example of what is meant by the term *serious performance analysis.* In this chapter you'll revisit the project and drill down on these topics:

- the way Bert conducted the NuPlant project
- reasons why NuPlant is one of my all-time favorite performance improvement projects
- some shortcomings of the NuPlant project
- generalizations performance consultants can take from the NuPlant project to any organization they are trying to improve
- The scalability of the anatomy of performance (AOP) framework and the results improvement process (RIP)
- The relationship of the AOP framework to the topics of culture and leadership

NuPlant Project Review

This review of Bert's work on the NuPlant project addresses three main topics: the application of the RIP, the project engagement model, and the application of the AOP framework.

Application of the Results Improvement Process (RIP)

To refresh your memory, figure 4-1 presents the phases of the RIP.

Bert accomplished all his phase I objectives. He was able to establish a critical business issue (beyond the initial request for "human relations training for production supervisors") and identify areas of results gaps, define a project to close those gaps, and generate an acceptable proposal.

The manner in which phase I was conducted was fairly typical. Bert had collected background information on the company, plant, and the request before his first visit to NuPlant. He was not able to identify specific numbers (current and desired) for the results areas in phase I, but that's not unusual for this type of project. He visited the plant site and probably made a few follow-up calls before beginning work on the project plan and proposal. Internal consultants usually have an advantage at this stage of a project, in that they should have more background initially and

Figure 4-1. Review of the results improvement process.

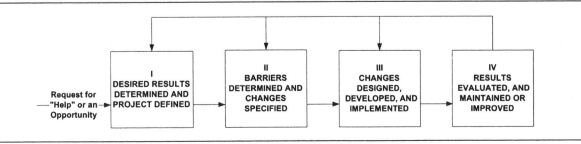

easier access to additional information on the situation.

After his visit to NuPlant, Bert had to make some key assumptions or hypotheses about the situation, project objective, and project scope, which were reflected in his project plan and proposal ("Study of the Effectiveness of Production Supervision" rather than "Training Needs Analysis"). As it turned out, his assumptions were good enough to get the proposal accepted. And, his hypotheses about the relationship between supervisor "attitudes" and plant productivity were accurate enough that his plan for conducting phase II was on target (According to Rummler [ATR] 4-1).

According to Rummler 4-1

Bert never explicitly mentioned evaluation during phase I of the NuPlant project. Nevertheless, the foundation of project evaluation, which is done formally in phase IV of the RIP, is laid in phase I, and I want to stress how important it is that this be done correctly.

Why is evaluation even necessary? It's needed to

- determine if you made a difference. You are in the business of improving results. Did you?
- demonstrate that clients received their money's worth. Did they?
- learn from your successes and failures. Did your intervention work? If not, why not? What else is required to close the gap in results? What can be learned to make you more effective next time?

If you are serious about performance improvement, then you are serious about evaluation. If you are serious about evaluation, you cannot exit phase I without establishing a CBI and related results improvement areas. At a minimum during phase I, you should identify results improvement areas and metrics, if not specific "is" and "should" data. If you have not done this and are then called upon to justify project cost and effort after the fact—you are in trouble. Avoid that ugly situation by establishing a CBI (ATR 4-2).

According to Rummler 4-2

I always want the CBI clear before I leave phase I because it assures me that I am working on something of value to the organization and that I can expect the support necessary for implementation of project recommendations.

In phase II, Bert accomplished what he set out to do, which was to

- learn the NuPlant "is" AOP including where NuPlant fits in the larger Big Auto system and the links among the production supervisors, production processes, and NuPlant productivity
- assess the NuPlant "is" AOP against the "should" AOP template
- find misalignments and evaluate their impact on the gap in results
- make recommendations to bring NuPlant into alignment and close the gaps in results

During this phase, Bert adhered to the tenets of *serious* performance analysis, including the following:

- He followed an effective, systematic process for conducting the analysis (i.e., testing the initial hypotheses).
- He determined through interviewing and close observation the detailed reality of the HPS for certain key positions he had identified, so that the root causes of undesired behavior could be understood and corrected.
- He identified an exemplary performer (Old Plant) to establish the difference between "is" and "should" performance and the cause.
- He relied on hard performance data to test hypotheses and support conclusions and recommendations.
- He conducted a comprehensive analysis of all factors that may be contributing to the gap in results.
- He specified a comprehensive solution set to address all significant factors that impacted the gap in results.

- He developed prototypes of key recommended solutions in order to illustrate their scope and value.
- He organized recommended changes to meet various client needs and priorities.

Bert definitely ended up where he needed to be in terms of findings and recommendations. He was able to build powerful prototypes so the client organization could carry out phase III without his assistance.

Bert did not participate in phase III. The original contract was for a study that encompassed phases I and II only. Bert had provided the necessary roadmap for improving plant performance, and the client believed it could take it the rest of the way—and it did (ATR 4-3).

According to Rummler 4-3

Bert felt comfortable handing the reins over to the client at the conclusion of phase II. I think a major reason why this worked at NuPlant was because a great sense of urgency existed. Resistance to change was not an issue. In fact, failure to change was the issue facing every employee, from plant manager to hourly worker. There was a high level of commitment to instituting change in the plant, and it was abundantly clear that the division was willing to provide the necessary resources. Implementation was not an issue. That is a wonderful position for Bert or any performance consultant to be in, but it is not the norm. Many situations require the performance consultant to guide the client through phase III—implementation.

Bert was not involved in phase IV either. The client did not carry out a formal evaluation of the project, but there was no doubt that the significant change in plant performance over the next six months was attributable to the changes made in accordance with Bert's recommendations. The client knew it had gotten its money's worth from Bert's study and from the subsequent internal changes.

The NuPlant case study is a good example of how the CBI can serve as a project beacon to keep everyone focused on the objective even though it

does not lead to a formal evaluation process that yields precise numbers to document the benefits of closing a gap in results (ATR 4-4).

Review of Engagement Models

Four basic engagement models for executing the RIP were discussed in the Introduction and depicted in figure I-2. They are:

A. The work in all four phases is done primarily by the performance consultant with input from members of the client organization.

B. The work in the first two phases is done primarily by the consultant with input from members of the client organization, and the last two phases are carried out by the client organization with little or no input from the consultant.

C. The work in the first two phases is done primarily by the consultant with input from members of the client organization, and the last two phases are carried out primarily by the client organization under the leadership of the consultant.

D. The work in all four phases is led by the consultant working with employees of the client organization, who usually are organized in teams or taskforces (ATR 4-5).

In the case of NuPlant, the work in the first two phases was done primarily by the consultant with input from members of the client organization consistent with models A, B, and C. This decision was dictated by two things: the time pressure to get a roadmap in place as soon as possible and the lack of available internal resources to participate on a team. If the project had included phases III and IV, Bert would have involved NuPlant personnel at whatever level could be tolerated under the circumstances, following model C or D.

Suppose the situation at NuPlant had been such that plant staff was available to work as a team led by Bert. How would that have worked? Bert's value wouldn't have been his process-consulting skills, although he has those. Bert's contribution was a robust analysis process—the results improvement process—and framework—the anatomy of performance—and related templates,

According to Rummler 4-4

You hear so much about evaluation in the field of performance consulting, yet it is not unusual that formal evaluation is not a part of a project.

Here is some reality around evaluating performance improvement interventions: Even with the best results data you can get, if you are working to improve the performance of organization units such as plants, stores, branches, and so forth, myriad other variables are at play. These confounding variables make it difficult for you to prove the value of your intervention.

For example, our friend Bert was involved in a massive redesign of a retail store management system at one point in his career. The changes were introduced during the quarter prior to a significant two-year recession that affected the entire retail industry. Consequently, he was unable to show any big jump in revenues or earnings as a result of the new system. And even numbers on management turnover were suspect because of the general business environment. Bert was able to show, however, that the client took less of a dip in earnings than its competitors and actually gained market share during the two-year period. Client management concluded that the new management system (with its new roles and responsibilities, better and more timely information, decision-making tools, and management training) was the major contributor to the gain in market share, which subsequently translated into major dollars.

Sometimes the client doesn't want highly visible evidence of closing a gap. Bert was involved in another situation where a general manager said, "I don't want any clear cost savings data identified. If the division managers see that, they will reduce my budget by that amount next year. Let's agree on some indicators in my unit so just you and I will know we have improved performance."

Few people in the real (business) world undertake an initiative that is sufficiently marginal at the outset that they feel the need to "prove" it. (As one corporate vice president said, "Sure, I'd like $300,000 to undertake this project—and another $35,000 to evaluate whether my idea made any difference or not. In my dreams!") Few real-world problems lend themselves to a classic experimental design with a single experimental variable and all other variables controlled for. It is rare indeed that a performance consultant will be able to generate clear, replicable performance data.

So, if it is so difficult to get reliable data around a performance intervention, how can you as a serious performance consultant show the value of your work? The key is to start with a sound CBI and specific gaps in results. If you start with that stake in the ground, there will always be fewer potential issues in phase IV.

According to Rummler 4-5

I think it's important for performance consultants to know that they have options as they plan how to improve performance. It is not a given in my book that the first thing you do is form a team. Participation of client personnel on performance improvement teams can be beneficial in terms of involving critical expertise and getting buy-in on subsequent changes. In that case, the value-add of the performance consultant isn't "meeting facilitation," but rather the deployment of a serious performance analysis methodology as described in the Introduction and chapter 2 and demonstrated in the NuPlant case study (chapter 3).

which he brought to the situation. He would have provided the team with a methodology/process and templates for getting agreement on the CBI and project scope, deliverables, evaluation, and methodology. In this case, Bert wouldn't provide the answers or the content, but he would guide the team as it formulated questions and followed a process for getting the answers. With the aid of the framework and templates, he would be helping them see what they should be looking for and where to look.

Bert could use a couple of approaches to accomplish these goals. He could work with the team to determine which questions to ask by

- having the team members gather the data and then work with them to analyze the data

and reach conclusions, using Bert's process and templates
- having Bert gather the data and then work with the team to analyze the data and reach conclusions, using his process and templates (ATR 4-6)

According to Rummler 4-6

The point here is that the key to improving results always relies on a robust performance analysis framework (the AOP) and process (the RIP), regardless of the particular engagement model.

Application of the AOP Framework

Chapter 2 (Performance Analysis Framework and Process) introduced the AOP and identified several things Bert was going to learn about NuPlant using the AOP template. He was going to use the AOP template to

- understand how NuPlant worked
- identify where NuPlant deviated from his "should" view of organization effectiveness and where improvements could be made ("is" versus "should" comparison)

Bert stuck to his plan. He used the AOP framework to generate initial hypotheses about the cause of NuPlant's results gap. These hypotheses guided the development of the phase II project plan. He then developed an AOP picture for NuPlant (customized the generic AOP), which helped him identify the key components of the NuPlant AOP. Next, he compared the NuPlant AOP against an exemplary performer (Old Plant) to see critical differences in key components. He was able to identify several critical differences, namely a superior scheduling system, availability of performance data, and an early-quit system that strongly influenced the HPS of hourly and supervisory personnel.

He carried out a rigorous analysis of why production supervisors did certain things that ran counter to the best interests of NuPlant. For example, the production supervisors would keep lines running even though they were not making "ship" parts, just "scrap" parts because of production problems. Nevertheless, as long as the line was producing parts—even of shoddy quality—the production supervisor would be able to stay "in the black" for the shift.

Finally, Bert used the NuPlant AOP as the framework for organizing his findings—the gaps between the "is" AOP and the "should" AOP template. And, the AOP guided Bert as he made recommendations—the actions required to close the gaps between "is" and "should" (ATR 4-7).

According to Rummler 4-7

The AOP application in the NuPlant project is a nice illustration of the power and utility of a sound theory and framework. It guided Bert and will guide you in carrying out performance analysis. You have seen how this basic framework has logically spawned a handful of templates and tools to help performance consultants do their job.

A recent trend described in several publications in the field of performance consulting is a disturbing one. The authors are merely offering collections of performance analysis and improvement models and tools without any unifying or underlying theory or framework. They look like an attempt to define performance consulting by the tools that might be used—a set of tools in search of a unifying theory.

 Top 10 Reasons Why the NuPlant Project Is My Favorite

10. It reinforces the necessity of pushing beyond a request for training to identify a CBI and results gaps.
9. The performance consultant must dig into the nitty-gritty of the business to understand the economics of the business, the operating system, the management system, and the reality of the HPS of key performers.
8. The plant is both a system and part of a larger super-system.
7. The power of fresh eyes is demonstrated: By applying an analytic framework and process and

by viewing the problem with professional distance, Bert could quickly identify several performance problems leading to results gaps.

6. Bert's approach brought about significant improvements in results (and plant working conditions) in six months. How easy it would be for the situation at NuPlant to have been interpreted by a consultant as a "culture" or "interpersonal" problem! But, no culture change or team-building exercises could have uncovered and corrected the multitude of system issues that were barriers to plant productivity.

5. Performance and results are the outcome of a system of factors, as described by the AOP. NuPlant illustrated that the causes of poor performance are many and varied.

4. Bert recommended a comprehensive solution set, demonstrating that there is no silver bullet.

3. The organization must be aligned in two directions: vertically (aligning the roles and responsibilities of three levels of production management) and horizontally (bringing support processes, such as plant engineering, material handling, and human relations, into alignment with the primary production process).

2. Bert identified causes and solutions at all three system levels: job, process, and organization.

1. And the number one reason the NuPlant project probably is my favorite performance improvement project of all time is because it illustrates nearly all of the most important aspects of performance analysis and consulting.

A Critique of the NuPlant Project

No project is perfect, the NuPlant project included. It was flawed in only a couple of respects. For example, specific results improvement goals for productivity and scrap were finally established with the client during phase II. Nevertheless, they were never formally documented and made part of the final report. No attempt was made by Bert to set a goal for direct labor/off-standard (DL/OS) because the phase II analysis showed it to be an inappropriate measure. Although the NuPlant manager was not interested in having the results gap information made public, it did serve as the target for the implementation of the recommendations.

There was no opportunity to demonstrate the use of data to determine the sources of performance variability in the plant (i.e., which day, shift, line, production supervisor, or part). Consequently, it was not possible to identify exemplary performance within the plant. Such data analysis, though, is a key technique in conducting *serious* performance analysis. The lack of an opportunity to perform such an analysis on this project was a function of the poor performance tracking system in NuPlant, the improvement of which was a major project recommendation.

Project Generalizations (ATR 4-8)

The Job Level

Many, many individuals are working in human performance systems that approximate that of the NuPlant production supervisors. In fact, the majority of first-line supervisory positions probably bear a profound similarity to this situation. The job expectations are inconsistent, confusing, conflicting, and unclear. Consequences are punishing. Inappropriate results are measured, and useful feedback is nonexistent. Resources and tools are inadequate. Lack of knowledge or skills on the part of the performer may be an issue.

An unfortunate generalization results when an organization has a problem, and some unlucky individual is identified as the cause or "bad guy." It is a sound performance analysis hypothesis that the individual is most likely the victim of a bad HPS and misaligned AOP. The performance problem may be manifest at the performer or job level, but the cause

According to Rummler 4-8

You have learned about many barriers to performance in this case study. Here are some fair questions you might be asking: "How many of the things I have seen in this case are typical and how many are unique to Big Auto? Am I likely to see things like this in other performance consulting projects?" In this section, I offer some points or lessons that can be taken from this project and generalized into sound analysis hypotheses for your future work.

and solution are going to be in the HPS and AOP, proving again that if you "Put a good performer in a bad system, the system wins every time."

Plant or Organization Level

Every organization is likely to have some variation on the misalignments you saw at NuPlant such as

- processes not aligned and at cross-purposes due to strong departmental "silo" behavior
- ineffective or inadequate processes or operating systems, such as the scheduling function at NuPlant
- faulty underlying operating models or algorithms, such as the way indirect labor allowances were calculated at NuPlant

Interplant Organization System

In the case study, you saw that NuPlant was a part of Big Auto's North American Vehicle Operations. At this level, Bert discovered predictable operational "silos"; vertical (silo) deployment of objectives and goals; and a general failure to see and manage the organization(s) as a system.

Performance Planned and Performance Managed

Sadly, almost every organization has misalignments in this area, including

- fragmented, uncoordinated planning
- measurement of inappropriate dimensions of performance
- unclear management roles and responsibilities
- lack of "memory" in the system and therefore no organizational learning

Initial Problem Statement

The problem statement that initiated this project ("We need human relations training for our first-line production supervisors") is fairly typical in that the requestor

- is making a major unsubstantiated assumption about a problem
- is describing the unarticulated problem in terms of a solution (training, in this case)

You can take away two important, generalizable lessons here. The first lesson is don't ever accept at face value either a proposed problem or a proposed solution. Your clients may try to steer you toward such diagnoses as poor attitude, low morale, ineffective communications, or a hostile organizational culture. Don't buy it. Neither should you automatically accede to proposed solutions such as, "We need training on . . ." Always respond to such proposed problems and solutions with questions:

- What tells you that this problem exists?
- What is not happening that you want to happen?"

Use this line of questioning to establish a results chain leading to a CBI and identification of specific gaps in results that must be closed.

The second generalizable lesson is to know the performance context—the anatomy of performance—behind every request for help. Performers do not operate in a vacuum; they are always in a system. Knowledge of this system enables the performance consultant to establish a link to a gap in results and discover the root causes of the poor performance of the individual and the organization.

Draining the Swamp

When you see a situation like the one at NuPlant, an obvious question is, "Why don't these people fix this mess?" Here are some generalizable observations on why this doesn't happen:

- Managers don't understand that they are part of a system and that the cause and solution of most of their problems lie in that system.
- Managers are trapped in their silos through a combination of system suboptimizing goals, measures, and consequences (i.e., their HPSs). This seriously reduces their chances of having any system perspective. This lack of perspective can clearly be seen in the NuPlant project by contrasting the findings and recommendations of Bert's team with the observations of NuPlant managers in table 3-3.

- No one has the energy to make the necessary changes. Everyone is paddling as hard as they can to keep their heads above water. It's hard to remember your objective is to drain the swamp, when you are up to your waist in alligators!

- Especially in manufacturing settings, individual heroics may prevail even if everyone in a unit knows that a given task or objective is pointless or impossible. But to point this out may be viewed as a sign of weakness, so people just tough it out.

- For lack of a better term, system stupidity may be at work. At Big Auto, for example, every year the individual plants negotiate next year's budget with the stamping division. And, each year, the division tightens the budget a little bit more. In the case of NuPlant, the belt was tightened too far to provide resources (plant engineering) to support the high level of automation. Rather than admit a mistake and make a midyear adjustment in the NuPlant budget, the division replaced the incumbent plant manager of several years and quietly provided the NuPlant manager with significant budget relief. The division waited for the plant manager to fail and then made the changes necessary for success. As a result of management moves like this, the plant limped along, barely meeting production expectations, and the underlying, systemic issues went unaddressed (ATR 4-9).

According to Rummler 4-9

All these lessons roll up into the most important generalization of all—the anatomy of performance. This view of the factors impacting performance and results applies to every organization under the sun, big or small, private or public, high-tech or low-tech, service or product. Three things you should never forget:

1. Every organization is a system.
2. Every individual is in a human performance system.
3. There are no exceptions to #1 and #2. You can take that to the bank!

Scalability of Models

Both the AOP framework and the RIP are scalable. That is, they apply to results improvement projects of any size.

The AOP framework applies to any organizational entity, ranging from a corporation to a department to a work unit. It works in any situation where there is a collection of people and processes that are expected to produce a defined result. Regardless of the size of the entity, the AOP template lays out the major variables that impact the results of that unit.

Likewise, the four-phase RIP applies to any size results improvement project. A practical way to think of the size, scope, or scale of a results improvement project is by the major links in the results chain:

- A project addressing a critical job issue (CJI) will be relatively small in scope and significance.
- A project addressing a critical process issue (CPI) will be considerably larger in scope and will have the potential for significant results.
- A project addressing a critical business issue (CBI) will necessarily have wide scope, ultimately involving several CPIs having a profound impact on organization results.

Table 4-1 summarizes how the RIP applies equally to projects at the CJI, CPI, and CBI levels. The first three rows of the matrix list the phases, objectives, and outputs of the generic RIP.

The objective and outputs of each phase remain the same regardless of the scope of the results improvement project. The bottom three rows of the matrix summarize the focus and major activities of each phase of the RIP for projects at each of the three major points on the results chain.

No matter how broad or narrow the scope of the project, the performance consultant should proceed through all four phases of the RIP. Let me illustrate using NuPlant as an example.

Table 4-1. The results improvement process and project scope.

		PROCESS PHASES			
		Phase I: Desired Results Determined and Project Defined	Phase II: Barriers Determined and Changes Specified	Phase III: Changes Designed, Developed, and Implemented	Phase IV: Results Evaluated and Maintained or Improved
RESULTS IMPROVEMENT PROCESS	Phase Objectives	• Determine if there is a significant results gap to be closed • Determine the feasibility of closing the results gap • Prepare a project plan for closing the results gap	• Identify factors that negatively impact the results gap • Specify the changes required to close the results gap	• Design, develop, and implement the interventions necessary to close the results gap and ensure continuous improvement	• Determine if the results gap has been closed and, if not, determine what must be done to do so
	Phase Outputs	• Project plan • Engagement model • Agreement to proceed • Project charter	• Recommendations for change that will close the results gap • Macro design and implementation plan	• Implemented changes	• Sustained results
PROJECT SCOPE	Critical Job Issue (CJI)	• Establish CJI • Establish job results gap • Expand to CPI, if possible	• Job focus with understanding of relevant AOP • Specify changes to improve job results • Expand to CPI, if possible	• Design and implement changes to improve job results	• Evaluate impact on CJI
	Critical Process Issue (CPI)	• Establish CPI • Establish process results gap • Expand to CBI, if possible	• Process focus with understanding of relevant AOP • Specify changes to improve process results • Expand to CBI, if possible	• Design and implement changes to improve process results	• Evaluate impact on CPI
	Critical Business Issue (CBI)	• Establish CBI • Establish organization results gap	• Maintain organization focus with an understanding of relevant AOP • Specify changes to improve organization results	• Design and implement changes to improve organization results	• Evaluate impact on CBI

Situation One

The CJI is expressed as one of the following:

- Train the production supervisor in troubleshooting press line problems and determining which maintenance section to call.
- Production supervisors don't know how to troubleshoot press line problems.

In phase I, the performance consultant tries to establish specific gaps in results. This is hard to do at the job level because it requires measuring the frequency and length of press downtime. Ideally, the performance consultant can convert the CJI to a CPI. If that can be done, then you are measuring press line or production process performance using such metrics as downtime, productivity, or scrap rates—all or which are assessed routinely by the plant.

Assuming the project stays at the CJI level, in phase II the performance consultant will

- identify exemplary performers and analyze their performance
- determine the factors that impact the results gap established in phase I
- specify the changes necessary to close the results gap

It is also possible that the data gathered in phase II will make a link to a CPI, suggesting that the project be expanded to analyze process performance. In phases III and IV, the performance consultant will design and implement the changes specified and evaluate the impact of the changes on the CJI or the expanded CPI and on the gap in results.

Situation Two

The CPI is expressed as one of the following:

- too much downtime
- scrap rate too high

In phase I, the performance consultant establishes specific gaps in results. This is relatively easy to do because the plant tracks these data continuously. The performance consultant should also test to see if the CPI can be linked to a CBI along with specific gaps in results.

Assuming the project stays at the CPI level, in phase II the performance consultant will:

- identify exemplary-performing press lines and analyze their performance
- determine the factors that impact the results gap established in phase I
- specify the changes necessary to close the results gap

It is also possible that the data gathered in phase II will connect to a CBI, suggesting that the project be expanded to analyze total plant performance. As before, in phases III and IV, the performance consultant designs and implements the changes specified and evaluates the impact of the changes on the CPI or expanded CBI and on the gap in results.

Situation Three

The CBI is expressed as one of the following:

- the plant is missing volume targets
- the plant has low productivity as measured by DL/OS

Similar to situation two, the performance consultant will establish specific gaps in results during phase I. Again, this will be relatively easy to do because the plant tracks these data continuously.

Phases II, III, and IV follow the same procedures as with the CPI. The only difference is that the relevant AOP that is explored may be broader in scope than was the case with the CPI (ATR 4-10).

According to Rummler 4-10

As you can see, phase I of the RIP is critical to determining the proper scope of a project. Always test the issue and see if it can be pushed further up the results chain. Remember, in the NuPlant case, Bert went from an initial "performer" issue to a CJI to a CPI to a CBI, as part of phase I. If your client is reluctant to agree to move the issue up the results chain in phase I, you may be able to generate data in phase II that will convince the client to expand the scope at this later point. The ability of the results improvement process to accommodate such a change in scope at that point is further evidence of its scalability.

The Anatomy of Performance and Culture

Organizational culture is a real, if elusive, phenomenon that must be contended with as part of serious performance analysis. Where does organizational culture fit into the AOP framework? Culture lies in the human performance system that encompasses all the variables that determine how individuals in an organization behave (ATR 4-11).

According to Rummler 4-11

In the current management environment, I think the word culture is frequently used as a smokescreen to avoid addressing more fundamental performance issues. It seems to be the catchall phrase used these days by executives trying to explain why things went wrong. But that aside, I've included my thoughts on culture and its relationship to performance analysis and performance consulting.

Defining Organizational Culture

But, just what is culture? Burke and Litwin (1989) define organizational culture as "the way we do things around here." Schein (1992) writes, "The culture of a group can be defined as a pattern of shared basic assumptions that the group learned as it solved its problems of external adaptation and internal integration, that has worked well enough to be considered valid and, therefore, to be taught to new members as the correct way to perceive, think, and feel in relation to those problems" (ATR 4-12).

In the context of an organization, if one is interested in going beyond *study* of a culture to *an attempt to alter a culture*, you need to understand the phenomenon at the more micro behavioral level than the macro anthropological level. Here is a behavioral view of the phenomenon of culture that pertains to the human performance system (Rummler and Brethower, unpublished notes):

- Anytime two or more individuals interact with one another on a frequent basis, a social relationship or dynamic is set in motion whereby the behavior of one

According to Rummler 4-12

Recently, I encountered the following definition of culture displayed as part of a natural history display at the University of Arizona: "To an anthropologist, culture is a 'shared system of beliefs, values, and traditions that shape a person's behavior and perception of the world.'" That definition or view of culture is sufficient for the anthropologist who is interested in studying, analyzing, and classifying the "is" behavior of a social group. That definition, however, does not offer any useful clues as to how to alter the "is" behavior of the social system, and it might lead people down the frustrating path of trying to alter the "is" state by manipulating such abstractions as values and beliefs.

affects (provides input to/has consequences for) the other(s). These relationships constitute a social system. Like any other system, these systems stabilize in a state of equilibrium. Key to this equilibrium is some predictability as to how these individuals will act toward one another in given situations (the norms, rules of the road, "the way we do things around here"). These patterns of predictable behavior, which are called *practices* by some visionaries (Tosti and Jackson, 1989; Lineberry and Carleton, 1999), generalize into values, which, in turn, are frequently generalized into the concept of culture.

- Organizational culture encompasses the prevailing expectation-consequence relationships that exist (per the HPS) in a particular work environment or work social system. It becomes the expectation-consequence fabric of a given society. Culture is a result of the reinforced behavior patterns (practices) within and between groups of individuals who, for whatever reason, must interact.
- Individuals learn these values, or behavior patterns, through explanations of the concept, by observation of the consequences to others, and by the rewards and punishments they experience for specific behaviors they exhibit.

This HPS-centric view speaks to how a culture is formed (i.e., expectation-consequence relationships that form reinforced behavior patterns). If you understand the elements that form a culture, then you have an understanding of what is required to change a culture. This understanding of behavior as the fundamental building block of culture is essential to developing an effective change methodology.

NuPlant's Organizational Culture

When Bert first visited NuPlant, it would have been easy for him to interpret the situation as one of culture; clearly, people were behaving badly toward one another. Remember the rat in the supervisor's lunchbox? Then, when Bert looked at the differences between NuPlant and Old Plant, there seemed to definitely be different plant cultures. Recall the differences between the environments of the respective scheduling departments. (See finding B2b in appendix A.)

Although culture appeared to be a variable in the NuPlant situation, Bert did not see it as the independent or driving variable, but rather as a dependent or resulting variable. Bert's bias was that the behavior of individuals that becomes generalized as culture ("the way we do things around here") in any organization is a function of the underlying system represented by the AOP. Individual behavior is always determined at the HPS level primarily by the expectation-consequence relationship (plus feedback, resources, knowledge/skill, and individual capacity), which, in turn, is determined by the larger organization AOP consisting of the organization's super-system, goals, strategy, business model, processes, systems, structure, and management. *The system is the driving variable, and culture is the dependent or resulting variable.*

No doubt about it: The culture of NuPlant clearly was bad. But, Bert went about changing it by making changes in the underlying, determining system. When it seems that organizational culture may be the cause of a performance or results gap, the following sequence provides a logical approach within the context of the RIP.

Phase I (Desired Results Determined and Project Defined). Determine the CBI and the gap in results that must be closed, as did Bert. This step alone will help put the issue of culture in perspective. Serious performance consulting must start with this crucial first step. Many "culture change" efforts neglect it.

Be aware of cultural issues, but design a project that will first analyze the AOP variables that impact the gap in results (ATR 4-13).

According to Rummler 4-13

Are there times when you would address culture first? Conceivably so, but I haven't encountered such a situation. It is possible that the relationship between senior executives is so acrimonious that you can't get them to agree on a CBI or a gap in results. Under these circumstances, one might be tempted to start the effort with some team building or a management culture change initiative. Nearly always, I have been able to get a senior management team to quickly agree on a CBI and a gap in results, at which point I had something solid to build on. Another consideration: If senior executives are unable to reach agreement on a CBI and gap in results, the key variable you may have to contend with is leadership, not culture.

Phase II (Barriers Determined and Changes Specified). Carry out the analysis of the AOP, in much the same way as Bert did. This analysis will capture all the misalignments impacting the gap in results, including identifying behaviors (à la the HPS) that are counterproductive to the desired results.

Specify the "should" AOP that would close the gap in results. This step includes the specification of new and different behaviors that are necessary to support the "should" expectations, systems, and processes, as well as changes to the HPSs necessary to support these new behaviors. For the most part, the specification of new or different expectations and supporting changes in the HPS variables constitute a blueprint for changing the culture (ATR 4-14).

Phase III (Changes Designed, Developed, and Implemented). Design and implement a comprehensive set of solutions, interventions, or initiatives that, among other things, address the behavior or practice changes required to support the system changes. The project outcome should be a closing of the targeted gap in organization results and a change in organization behavior most likely described as a "culture change."

A Final Word About Culture

Culture is a phenomenon that needs to be considered by the performance consultant, but culture change is never the goal of the serious performance consultant. Closing the gap in results is the goal. The driver in closing the gap in results is the design and implementation of the appropriate "should" AOP, including a "should" HPS that supports the desired individual behavior. In some circumstances it may be necessary to also engage in a broader program of behavior or culture change to support the successful implementation of the "should" AOP. Nevertheless, such an effort must be executed within the context of implementing the "should" AOP and closing the gap in results.

The Anatomy of Performance and Leadership

Leadership was not considered in the NuPlant case study. What is the relationship of leadership to the

AOP? Like organizational culture, leadership is a much published and discussed topic these days. Unlike culture, leadership always has the potential to be a significant variable in the AOP formula for results. Where is leadership in the AOP framework? It appears in the form of the behavior of key executives in the management box of the AOP (see figure 2-3) (AR 4-15).

The distinction made in the literature between management and leadership, which is illustrated in figure 4-2, is a useful one. Both management and leadership are needed at the top of an organization. Management is about getting the necessary AOP in place to achieve the desired organizational results and then fulfilling the roles dictated by the Performance Planned and Performance Managed System (see figure 2-13). Basically, the operating and management systems are in place and working.

Leadership is about setting an appropriate direction or course for the enterprise and getting the troops to effectively follow and implement that course. The notion of leadership is paradoxical because it is often most made apparent by its absence. You only have to spend a day at a site (field office, plant, or store) or a few days at the corporate level to reach the conclusion, "There is no leadership here" (ATR 4-16).

Leadership is relevant to the work of the performance analyst in two ways:

1. the extent to which the current gap in results is a function of leadership
2. the presence of leadership willing and able to ensure successful implementation of the specified changes necessary to close the gap in results

Following are some thoughts on both these points, starting with number 2.

Figure 4-2. Management and leadership algorithm.

Is the Issue Management? Ask These Questions:		Is the Issue Leadership? Ask These Questions:
1. Is the organization system aligned from the super-system level down to the job level? 2. Are the HPSs aligned? 3. Is management doing the necessary aligning?	**Any Business**	1. Are the direction and strategy appropriate? 2. Do employees (and customers and suppliers) know and understand the direction and goals? 3. Do employees (and customers and suppliers) know and understand the strategy? 4. Do employees (and customers and suppliers) have confidence in the direction and strategy? 5. Are employees committed to and supportive of the direction and strategy? 6. Is it clear to employees what they are supposed to do to meet the goals?

According to Rummler 4-16

Management and leadership are both required for sustained results. You and I have seen organizations with great operating and management systems and no leadership. They fail. Conversely, I have seen seemingly great charismatic leaders who manage by relationships but who ultimately fail because they were blind to the need for effective operating and management systems. The algorithm in figure 4-2 can be used to determine if a poor performing organization is suffering from a lack of management, leadership, or both.

Lack of Necessary Change Leadership

This point is being addressed first because, in the final analysis, it is potentially the most critical leadership gap for the performance consultant. For a results improvement project to be successfully implemented, there will need to be management leadership. From the outset of a project—indeed, starting with the decision to propose on a project or not—you need to know if your client will provide the necessary leadership to implement your recommendations. If not, will you be able to garner the necessary leadership from elsewhere in the organization—perhaps from the client's superior, peers, or subordinates (ATR 4-17)?

Management as a Cause of a Results Gap

If the current results gap is at least partly attributable to management, then the issue becomes what is the exact nature of their contribution to the gap. If the issue is an inability to manage, then the performance consultant can usually address this issue through the improvement of the management system—both the design of the management processes or infrastructure and training in the use of the redesigned system. For example, at NuPlant much of the variability in the quality of production management was going to be corrected by the change in the roles of the production management hierarchy, better information for making decisions, and a totally revamped production scheduling system.

If the issue is lack of leadership, either as a cause of the gap or through the leadership's unwillingness to provide the necessary support for implementing subsequent changes, you have a challenge. There is no easy solution.

If you are an external consultant, you need to work closely with people in the internal organization development or organization effectiveness department. They will be able to call on internal resources to support the executive or facilitate the executive's reassignment. If you are an internal consultant, you usually would know the limitations of such an executive in advance and have already lined up the internal resources to take the necessary action.

In the case of NuPlant, Bert was pretty lucky. Lack of leadership at the plant level was not a major contributor to the gap in results, compared to the misalignments in the AOP. The greatest leader in stamping plant history would have had little impact on plant performance, given the overwhelming company-driven system issues. In fact, it appears that the critical leadership issue was at the stamping division level, well out of the scope of Bert's project.

The biggest potential problem was whether the NuPlant manager would exercise the leadership necessary for the implementation of Bert's recommendations. Fortunately for everyone, he did. He publicly embraced the recommendations, drove the necessary changes in the plant, and aggressively lobbied for changes at the division level. Three years later he was promoted to turn around another plant because of his leadership skills. The critical unknown is to what extent he knew how to use the AOP to diagnose the changes that had to be made at NuPlant.

In summary, the leadership issue for the performance consultant is really the *lack* of leadership. It may be part of the reason for the gap in results and it may cause a project to flounder during implementation. I have never seen any convincing evidence that you can change an adult non-leader into a leader. Given that reality, the choices for the performance consultant are to avoid situations where poor leadership is a factor, get help reassigning the non-leader, or minimize the impact of the non-leader by (1) building or modifying systems so as to make results less dependent on the individual, (2) helping peers and subordinates fill the leadership vacuum, or (3) both.

Wrapping up the Case Study

This chapter completes your look back at the NuPlant project. In conclusion, the project

- illustrated the application of the AOP template and the first two phases of the RIP.
- demonstrated a rigorous analysis and the development of a range of recommended changes.
- illustrated a number of points that the performance analyst or consultant can generalize to other results improvement situations.
- reinforced the central tenet of serious performance consulting: Every organization is a system and every individual in an organization is in an HPS.

According to Rummler 4-17

From the get-go, I am always assessing the prospective client's ability to provide change leadership from the moment I first meet him or her. I believe a good client is someone who

- *says "I want this accomplished" and either identifies or agrees to the gap in results that is to be closed*
- *is accountable for the results of the project*
- *will say yes or no to the recommended changes*
- *will drive the implementation of the recommended changes*
- *will judge the success of the project and sign the check*

If the prospective client meets these criteria, he or she most likely will provide the project leadership I seek. If these criteria are not met and I suspect that it is more than likely that the client will "wimp" out on me, I can either bail out of the project, look for another client in the organization, or bet that I'll be able to build the necessary leadership support for implementation from above, around, or under this individual.

Even though the project did not demonstrate the scalability of the AOP and RIP, they are indeed very scalable. Likewise, you saw how the AOP addresses the issues of culture and leadership. Now you should be able to see the potential impact you can have as a serious performance consultant.

CHAPTER 4 HIGHLIGHTS

1. A number of points and lessons from the NuPlant project can be generalized into sound analysis hypotheses for other performance consulting work.

2. Both the AOP framework and the RIP can be effectively scaled to address a critical job issue, a critical process issue, or a critical business issue.

3. Anthropologists have a general definition of culture related to beliefs and values that is adequate for studying cultures. But, to change a culture, it is necessary to go deeper, to understand the behavioral elements that form a culture.

4. Culture is a variable in organization performance. It is not, however, an independent, driving variable, but rather a dependent or resulting variable. Culture is the result of behavior, not the driver of behavior. The behavior of individuals that becomes generalized as culture in an organization is a function of the underlying system represented by the AOP.

5. Both management and leadership are required for sustainable organization results. Leadership is required to set an appropriate direction and to enlist the troops. Management is required to see that the organization system remains aligned, from top to bottom, so that the troops can achieve the desired goal.

6. The performance consultant is concerned about leadership in two ways:

- the extent to which the current gap in results is a function of leadership
- the presence of leadership willing and able to close the gap in results

---

Part Two

The Craft of Serious Performance Consulting

Now it's time to swing the spotlight away from Bert and NuPlant and onto you. The two chapters in Part Two are devoted to the craft of serious performance consulting.

In reality, a performance analysis, such as that demonstrated in the NuPlant case study, is done selectively and in degrees as circumstances permit. Chapter 5 presents guidelines on when to attempt serious performance analysis and when not to—and why. It is geared mainly toward internal consultants, but externals will find strategies and tools that will be valuable in their practices. This chapter also provides an example to show how internal consultants can apply the principles of serious performance consulting in their organizations.

Chapter 6 speaks to serious performance consulting as a craft and a career. It presents a framework for negotiating the serious performance consultant learning curve and offers guidance on how to learn, practice, and grow as a serious performance consultant.

Let's go!

Performance Analysis and the Internal Consultant

The NuPlant case study is an example of a serious performance analysis conducted by Bert, an external consultant. Internal consultants also need to do serious performance analysis, but they face unique challenges when they are attempting to conduct results improvement projects. This chapter describes some of these challenges and presents some ideas and tools to assist the internal consultant in meeting these challenges and making a difference in his or her organizations (According to Rummler [ATR] 5-1).

This chapter opens with a recap of some fundamental assumptions about performance consulting and then discusses some realities of being an internal performance consultant, suggests some notions and tools for overcoming obstacles to internal performance consulting, and then ties these notions together with an example.

Serious Performance Consulting on the Inside

The following are some fundamental points discussed so far that are basic to the discussion of the internal performance consultant. First, the internal performance consultant is usually confronted with the situation depicted in figure 5-1, which was first presented in the Introduction. More often than not, the performance consultant is responding to a request for assistance.

Second, when in this situation, it is essential for the internal performance consultant to have the same AOP mental model Bert employed on the NuPlant project, shown in figure 5-2.

Third, it was established in chapter 4 that the AOP framework and the RIP are scalable; they can be applied to situations initiated at the job, process, or organization level. In the case of NuPlant, the initial problem was stated at the job level, but ultimately was treated as an issue involving all three levels. The ability to scale these models applies equally to the situations faced by the internal consultant.

So, the basic AOP framework and RIP clearly apply to the world of the internal performance consultant. However, there are some organizational realities in the world of the internal performance consultant that distinguish that operating environment from that of the external performance consultant.

The Organizational Reality of the Internal Performance Consultant

The challenges faced by those who strive to carry out serious performance consulting inside their organizations can be daunting. You need to be

Figure 5-1. Typical performance consulting situation.

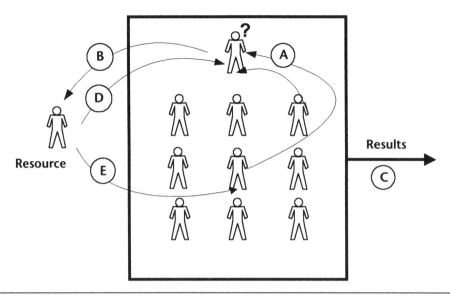

Reprinted with permission of Geary A. Rummler, Performance Design Lab, 2004.

aware of three organizational realities you're likely to come up against.

The Reality of Client Management

The first reality of internal performance consultants is that they have a multilevel challenge in regard to client management, as depicted in figure 5-3. At the highest level (1), they need to establish a long-lasting, strategic partnership with their client organization. On the way to accomplishing that, they must develop strong working relationships with key individual managers (2). However,

Figure 5-2. Bert's anatomy of performance mental model.

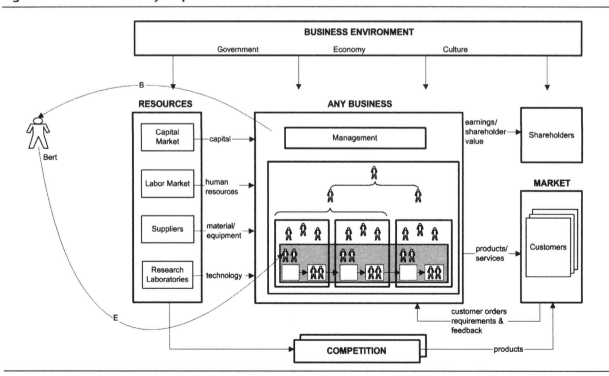

Reprinted with permission of Geary A. Rummler, Performance Design Lab, 2004.

all this is accomplished (or not) by the work they do—the specific improvement projects (3).

Therefore, the ultimate goal of the internal consultant is to deliver valued results and thereby establish a business partnership with client organizations. Internal performance consultants must always be working toward this ultimate goal by delivering results. In addition, they must also be thinking specifically about the project on which they are currently working or considering working.

The Reality of Client Requests

The second reality of internal performance consultants is that they are usually part of a function that is perceived as a solution provider—an entity that is looked to for training, process reengineering, Six Sigma, organization development, and so forth. Whatever the function is called, its name usually does not sound solution-neutral. As a result, most requests for help are going to be in the form of a request for a specific solution. This reality puts two demands on the internal performance consultant:

- It is frequently necessary to push back on, or question, the initial request to determine what the problem is that led the requestor to the conclusion that the requested solution is necessary. It's not easy to be in this position

because you want to be respectful of the requestor and responsive to the request. At the same time, though, you want to deliver results and make a difference. The challenge frequently is to strike a balance between being responsive and doing the right thing.

- It is necessary to continuously educate the client about the factors that impact performance and results and why it is a prudent *business* practice to determine which factors are deficient before implementing a costly and inappropriate solution.

The Reality of Internal Performance Analysis

The third reality is that internal performance consultants are not going to do serious performance analysis on all requests that come their way. In fact, they will do serious performance analysis on only a fraction of those requests. For one reason, many of the projects they are asked to undertake will not impact measurable organization results in any significant way ("I want to expose my people to that new Four-Quadrant personality classification exercise"). If that is the case, there is no value in doing a performance analysis. In such circumstances, your alternatives are to try to talk the requestor into dropping the request or to take a deep breath and just deliver what's requested.

Figure 5-3. The internal performance consulting model.

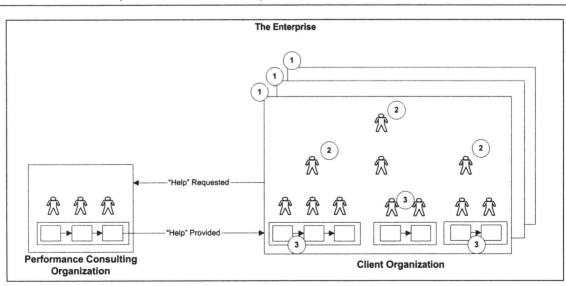

Reprinted with permission of Geary A. Rummler, Performance Design Lab, 2004.

Oftentimes internal performance consultants lack the time and money to carry out a rigorous analysis. In other cases, the requestor is too impatient to wait for a performance analysis or to consider alternative solutions. The key here is for the internal performance consultant to *know when and where to do serious performance analysis.*

Dealing with Organizational Realities as an Internal Consultant

1. Internal performance consultants must be selective about when and where they do serious performance analysis. Balance responsiveness with doing the right thing.
2. Continually educate your clients on the right thing. This means turning every project into a chance to move clients up the AOP learning curve. Be patient. Educating clients is part of a long, continuous selling process.
3. Test every request for help. "What tells you there is a problem?" "Why is this a problem now and not six months ago?" "How will you know when this problem is solved?" Push back gently, but firmly, on the request and the requestors.
4. Accept that, as an internal consultant, you can't always do the right thing (ATR 5-2). After you have tested the request and determined that there is no gap in results or no time or tolerance for analysis, deliver the requested solution in your best professional manner and learn from the experience. Every project is an opportunity for you to educate your client and to learn more about the client's relevant AOP.

According to Rummler 5-2

In my opinion, external *performance consultants should* always *do the right thing for two reasons:* First, doing the right thing is what the client is paying for. Second, external consultants have the ability to walk away from a request for a specific solution. Internal consultants rarely have the luxury to decline such a request.

Tools to Assist the Internal Performance Consultant

This section equips you with some notions and tools that a number of internal performance consultants have found helpful in the wise application of performance analysis. The 10 items are presented individually and then illustrated with an example.

One: An Important Notion

Always keep the internal performance consulting model (figure 5-3) in mind and remember to be thinking on both levels: doing the right thing on any given project while building and maintaining a business partnership with the client. To support this notion, you can think of each client group as an "account" and develop an account strategy for each. Include a statement of the long-term goals for the account, a multiyear plan for how to achieve those goals, and the names of key managers whose support needs to be cultivated along the way. Each project opportunity should be assessed against the account goals and strategy.

Two: Another Notion

Tom Gilbert's (1996) First Leisurely Theorem, which was first published in 1978, reads thus:

$$W = A/B$$

meaning that worthy performance (W) is a function of the ratio of valuable accomplishments (A) to costly behavior (B). This formula can be recast as:

$$W = V \text{ (or R)}/C$$

where W, the worth of doing a project, is a function of the value (V) or results (R) of the project divided by the cost of the project (C). Of course, the goal is for W to be much greater than one.

This equation can be used to approximate a return-on-investment for a project, but perhaps it is more useful as a talking point with a manager when reviewing a request for a solution: "What do you think the return will be on this effort? I can tell you roughly what the cost of the solution will be. Do you think the value will exceed that cost? Could you get a bigger bang for those bucks working on something else? If we go ahead with this, where will the funding come from?" Even a casual discussion around the worth of a solution can cause the requestor to think twice.

Three: A Tool

Build a business case. Figure 5-4 contains a generic business case template that can be applied to any request for help or proposed initiative an internal performance consultant (or external consultant, for that matter) is likely to receive (ATR 5-3). You can use this tool to support the discussion you might start around a solution's worth (as per point two, above).

According to Rummler 5-3

The template in figure 5-4 is quite self-explanatory. However, let me point out that the real business case ("Is this worth doing?") is captured in sections III, V, and VI. One subtlety to note: Often requestors of training (and other interventions) do not take into account the cost of their people undergoing training, the direct cost of the trainees' labor, or the indirect opportunity cost of the trainees being offline. Section V is designed to make both the provider's (your) costs and recipient's costs explicit. Section IV gets into some important non-economic factors that should be evaluated in deciding to move ahead on a project or not. I have seen this document used to cause some requestors to withdraw frivolous or knee-jerk reaction requests and others to understand the size of the investment and the commitment needed from them to make it pay off.

Four: Another Tool

Systematically assess the feasibility of undertaking a performance analysis project. Figure 5-5 contains a checklist and decision guide that can help the performance consultant (internal or external) decide whether to undertake a project. The questions are generic, so you might need to modify them to meet your needs. This tool might be used as part of the strategic assessment that is discussed under point eight, below.

Five: A Notion and Tools

The NuPlant project was an example of a fairly rigorous performance analysis. But, you can make quick and dirty approximations to performance analysis while you are first learning about the request. Figure 5-6 contains some questions that you can ask to quickly identify a gap in results and decide where you can begin some preliminary analysis.

Figure 5-7 contains a worksheet and some questions that can help you quickly test the soundness of the HPS of an alleged "broken" performer. (Note: This tool is most effective when you ask and answer the question around a specific performer and an identified gap between desired and undesired output or performance.) Of course, these performance analysis approximation tools are most effective when the internal performance consultant understands the larger framework of the AOP.

Six: A Notion and Tools

Develop a profile of each of your client organizations (e.g., division, region, line of business, plant, store, department). Such a profile supports notion one and should be part of an account strategy. A profile might consist of your long-term objectives or goals for your working relationship with this entity, as well as an organization chart showing all the functions and key players in the organization. You'll also want to include in the profile some approximation of the macro AOP of the organization, supported by more detailed process maps you have developed on past projects. Every client organization you're serving looks something like NuPlant on the inside. Begin to develop a picture like the one that Bert did for NuPlant (see figure 3-8).

Your profile should include a business summary of the unit consisting of

- mission, vision, or both
- products and services
- markets
- business model
- goals
- strategy
- key variables impacting unit performance
- approximate annual operating budget

Finally, the profile you develop for your client organization should include a brief history of each project undertaken with this organization and notations about where to access complete project

Figure 5-4. Business case template.

I. BACKGROUND	

Requestor:
  Name:
  Title:
  Organization:
Funding:
  Cost of preparing initiative charged to:
  Cost of recipient time charged to:
	Request No.:
	  __ Initial:
	  __ Revision No.:
	Date Request Received:
	Date Business Case
	  Completed:
	Date Decision Made:
	Project No.:

II. REQUEST:

III. BENEFITS OF REQUESTED INITIATIVE

A. How will this proposed initiative benefit the business?
  1. More *revenues* because:

  2. Less *cost* because:

  3. *Other* because:

B. How will this/these benefit(s) be measured?

C. Regarding the measurement identified in (B), above,
  a. What is the current performance?

  b. What is the desired performance after this intervention?

D. In summary, the anticipated economic benefit of this Initiative over the next three years is:
  1. Year One $ _____
  2. Year Two $ _____
  3. Year Three $ _____

IV. INITIATIVE DETAIL

A. Why this initiative now?

B. What is the evidence that this initiative is required?

C. What are the objectives of this initiative?

D. What measurable results are expected from this initiative?

E. Who are the recipients of this initiative?

    1. Organization(s)

    2. Individuals

F. Who is the sponsor of this initiative?

G. Who is *accountable* for achieving the desired results from this initiative?

    1. Representing the recipient organization?

    2. Representing the provider organization?

H. Who are the relevant stakeholders for this initiative?

I. What is required for this initiative to achieve the desired results?

J. By when must this initiative be implemented?

K. By when must the results of this initiative be evident?

(continued on page 102)

Figure 5-4. Business case template (continued).

V. COST OF REQUESTED INITIATIVE

	Costs to Provider Organization	Costs to Recipient Organization
A. Analysis		
B. Design/Development		
C. Production		
D. Delivery		
E. Initiative Maintenance/Support		
Year One		
Year Two		
Year Three		
F. Evaluation		
G. Management Support		
Year One		
Year Two		
Year Three		

VI. POTENTIAL RETURN ON THIS INITIATIVE

	Year One	Year Two	Year Three
Benefit			
Cost			
Net			
Cumulative Net			

VII. DECISION and ⟶ NEXT STEP(S)

____ A. Proceed with the proposed initiative, as requested	1. Prepare project plan to develop proposed initiative
____ B. Conduct brief analysis to clarify need and appropriate action	1. Prepare project plan for analysis
____ C. Not a good use of resources at this time	1. Put proposed initiative on hold 2. Requestor strengthen business case
____ D. Rethink proposed initiative and business case	1. Requestor reexamine apparent need
____ E. Other	

VIII. CONCURRENCE ON DECISION

1. Signature of Requestor:	Date:	Comments:
2. Signature of Provider Representative:	Date:	Comments:

Reprinted with permission of Geary A. Rummler, Performance Design Lab, 2004.

Figure 5-5. Project feasibility checklist.

I. FEASIBILITY QUESTIONS

QUESTIONS/CRITERIA	ANSWER			DISCUSSION
	Yes	No	Not Sure	
A. The Problem/Opportunity				
1. Is the perceived need the real need?				
2. Is there a clear results gap?				
3. Is this the right gap to be working on?				
4. Is the results gap tied to a strategic issue or critical business issue?				
5. Is the gap significant enough to ensure an adequate ROI for an intervention?				
6. Is the gap significant enough to ensure implementation of recommended changes?				
7. Will it be possible to measure the closing of the gap?				
8. Will we be able to demonstrate that the gap in results has been closed?				
B. The Client				
1. Does client management agree with what has been identified as the real need? With the results gap to be closed?				
2. Does client management agree on the value of closing this gap at this time?				
3. Does client management have a bias toward a particular solution or approach that is contrary to our likely solution set and approach?				
4. Is client management supportive of our approach to this project?				
5. Will the client management provide the necessary leadership, resources, and support to make the project a success?				
6. Have we identified the individual client who assumes accountability for closing this gap in results?				
7. Do we have the right client?				
8. Is the client organization ready for the level of change required to close the gap?				
C. The Project Environment				
1. Are the constraints on conducting this project acceptable?				
2. Are the risks to a successful project acceptable?				
3. Is the organization sufficiently stable to support a successful project?				
4. Is the organization's culture supportive of a project such as this?				

(continued on page 104)

Figure 5-5. Project feasibility checklist (continued).

I. FEASIBILITY QUESTIONS

QUESTIONS/CRITERIA	ANSWER			DISCUSSION
	Yes	No	Not Sure	
D. Project Design				
1. Do we have a sufficient understanding of the performance anatomy associated with the gap?				
2. Do we have a good hypothesis as to the cause of the gap?				
3. Is the scope of the project sufficient to close the identified gap?				
4. Will we have access to the data and people necessary to test our hypotheses and close the gap?				
E. Us				
1. Do we have the capability and capacity to successfully complete this project in an acceptable timeframe?				
2. Can we get the business with a reasonable amount of effort?				
3. Will this project yield our target margins?				
4. Are we likely to be able to use this client, by name, as a reference for future work?				
5. Are we likely to learn something we can use elsewhere?				
6. Is it likely that this project will lead to other business with this client?				

II - CONCLUSIONS

QUESTIONS/CRITERIA	ANSWER		DISCUSSION
	Yes	No	
1. Is there the potential to make a difference?			
2. Is there a reasonable chance we will be successful at making a difference?			
3. Is there a reasonable chance we can obtain this business?			

III - PROPOSAL DECISION

DECISION	COMMENT
____ "YES"	(No explanation necessary.)
____ "YES, BUT...."	(Explain concerns and proposed actions to reduce risks.)
____ "NO"	(Why?)

Reprinted with permission of Geary A. Rummler, Performance Design Lab, 2004.

Figure 5-6. The problem analysis pentagon.

Is there a problem?
What do you observe that indicates there is a problem?

Acceptable Response	Unacceptable Response
Reports are rarely submitted on time.	Morale is low.

For further analysis, ask:	Probe further for identification of deficiency:
What do you mean by rarely—2 out of 10; 5 out of 10? Can you give me a specific number or range?	Give me an example of what someone does that indicates to you that morale is low.

How will you know when the problem is solved? (What will be different?)

Acceptable Response	Unacceptable Response
• The accident rate will decline by X%. • The grievances will decrease by X number. • The rejects will decrease by X%. • The production will increase by X%. • Customer complaints will be reduced by X%. • Sales will increase by X dollars. • The time required will be reduced by X%. • The index will reach objective.	Things will run smoother.

Probe with:

What do you mean by smoother? That is, if you have two departments one running smoothly and one not so smoothly, how do you know the difference? What do you look at that tells you there is a difference?

How general a problem is it?
1. Where does it occur (e.g., region, department)?
2. Is it restricted to a particular place within the area?
3. Is that the only place it occurs?
4. Where doesn't it occur?

When is it a problem?
What do you observe that indicates there is a problem?

1. When does it occur (e.g., third shift, start-up, new product introduction)?
2. Does it always occur at the same time?
3. When doesn't it occur?
4. How frequently does it occur (e.g., once a day, week, month, year)?
5. How long has this been a problem?

(continued on page 106)

Figure 5-6. The problem analysis pentagon (continued).

WHO

Whom should we look at?

1. Who is the performer in question?
2. What is the desired performance?
3. What specifically is the performer doing wrong?

Acceptable Response	
PRESENT INCORRECT BEHAVIOR	DESIRED BEHAVIOR
Not answering customer questions.	Answer customer questions or refer to supervisor who can answer questions.

Unacceptable Response	
PRESENT INCORRECT BEHAVIOR	DESIRED BEHAVIOR
Has poor attitude toward customer.	Have good attitude toward customer.

Probe with:

Assume we have two sales clerks, one with what you describe as a good attitude and one with a poor attitude. I approach them as a customer. How would each sales clerk respond?

4. Does the performer ever perform correctly? If **YES,** when?
   If **NO,** has anyone ever performed correctly?

   WHO? WHEN? WHERE?

WORTH

Is it important?

1. Does the incorrect performance impact the following:

   The product or service?
   ☐ Quality
   ☐ Cost
   ☐ Quantity

   The performer or his or her department?
   ☐ Safety
   ☐ Ease of work
   ☐ Performance measures

   The organization?
   ☐ Procedures
   ☐ Image
   ☐ Revenue
   ☐ Profitability

   Other workers or department?
   ☐ Safety
   ☐ Ease of work
   ☐ Performance measures

2. How much is the problem costing the organization per year?

IS THE PROBLEM WORTH PURSUING?

Reprinted with permission of Geary A. Rummler, Performance Design Lab, 2004.

records and deliverables. The idea is to reduce the amount of time it takes you to respond to requests. If you have compiled good client profiles, you won't have to spend much time getting up to speed when an opportunity comes your way.

For example, think about the position Bert would be in now if he were an internal perform-ance consultant on the Big Auto corporate or stamping division staff. Because of what he knows about stamping plants, he could respond quickly to future requests for help from stamping plants (and, to a degree, all plants) and the stamping division because he knows where to look to link to results, and he has models and an understanding

Figure 5-7. Human performance system (HPS) worksheet.

HPS COMPONENTS	CHARACTERISTICS OF THE IDEAL HPS	HPS TROUBLESHOOTING QUESTIONS AND ANSWERS				HPS IMPROVEMENT ACTIONS
		QUESTIONS	Yes	No	?	
OUTPUT	Adequate and appropriate criteria (standards) with which to judge successful performance	A. PERFORMANCE SPECIFICATION				
		1. Do performance standards exist? (If "yes," complete items 2 and 3.)				
		2. Do performers know the desired output and performance standards?				
		3. Do performers consider the standards attainable?				
INPUT	1. Clear or sufficiently recognizable indications of the need to perform	B. TASK SUPPORT				
		1. Can the performer easily recognize the input requiring action?				
	2. Minimal interference from incompatible or extraneous demands	2. Can the task be done without interference from other tasks?				
		3. Are the job procedures and workflow logical?				
	3. Necessary resources (budget, personnel, equipment) to perform	4. Are adequate resources available for performance (time, tools, staff, information)?				
CONSEQUENCES	1. Sufficient positive consequences (incentives) to perform	C. CONSEQUENCES				
		1. Are the consequences aligned to support desired performance? (If "yes," complete item 2.)				
	2. Few, if any, negative consequences (disincentives) to perform	2. Are consequences meaningful from the performers' viewpoint?				
		3. Are the consequences timely?				
FEEDBACK	Frequent and relevant feedback as to how well (or how poorly) the job is being performed	D. FEEDBACK				
		1. Do performers receive information about their performance? (If "yes," complete item 2)				
		2. Is the information they receive:				
		a. Relevant?				
		b. Timely?				
		c. Accurate?				
		d. Specific?				
		e. Constructive?				
		f. Easy to understand?				
PERFORMER	1. Necessary understanding and skill to perform	E. KNOWLEDGE/SKILL				
		1. Do the performers have the necessary skills and knowledge to perform?				
	2. Capacity to perform, both physically and emotionally	2. Do the performers know why desired performance is important?				
	3. Willingness to perform (given the incentives available)	F. INDIVIDUAL CAPACITY				
		1. Are the performers physically, mentally, and emotionally able to perform?				

Performer:
Desired Performance:
Undesired Performance:
Situation/Input:

Reprinted with permission of Geary A. Rummler, Performance Design Lab, 2004.

of the business and organization that make it possible to quickly generate and test hypotheses about causes of poor performance. He wouldn't easily be misled into delivering a solution or activity that would not have a positive impact on a plant. Bert would also be able to look proactively for opportunities to improve plant and division performance. By relating trends in division and plant results with his knowledge of the plant's AOP, he can convert his hypotheses for improving performance into proposals to improve results.

Really, the goal is to *know the client's business*. If performance consultants don't know the business, they are at the mercy of the requestor. If they know the client's business, they will be much more effective at pushing back on inappropriate requests, asking better questions, posing alternative explanations of cause, and suggesting alternative solutions. Knowing the business is essential to building credibility with clients.

These client organization profiles are also very useful in orienting new internal consultants to client organizations.

Seven: A Notion and Tool

You need to keep pushing your client managers along a learning curve. Consider the client manager relationship model shown in figure 5-8 as a way of tracking your progress.

The model goes beyond a single learning curve and assesses four dimensions essential to a successful performance consulting relationship with client managers. The idea is to continuously evaluate where you think you are with any particular key manager.

Related to this notion, look for opportunities to educate key managers in what you believe and how you look at performance and results. Introduce them to portions of this book. Send them articles pertaining to results and the practice of performance consulting. Look for early adopters of performance improvement ideas, and invite them to sit in on selected training courses or briefings. Maintain a list of managers who support your approach to improving results and who would be receptive to new but appropriate results improvement strategies or interventions.

Figure 5-8. Client manager relationship model.

Manager Name:
Manager Title:
Organization Unit:
Date Relationship Established:
Assessment of Current Relationship:

Item	Rating						
	1 (Low)	2	3	4	5	6	7 (High)
A. Trust in the performance consulting (PC) unit							
B. Understanding of what the PC unit is doing and why							
C. Understanding what they must be doing and why							
D. Demonstrated results							
Comments (Date)							

Eight: A Notion and Tool

As pointed out earlier, it is not appropriate to do a serious performance analysis on every request. How do you decide when a performance analysis is in order? Every request received by the performance consulting function should be subjected to a strategic assessment (figure 5-9) to determine which of four categories (*A, B, C, D*) the request for help should be assigned. Depending on the classification, the performance consultant can take appropriate action on the request (table 5-1).

In your strategic assessment, you should consider these questions:

- Where do the request and requestor fit in the internal performance consulting model (figure 5-3)? Think about whether political or power considerations must be taken into account and how the request fits with your client partnership strategy.
- Where does the request fit in the AOP and the results chain for the entity in question? Assess the likelihood that you will be able to make a difference, and estimate the client organization's tolerance for "looking" and openness to modifying the problem or solution.

Such a strategic assessment can be a powerful management tool for the leader of the performance consulting unit. It makes it possible to track, by client,

- the number of requests received and actions taken

- the number and percent of each category of request or project
- the distribution trend of types of projects over a period of years

Tracking distribution trends makes it possible to assess the progress the consulting unit is making in getting clients to ask for help in solving problems and improving results rather than continually asking for questionable solutions.

Nine: A Notion and Tool

This notion picks up from notion eight. If a request falls under classification *C* (a request that is to be tested), then it might end up following the roadmap in figure 5-10, which shows some recommended questions, decisions, and actions.

Let's take a closer look at the main decision points in the request roadmap. The following numbered items correspond to figure 5-10.

1. The first question to ask the requestor is "Can we go take a look?" If possible, you want to observe and interview to get a firsthand understanding of the supposed problem leading to the proposed solution.

2. If the answer is no, then the next issue is about the probability that the proposed solution will close a gap in results. Because you can't look for yourself, you'll have to rely on what the client tells you and your experience. You can use the questions in figure 5-6 to get some insight into the potential for the proposed solution to close a gap in results.

Figure 5-9. A process for strategic assessment.

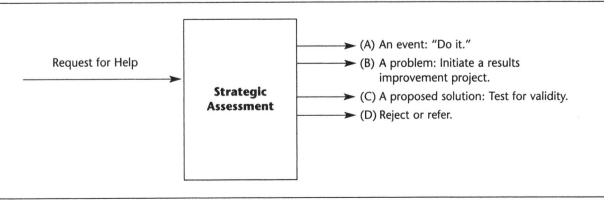

Request for Help → Strategic Assessment →
- (A) An event: "Do it."
- (B) A problem: Initiate a results improvement project.
- (C) A proposed solution: Test for validity.
- (D) Reject or refer.

Reprinted with permission of Geary A. Rummler, Performance Design Lab, 2004.

Table 5-1. Classifying and acting on internal clients' requests for help.

Request Classification	Description of Request	Recommended Action
A.	The request for an activity involves some combination of the following: • It is a one-time event, such as a meeting, conference, brief training program. • Per Gilbert's (1996) First Leisurely Theorem, the requested activity has little potential for results. • There is no time or money for any analysis. • There is no tolerance for any analysis.	1. If there is little potential for results, try to talk the requestor out of doing the project. You can apply the business case tool provided in figure 5-4. 2. If you can't talk the requestor out of the project, deliver the project (as inexpensively as possible, given the lack of results) and learn as much as you can about the organization in anticipation of the next request. Remember to add whatever you learn to the client organization profile.
B.	The request identifies an apparent real problem, with no proposed solution. This type of request is about as good as it gets for the performance consultant.	The recommended action is to propose phase I of a results improvement project to determine the gap in results and define a possible project.
C.	The request comes with a proposed solution. It is not clear what the problem is that the solution is supposed to correct, what the gap in results is, or both.	The recommended action is to test the request with some questions in an attempt to reclassify the request as A, B, or D.
D.	Upon some questioning, it becomes clear the request has no merit or is a need that can be better met through some other resource, internal or external.	If the request has no merit, try hard to get the requestor to withdraw the request. If the request could be better met some other way, refer the client to a more appropriate resource.

3. If you believe some potential exists to impact results, you may feel justified in delivering the requested activity and learning.

4. If, however, there is no evidence that the proposed solution will impact results, the recommended action is to persuade the requestor to drop the request. You might use Gilbert's 1996 First Leisurely Theorem or the business case tool in figure 5-4 to help your argument.

5. If you are able to convince the requestor to drop the request, then the project stops here. Hooray!

6. If you are unable to convince the requestor to drop the request, then it is time to deliver and learn. Given that there is no evidence this solution will impact results, consider designing and delivering a solution as inexpensively as you can (ATR 5-4).

7. However, if you are going to be able to take a look at the situation, conduct a preliminary

According to Rummler 5-4

Rummler's rule of performance economics: If you aren't going to improve performance, don't improve it just as cheaply as you can.

analysis, which may take from a half a day to three days to accomplish. Ideally, you have the AOP framework in mind and a good idea about what to look for. You might also use the questions shown in figures 5-6 and 5-7. This preliminary analysis will be made easier if your performance consulting unit has developed the client organization profiles described in notion six.

8. Following the preliminary analysis, the next question is "Does a results gap exist?" If the answer is no, then you should try to persuade the requestor to drop the request (9).

Figure 5-10. Project roadmap for category C requests.

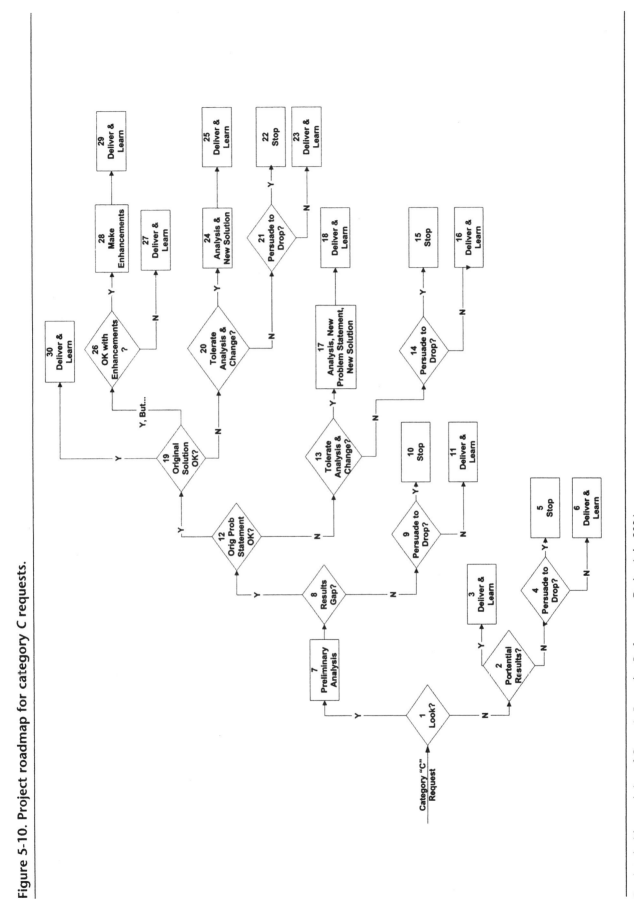

Reprinted with permission of Geary A. Rummler, Performance Design Lab, 2004.

Depending on the success of that action, either you stop (10) or you deliver and learn (11).

12. If there is a viable gap in results identified in the preliminary analysis, the next question is "Did the preliminary analysis support the original problem statement or problem assumption underlying the request for the solution?"

13. If the answer is no, then the question becomes "Will the requestor tolerate a more extensive performance analysis to identify the real cause of the gap in results?" That was exactly the situation Bert faced at NuPlant.

14. If the requestor is unwilling to undertake a more extensive performance analysis, then the appropriate action is to try to persuade the requestor to drop the request. Depending on the success of that action, you stop (15) or deliver and learn (16), as before.

17. If the requestor's answer is yes to analysis and change, and there is a serious gap in results, then undertake a serious performance analysis and deliver the specified solution set and learn (18).

19. If the original problem statement was OK, then was the original solution proposed by the requestor OK?

20. If the answer is no or not sure, then the question is whether the requestor will tolerate a more extensive performance analysis to identify an appropriate solution set for the problem.

21. If the answer is no, then it is best if you can persuade the requestor to drop the request. Depending on the success of that action, you either stop (22) or deliver and learn (23).

24. If the answer is yes to analysis and change (20), and there is a serious gap in results, then undertake a serious performance analysis (24) and deliver the specified solution set and learn (25).

26. If the answer is "Yes, but . . ." to the question "Is the original solution OK?" (19), the solution could benefit from some enhancements to be more effective (e.g., job aids, an improved performance feedback system, additional tools), then the question becomes

whether the requestor is OK with the proposed enhancements.

27. If the answer is no, then deliver and learn.

28. If the answer is yes, make the enhancements and deliver and learn (29).

30. If the answer at decision point 19 is yes, then deliver and learn (30).

Don't get turned off by this seemingly complex roadmap. With a little experience, you will be making these decisions automatically if you aren't already.

Ten: A Notion and Tools

An unfortunate reality of the internal performance consultants is that most of their resources are consumed responding to requests for help that involve all the issues outlined on the roadmap (figure 5-10). It is a real challenge for an internal performance consultant to get ahead of the curve and apply his or her expertise and energy in areas that will have significant long-term benefits to the client.

An underutilized tactic is for the internal consulting group to proactively identify opportunities to impact results. The AOP framework and its related templates provide the tools for the internal performance consultant to learn the client's business and uncover opportunities to make a difference.

How can internal performance consultants identify such opportunities? First, know your internal performance consultant model (figure 5-3) and account strategy (with client profile, per notion six) for each target client. Ask yourself these questions:

- What are you trying to accomplish with a given client organization?
- Who are the key people you would like to have as clients?
- What are they talking and worrying about?

Second, for your key client targets, use your knowledge of their AOPs to look for opportunity areas:

- Look for events happening in the client's super-system that may constitute potential critical business issues or critical process issues.

- Review proposed executive initiatives to see how they relate to possible CBIs and potentially impact CPIs and CJIs.
- Be sensitive to changes in strategy and the implications for possible CBIs, CPIs, and CJIs and related results gaps you can impact through performance analysis and the design of appropriate solution sets.
- Check out annual operating plans of client executives and look for potential CBIs and CPIs and related results gaps you can impact.

Then, when you have located a potential opportunity in a client organization,

1. Build a business case and a possible plan of attack.
2. Find an executive (i.e., potential client) who is committed to closing the gap you have identified.
3. Adjust the scope of the project and plan to fit the client executive's sphere of influence and interest, or if there isn't a fit between your opportunity and the client, then...
4. Identify a different, better client.

Internal Performance Consulting: An Example (ATR 5-5)

According to Rummler 5-5

I've introduced to you the unique challenges faced by internal consultants and offered some strategies for overcoming those challenges. In addition, your personal arsenal is now equipped with notions and tools that you can apply in service to your client organizations. Now let me put these notions and tools in context by describing how Mark, the head of an internal performance consulting team, implemented some strategic changes in his department to move from delivering solutions to improving results. Then, I'll show you how Zoe, an internal performance consultant in the department, put these strategies, notions, and tools to work as she serves her client organization.

Mark is the head of an internal performance consulting organization that might be called the organization development, organization effectiveness, or the training and development department. The name of Mark's department isn't important because serious performance consulting is more a mission or state of mind, than it is a function.

What's important is that in the three years he has led the unit, he has shifted the mission of the department from just providing a narrow set of solutions (largely training) to a commitment to delivering results, conducting serious performance analysis where feasible, and coordinating the delivery of a broad set of results improvement solutions. Like many internal performance consultants, this transition in mission is a challenge to implement because client managers still see the function as a solution provider and continue to seek solutions rather than improved results.

Mark and his team of performance consultants guide requestors with diplomatic push-backs and strive to continually educate requestors about the importance of improving results. The effectiveness of the individuals in Mark's unit has also been enhanced by implementation of some of the notions, processes, and tools provided in this chapter. In short, Mark has helped his performance consulting organization evolve in ways both *strategic* and *tactical*.

Strategic Level

Mark has done a number of things at the strategic level to stipulate how his function operates to serve its clients.

Stated Beliefs. Mark has developed a set of stated beliefs to reinforce the performance improvement mindset that prevails in his department:

1. Our ultimate goal is improved results for our employer.
2. For any given client group, our goal is to establish and maintain a business partnership through the demonstration of improved results. (An approximation of the internal consulting model in figure 5-3 is posted on the wall.)
3. Our performance improvement work is based on serious performance analysis, which in turn is based on the AOP framework and RIP.

(A common analysis approach is important for the unit, as the various performance consultants in the unit have backgrounds in such areas as organization development, organization behavior, total quality management, training, process reengineering, and human relations.)

Market Identification. Mark clarified for himself and his staff just who their client organizations are. Although his unit reports to the corporate vice president of administration, he segmented his "market" as the three business units and the corporate finance, IT, and marketing units. Each of the business units has its own engineering design, sales, customer support, and manufacturing operations. Mark wants to establish a strategic business partnership with each of the business units and the three corporate staff units.

Plans. Within six months on the job, Mark had developed multiyear plans for establishing the desired business partnership with each client group. Because this partnership would only result through demonstrated results, these plans influence the projects carried out by Mark's group during the year. The plans are reviewed and modified annually.

Customer Focus and Accountability. Mark designated members of his leadership team to be the primary liaison (relationship manager) for each client group. These individuals are responsible for the strategic assessments of all requests from their clients (per notion eight) and for overseeing the quality of work done for their client group.

Organization Profiles. The relationship managers are responsible for overseeing the development and maintenance of a comprehensive organization profile (per notion six) of their client group.

Strategic Assessments. All potential projects—either requested or generated proactively by Mark's group—are subjected to a strategic assessment per notion eight. Some of the features of this process include the following:

- Because every request is a potential demand on the scarce resources in Mark's unit, each one is documented, assigned a request number, and entered into a database for tracking and analysis.
- The strategic assessment involves, among other things, the review of a request against the overall plan to support the client group and available resources to perform the work.
- After the strategic assessment and request classification, each project is assigned a project number, and the database is updated with a project plan and budget.

Management. Mark and his leadership team continually monitor and manage the performance of individual projects against their plans and budgets. They also track the achievement of the individual client group plans for demonstrated results and a business partnership. They monitor the categories of projects carried out for each client group each year and analyze trends over the years.

Tactical Level

At the tactical level, the following example demonstrates how performance consultants in Mark's organization go about responding to requests, educating clients, and delivering and learning.

Lou is a regional sales manager in one of the business units supported by Mark's organization. He asks the performance consulting liaison to his business unit for some help in locating and presenting a particular video on coaching at his next district sales managers' meeting. Lou had seen it at a conference and thought it was great. The relationship manager guides the request through the strategic assessment process, where it is categorized as *A,* an event.

The request is then turned over to Zoe, a performance consultant who has some experience around sales organizations. Zoe knows that the business unit is struggling with flat sales, and she knows enough about business in general and sales in particular to know that a 30-minute video plus facilitated discussion isn't going to have any impact on district manager behavior or sales rep performance. In a brief conversation with Lou, Zoe can see that he is committed to showing this video and has no tolerance for considering any alternatives.

So, she responds to Lou this way: "Lou, that's a great idea. I've heard about this film, and this looks like a great opportunity to do two things. First, we will meet your needs by getting the video and showing it at your district managers' meeting. Second, showing the video provides me with a chance to evaluate its effectiveness. I'd like to make a deal with you: I'll get the video and facilitate the presentation at your district managers' meeting if you will let me interview three or four of the district managers back in the field over the next few weeks to determine the effectiveness of the video. The interviews will take less than 30 minutes each. Deal?"

Lou says, "Sure." Zoe facilitates the session and gets to know several sharp district managers, whom she subsequently interviews. She visits two in the field and talks with two on the phone. During the interviews, she uses the film as a starting point to ask how the district managers oversee their sales reps, what they believe the major issues are regarding sales, and what they think the business unit needs to do to increase sales. She also asks them what they thought of the video and gets the response, "It was OK. Lou likes that sort of thing."

Zoe uses this information to begin to build a model of what the sales process is, what the sales management process is, and what the current sales management measurement process is. In short, she begins to build her own "is" AOP picture of the business unit sales organization.

After her brief foray into the field, Zoe can now do a couple of things. If she could see that a particular intervention, say, a customer qualification checklist, would make a difference, she could move to the proactive mode by approaching Lou with something like this: "Lou, thanks for letting me have some time with your district managers. As you predicted, they seemed to find the video on coaching helpful. But, I learned some other things. They pointed out that one of the critical areas in which they have to continually coach new sales reps is properly qualifying potential customers. I asked about the possibility of providing new sales reps with a customer/lead qualification checklist—sort of a job aid. Every district manager thought that would be great! So, I was thinking, would you be OK with my developing such a job aid? It would keep the momentum going from your sales meeting."

The other thing Zoe can do is just file away the models she's developed (e.g., the updated organization profile for the business unit) and wait for an opportunity to be "proactively reactive." Such an opportunity might work like this: About three months after Zoe's visit with the district managers in Lou's region, the VP of sales for the business unit approaches Mark's organization and makes a request for sales training as a way to provide a uniform sales process across all regions. Zoe is assigned to a team to respond to the request.

Armed with her models of the sales organization, her understanding of the issues in the field, and the reality of the business unit's flat sales for the past 18 months, Zoe meets with the sales VP and establishes that the CBI is really "no sales growth" and that the goal (results gap) is to get back to an annual growth in sales of 8%. Based on her earlier work with the district managers, Zoe is convinced that pieces of the puzzle include the following:

- In an effort to meet shifting customer needs, the business unit has overwhelmed the field sales organization with a barrage of new products.
- There is no uniform sales process for integrating and successfully selling the growing portfolio of products.
- The system for managing the salesforce is fragmented and lacks uniformity.
- The sales performance data are inadequate for managing the increasingly complex product portfolio.

During her meeting with the sales VP, Zoe raises some of her concerns about the various factors that might be influencing the CBI and indicates that "sales training" by itself will have little impact. The VP is impressed with Zoe's knowledge of the issues, and they agree that the next step is for Zoe and her team to conduct a quick four-week performance analysis to identify the major variables impacting the CBI. Next, they will develop and present a comprehensive plan for getting the business unit's sales back on track (ATR 5-6).

In summary, the internal performance consultant has some significant challenges in applying serious performance analysis, in balancing being responsive, and doing the right thing. Nevertheless, the AOP framework and the RIP can help with that challenge, as illustrated by the work of Mark and Zoe.

According to Rummler 5-6

I think you can see how Zoe was able to integrate some of the notions and tools provided in this chapter into her internal performance consulting practice. This example illustrates

- *the value of delivering and learning, even if the initial request lacks much merit in and of itself*
- *that your fundamental objective is to make a difference (impact results), which requires that you continually learn more about the AOP of your client organizations*
- *that, with your understanding of the AOP of a client organization, you can find opportunities to propose a performance improvement project, and you can be ready to respond proactively to a request for help*

CHAPTER 5 HIGHLIGHTS

1. The AOP framework and the RIP are equally applicable to the performance analysis work of both internal and external performance consultants.

2. Internal performance consultants must operate on two levels simultaneously. They must be responsive to a particular request for help, while at the same time building a long-term business partnership with a client organization by demonstrating results.

3. Internal performance consultants are part of a function perceived as a solution provider, requiring them to have to push back on requests for help and educate the requestor on alternative solutions.

4. Internal performance consultants are unable to do serious performance analysis on many of the requests they receive.

5. Given the realities faced by internal consultants, they must:
   - Be selective when they are to do serious performance consulting.
   - Balance being responsive with doing the right thing.
   - Continually educate their clients on the right thing.
   - Test every request for help to see if there is a possibility of closing a gap in results, test the soundness of the client's statement of the "problem," and assess the validity of the proposed solution.

6. Be prepared to not do the right thing. In some circumstances, the only option is to deliver and learn.

7. A number of notions and tools can help the internal performance consultant carry out effective performance analysis and improve organizational results.

A Path to Becoming a Performance Consultant

According to Rummler 6-1

It is my hope that your interest in the craft of performance consulting has increased a hundredfold after all you've learned in the preceding chapters. This final chapter presents my thoughts on how to continue to build your capabilities in terms of performance analysis and serious performance consulting.

The focus of this chapter is what it takes to be able to perform *serious* performance consulting. First, a brief recap:

In the Introduction, serious performance consulting was distinguished from performance consulting "lite" by the following:

- the objective of closing the measurable gap between "is" and "should" results
- the application of a systematic results improvement process
- a sound, rigorous performance analysis

You also learned in the Introduction that performance consultant "right stuff" includes

- being committed to improving measurable results
- remaining solution-neutral
- being capable of using a validated, robust methodology for determining desired results; systematically identifying barriers to desired results; specifying changes necessary to achieve the desired results; and eval-

uating the impact of the specified changes on results

- having a broad repertoire of results improvement strategies and tactics

Chapter 2 introduced a framework for conducting performance analysis, the key to serious performance consulting. The results of a performance improvement project are only as good as the underlying performance analysis.

In chapter 3 serious performance consulting was demonstrated with an example—the NuPlant case study. You watched as Bert transformed a request for human relations training for supervisors into a CBI of plant productivity. He recommended changes in job design, plant management systems, plant production systems, and the production measurement system.

Chapter 4 showed that the performance analysis lessons from the NuPlant case study can be generalized to most results improvement situations. Chapter 5 discussed the reality of trade-offs between doing the right thing versus doing the smart thing vis-à-vis the application of serious performance consulting.

Dimensions of Serious Performance Consulting Capability

First, let's look at a framework for defining the serious performance consultant developmental task. In chapter 4 you learned about the scalability of the AOP framework and the RIP as the performance consultant moved from addressing CJIs to CPIs to CBIs. The same AOP principles and the same RIP phases and objectives apply at all three levels of the results chain.

The realization that the fundamentals of performance consulting are scalable raises some interesting questions: Is the performance consultant scalable? Are *you* scalable?

Figure 6-1 shows the two dimensions of serious performance consulting and the two dimensions of a performance consultant's scalability. One dimension is the scope of the engagement or endeavor—where the performance consultant entered the results chain. The performance analyst's challenge increases as he or she moves up the results chain scale (see table 4-1). A second dimension is the rigor of analysis, specifically:

1. *The application of all phases of the RIP for whatever critical issue is being addressed:* Of course, the quality of the scoping and project definition work done in phase I determine the rigor and effectiveness of the remaining phases.

2. *The depth of the analysis conducted (phase II):* To what extent were all potentially relevant factors of the AOP systematically examined for "root cause"? Did the investigation involve a 50,000-foot fly-by or a close scrutiny of actual performance data?

3. *Comprehensiveness of solutions specified in phase II and developed and implemented in phase III:* Are the recommended changes an appropriately comprehensive solution set or just some predetermined solution designed to pick only low-hanging fruit?

Figure 6-1. Dimensions of serious performance consulting.

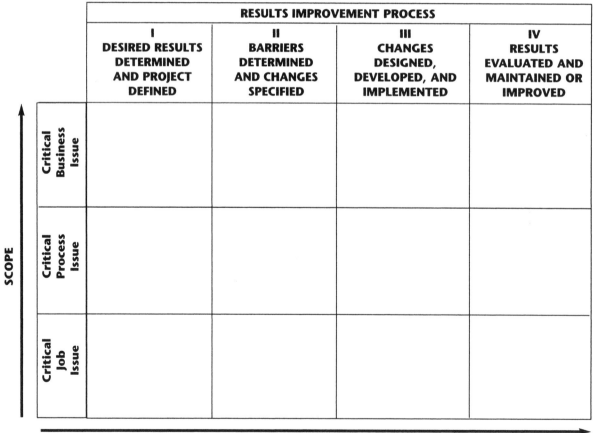

You can appreciate some implications of this view of serious performance consulting. The higher up the results chain scale you go, the greater the *potential* for improving organization results or really making a difference. The greater rigor employed at each level in the results chain scale, the greater the *probability* of achieving those potential organization results.

Bottom-line, serious performance consulting requires going beyond the job level or addressing just CJIs. Improving human performance is *interesting* work, but it is only *important* work when it is done in the context of improving process and organization results. Be assured that increasing your performance analysis capability to address CPIs and CBIs doesn't in any way diminish your capability at the job level. Effectively closing gaps in CPIs and CBIs will almost certainly also entail changes at the job level. Increasing the scope of your competence is about accumulating capability; it's not about considering alternative capabilities (According to Rummler [ATR] 6-2).

According to Rummler 6-2

Becoming (and remaining) an effective serious performance consultant means continuously increasing your capability to operate effectively at all levels of the results chain scale and to apply the appropriate amount of rigor to the task at hand. Even after 35 years, I still continue to look for ways to be more effective in each cell of the matrix in figure 6-1.

Building Your Serious Performance Consulting Capability

So, what do you have to do to master the scope and rigor dimensions of serious performance consulting? You can build your serious performance consulting capability by

- knowing how business in general works
- knowing how *your* business works
- learning the craft of serious performance consulting
- practicing your craft

Know How Business Works

Business in this context means how for-profit and not-for-profit organizations go about delivering their products or services. To do serious performance consulting, you need to move away from the job level and toward the process and organization levels. That means you need to understand

- *How organizations work:* What are the pieces, how do they fit together?

  Of course, the AOP is a great framework to guide this way of thinking. Starting with the super-system, ask these questions: Who are the organization's customers? Who are the competitors? What are the financial requirements? What are the critical resources needed to make it work? What factors in the general business environment impact this business? Then explore inside the AOP framework: What are the basic processes that produce the products or services? How do they fit together? What are the roles or functions necessary to perform or support the processes? How is this thing managed (ATR 6-3)?

- *The basic economic principles of business (indeed of any organization, for-profit or*

According to Rummler 6-3

An engineering professor of mine told the class that if we were serious about engineering we needed to develop a curiosity about how things work. He said we should start by taking apart doorknobs, locks, and cabinet latches to understand what the pieces are, how they fit together, and what mechanical relationships make the thing work. His objective was to have us begin to build a mental repertoire about how things work so that in the future we would be able to both diagnose problems and design gizmos to accomplish certain tasks. Subsequently, my curiosity shifted from cabinet latches to organizations, and I moved from engineering school to business school. But, to this day, I am fascinated by how organizations work. How does this restaurant work? How does this hotel work? How does this hospital work?

---

nonprofit, product, or service: Where does the cash come from to operate the business (customer, investors, loans, charitable grants)? Where does the cash go to operate the business (employees, materials, facilities, marketing)? What happens to the difference between cash-in and operating expenses (taxes, reinvestment, investors)?

- *The many languages of business:* The primary and most pervasive is the language of finance. There are specialized languages for functions (e.g., sales, marketing, manufacturing, information technology) and industries (e.g., retail, financial services, health services). For purposes of learning business, you may want to look into a rigorous master's of business administration (MBA) program that offers a strong dose of strategy, finance, marketing, and production. A starting point might be Silberger's (1999) book, *The Ten-Day MBA.*

Know How Your Business Works

You must learn the business of your employer and the business of your client (ATR 6-4). Learn it as well as most managers in the business. This specific business knowledge will keep you from being misled by a manager into chasing after a "nonproblem" and lead you to high-return opportunities that can make you a hero. Knowing your business is the way to gain credibility and earn respect.

When learning *your* business, focus first and foremost on how work gets done. Learn how the organization produces its products or services and which processes are critical. Then you have a foundation from which to interpret questions of culture, social dynamics, and so forth. Of course, the AOP framework is a great guide for learning how your business works.

Learn Your Craft

In addition to knowing business in general and knowing your business in particular, what is involved in learning the craft of the serious performance consultant (ATR 6-5)? There is an almost endless list of things that would be helpful to know and skills to have that could benefit the serious performance consultant. But, what is absolutely necessary in terms of accomplishments to fill the role of a serious performance consultant?

According to Rummler 6-5

I like to think of what we performance analysts, performance consultants, and performance improvers do as a craft rather than as a field or discipline. We draw from many fields and disciplines and apply different techniques and tools. In that regard, we are like engineers who base their work on a variety of scientific fields and areas of research to meet real-world challenges. I have maintained for 30 years that we are performance engineers *although that label has not been widely accepted.*

Table 6-1 is an extension of the RIP and results chain matrix shown in figure 6-1. This grid lists *possible* accomplishments or deliverables that *might* be involved in a serious performance consulting engagement, depending on the situation and which level of critical issue is being addressed. Implicit in the grid is the assumption that aspiring serious performance consultants have a firm understanding of the AOP framework, that they know what Bert knows as described in chapter 2.

This list is not exhaustive, and it is likely the content of the grid will expand as there are new developments in organization effectiveness. This framework should be useful in classifying and positioning such changes.

According to Rummler 6-4

One of my colleagues recently became an internal consultant within the organization development function of a high-tech company. Within three months of joining the company, she was being invited by engineering vice-presidents to attend their staff meetings because she seemed so interested in the business. Another performance consulting colleague recommends what he calls informational interviews. He asks key managers, "Could you give me 45 minutes? I need to learn more about your business and what you do, so I can do a better job of supporting you." Few managers can resist a request like that!

Table 6-1. Serious performance consulting accomplishment grid.

		RESULTS CHAIN		
		Critical Job Issue	Critical Process Issue	Critical Business Issue
RESULTS IMPROVEMENT PROCESS	**I** Desired Results Determined and Project Defined	**(A) Project Scoped—Correct issue identified and gap in results articulated** **(B) Project Designed—Deliverables specified, engagement model selected, relevant AOP identified, data sweeps planned, and budget prepared**		
	II Barriers Determined and Changes Specified	**(A) Relevant AOP Analyzed and Barriers to Results Identified**		
		1. Performance Improvement Potentials (PIPs) and Stakes Analyzed 2. Exemplars Identified 3. Job/Tasks/HPS/Practices Analysis Conducted 4. Process Analyzed 5. Job PPMS Analyzed	6. PIPs and Stakes Analyzed 7. Cross-Functional Processes Analyzed 8. Roles and Responsibilities Analyzed 9. Process PPMS Analyzed	10. Super-System Analyzed 11. Business Direction Analyzed 12. PIPS and Stakes Analyzed 13. Value Chain Analyzed 14. Organization PPMS Analyzed
		(B) Changes Specified		
		1. Jobs Specified 2. Roles and Responsibilities Specified 3. Practices Specified 4. HPS Specified 5. Job PPMS Requirements Specified 6. Solution Design Resources Identified	7. Cross-Functional Processes Specified (expectations/flow/ policies/resource allocation) 8. Roles and Responsibilities Specified 9. Process PPMS Requirements Specified 10. Process Solution Design Resources Identified	11. Super-System Monitoring System Requirements Specified 12. Strategy Requirements Specified 13. Value Chain Alignment Requirements Specified 14. Organization Structure Requirements Specified 15. Organization PPMS Requirements Specified 16. Organization Solution Design Resources Identified
	III Changes Designed, Developed, and Implemented	**(A) Changes Designed and Developed**		
		1. Job Models Developed 2. Role/Responsibility Matrices Developed 3. Performance Support Developed 4. Job PPMS Developed 5. Solution Design Resources Managed 6. Evaluation System Developed	7. Cross-Functional Processes Developed (expectations/flow/ policies/resource allocation) 8. IT Support Developed 9. Role/Responsibility Matrices Developed 10. Process PPMS Developed 11. Process Solution Design Resources Managed 12. Evaluation System Developed	13. Super-System Monitoring System Developed 14. Strategy Formulated 15. Value Chain Aligned 16. Organization Structure Redesigned 17. Organization PPMS Developed 18. Organization Solution Design Resources Managed 19. Evaluation System Developed
		(B) Changes Implemented		
		(C) Evaluation System Implemented		
	IV Results Evaluated and Maintained or Improved	**(A) Performance Data Gathered and Analyzed** **(B) Results Analyzed and Changes Made as Required to Close Gap in Results**		
	OTHER	**(A) Project Managed**		
		(B) Engagement Managed		
		(C) Client Relations Maintained		
		(D) Project Teams Guided/Managed		

Additionally, table 6-1 is a useful roadmap for self-development. It can be used as a template to answer such questions as "What are my current capabilities?" and "What capabilities do I need to achieve my serious performance consulting aspirations?" It is a framework for building a developmental plan: "How can I close the gap between the capability I have and the capability I need to be proficient at addressing particular critical issues?" The grid can help you plot your self-development progress: "How am I doing against my goal?"

Finally, the accomplishment grid reinforces the notion that the path to becoming a serious performance consultant is a journey—a continuous learning process. Table 6-2 describes in some detail each serious performance consulting accomplishment in the grid.

Practice Your Craft

People who successfully move up the serious performance consulting scale work very hard to both learn and practice their craft. They don't wait to be asked to do something. They find or make opportunities to expand their capabilities—both inside and outside of their organizations. Following are some the things I have seen help the aspiring serious performance consultant practice his or her craft and learn.

Decide What You Want. You need to want to do this work—to make a measurable difference, sometimes against overwhelming odds. You need to be excited about the challenge of swimming upstream and overcoming significant organizational obstacles. Passion is important because it will have to carry you over the rough spots as you learn to do the right thing and make a difference.

The potential to make changes in an organization and impact results is almost unlimited depending on your vision, skills, and the right opportunities. But, being a serious performance consultant is not for everyone. Reading the NuPlant case can help you determine if this kind of work is for you.

Make Opportunities to Learn and Practice. You must seize chances to practice your craft and

develop your skills both inside and outside of your own organization. If necessary, try doing some pro bono work with for-profit and nonprofit institutions. Offer to help a small business with whom you do business in the course of running your household. Start by showing interest in the business, how it works, how well it is doing. And, there is no shortage of opportunities to do volunteer work for nonprofit organizations.

Realize You Are on a Learning Curve. Most likely, you will not make a big impact for awhile. You will progress from small projects and small successes to big projects and big impact. Maximize your learning from each project along the way. Remember that you are on a journey. Manage your way up that learning curve. Use table 6-1 to help you. Know where you are going and establish a plan for getting there. Ask yourself, "What kind of project do I need next?" "What do I need to practice or learn from that project?"

Apply the Notions and Tools Offered in This Book. Chapter 5 presented you with an abundance of notions and tools that you can apply in your practice, including the strategic assessment process (see figure 5-9) and the project roadmap (see figure 5-10). Ideally these notions would be implemented as part of the formal performance consulting process within your unit, but you can use these notions offline to review and critique projects.

Maximize Your Learning. You can apply some tactics to get the most learning out of every attempt to practice your craft. Here are some ideas:

- Consider collaborating with a colleague in a buddy system as you undertake this journey.
- Keep a journal of all your projects, listing your hypotheses about problems and solutions and the eventual reality and outcomes. Write out a postmortem of all the projects, noting lessons learned and what you'd do differently next time. Review your journal with your buddy.
- Conduct formal project debriefings, or lookbacks, with your buddy to capture learning.

Table 6-2. Serious performance consulting accomplishments.

Results Improvement Process (RIP) Phase	Serious Performance Consulting Accomplishment	Accomplishment Description	Comment
I	**(A) Project Scoped**		
	Correct issue identified and gaps in results articulated (cutting across all three levels of the results chain)	• Determine the issue. • Identify where the issue lies in the results chain (e.g., job, process, or organization level). • Establish a link to a critical business issue (CBI). • Identify results gaps. • Determine relevant anatomy of performance (AOP).	The complexity of this accomplishment increases as the scope of the project increases from a critical job issue (CJI) to a critical process issue (CPI) to a critical business issue (CBI). Accordingly, so must the skill of the serious performance consultant. This accomplishment was illustrated in the NuPlant case study.
	(B) Project Designed		
	Deliverables specified, engagement model selected, relevant AOP identified, data sweeps planned, and budget prepared (cutting across all three levels of the results chain)	Given the issue, gap in results, and relevant AOP, design a project that will close the identified gap in results: • Specify project deliverables • Select an appropriate engagement model • Plan data sweeps • Develop project plan and budget	The complexity of this accomplishment increases as the scope of the project increases from a CJI to a CPI to a CBI. Accordingly, so must the skill of the serious performance consultant. This accomplishment was illustrated in the NuPlant case study.
II	**(A) Relevant AOP Analyzed and Barriers to Results Identified**		
	1. Performance Improvement Potential (PIPs) and Stakes Analyzed	• PIP: Determine where there is the greatest variability in performance and, therefore, the greatest opportunity for performance improvement (e.g., variability between jobs, supervisors, shifts, districts, stores). • Determine the economic stakes involved in the issue (e.g., scrap cost, labor cost, material cost).	Note that this accomplishment is required at all three results chain levels. This is one of the first analyses applied during a serious performance analysis project because it points the way to determining why some units are performing better than others. The notion of "PIPs and stakes" comes from Gilbert (1996), who excelled in this area of analysis. This particular form of analysis was not illustrated in the NuPlant case study.
	2. Exemplars Identified	Identify individuals or units that consistently produce all or part of the desired behavior, performance, or results. The exemplars can then be studied or analyzed to determine why they perform better than other individuals/units, providing insight into "should" methods. Ideally, exemplars are identified by objective performance data.	Identifying and analyzing exemplars is a fundamental principle and accomplishment for the serious performance consultant. For more information on this topic, see Gilbert (1996). In the NuPlant case study, Old Plant was considered an exemplar, and Bert studied its AOP.

(continued on page 124)

Table 6-2. Serious performance consulting accomplishments (continued).

Results Improvement Process (RIP) Phase	Serious Performance Consulting Accomplishment	Accomplishment Description	Comment
II (continued)	(A) Relevant AOP Analyzed and Barriers to Results Identified		
	3. Job/Tasks/Human Performance System (HPS)/ Practices Analysis Conducted	This is the basic "is" and "should" analysis of a job, including • What are the job accomplishments, outputs, outcomes? • What are the tasks to produce the accomplishment, outputs, and outcomes? • What is the HPS for the "is" job, and what is the desired HPS for the "should" job? • What are the "is" and "should" practices (behavioral patterns per Tosti and Jackson, 1989)?	This is the basic "blocking and tackling" of serious performance consulting. This was illustrated in the NuPlant case study.
	4. Process Analyzed	Identify, document, and analyze the process or processes that a job is part of. No job exists in a vacuum; all are (or should be) part of a process that ultimately delivers value to external customers. No job analysis is complete without understanding the context of the processes it performs. This is the only way that the value of job accomplishments, outputs, or outcomes can be established.	This accomplishment was illustrated in the NuPlant case study.
	5. Job Performance Planned and Management System (PPMS) Analyzed	Determine the components and effectiveness of the "is" job-level PPMS. (Refer to the discussion of management in chapter 2.)	Examples of job-level PPMS analysis in the NuPlant case study include findings A2, B3, and B9.
	6. PIPs and Stakes Analyzed	Same as (1), except the analysis would focus on processes (stakes and variability between and within processes).	This particular form of analysis was not illustrated in the NuPlant case study.
	7. Cross-Functional Processes Analyzed	Document and analyze the flow of a major process as it moves across multiple functions.	This is a basic requirement for SPC. However, it was not illustrated in the NuPlant case study. For more information on the topic, see Rummler and Brache (1995).
	8. Roles and Responsibilities Analyzed	Determine the "is" roles and responsibilities of a hierarchy of individuals, usually in reference to a particular cross-functional process.	Case study finding B9 is an example of this accomplishment, although on a limited scale.
	9. Process PPMS Analyzed	Determine the components and effectiveness of the "is" process-level PPMS. (Refer to the discussion of management in chapter 2.)	Examples of process-level PPMS analysis in the NuPlant case study include findings B1, B2, B3, B4, and B5.

Results Improvement Process (RIP) Phase	Serious Performance Consulting Accomplishment	Accomplishment Description	Comment
II (continued)	**(A) Relevant AOP Analyzed and Barriers to Results Identified**		
	10. Super-System Analyzed	Identify the relevant components of the super-system of the organization in question and determine if they have or are likely to have any impact on the issue and gap in results.	For more on the super-system, see Rummler and Brache (1995). The super-system of NuPlant was illustrated to a limited extent in the case study.
	11. Business Direction Analyzed	• Determine the organization's goals, strategy, and operating plan for implementing the strategy. • Assess the appropriateness of the direction, given the reality of the organization's super-system and existing internal capabilities.	This accomplishment was not formally illustrated in the NuPlant case study.
	12. PIPs and Stakes Analyzed	Same as (1), except the analysis would focus on the organization (stakes and variability between and within operating units, products, markets, etc.).	This particular form of analysis was not illustrated in the NuPlant case study.
	13. Value Chain Analyzed	Document and analyze the primary processes that make up the organization's value chain (the internal processes that deliver value to the external customer).	This particular form of analysis was not illustrated in the NuPlant case study.
	14. Organization PPMS Analyzed	Determine the components and effectiveness of the "is" organization-level PPMS. (Refer to the discussion of management in chapter 2.)	This particular form of analysis was not illustrated in the NuPlant case study.
	(B) Changes Specified		
	1. Jobs Specified	• "Should" jobs specified, including accomplishments, outputs, outcomes. • Critical dimensions, measures, and standards developed for "should" accomplishments. • Supporting tasks for "should" accomplishments developed.	The recommended format for this work is the job model described by Gilbert (1996). The NuPlant case study did not illustrate "jobs specified" in a formal way.
	2. Roles and Responsibilities Specified	Determine and document the "should" roles and responsibilities of functions and individuals required to support a "should" process.	An approximation of a roles and responsibility matrix appears in the NuPlant case study. Rummler and Brache (1995) provide examples.
	3. Practices Specified	Identify the "should" practices or behavior patterns of key individuals necessary to support the "should" AOP being developed (e.g., "Demonstrates an understanding of the customer's business"). (Refer to the discussion of organizational culture and practices in chapter 4.)	For more information on practices, see the discussion in chapter 4 as well as Tosti and Jackson (1989) and Lineberry and Carleton (1999).

(continued on page 126)

Table 6-2. Serious performance consulting accomplishments (continued).

Results Improvement Process (RIP) Phase	Serious Performance Consulting Accomplishment	Accomplishment Description	Comment
II (continued)	**(B) Changes Specified**		
	4. HPS Specified	Determine the "should" HPS components required to support the "should" performance of key individuals to support the "should" AOP being developed.	Recommendations 1, 2, 3, 4, 8, 9, and 10 in the NuPlant case study are all examples of specifying the "should" HPS.
	5. Job Performance PPMS Specified	Specify the "should" job-level PPMS necessary to support the execution of the "should" jobs. (Refer to the discussion of management in chapter 2.)	This work is implied throughout the NuPlant case study, although there are no clear examples as such.
	6. Solution Design Resources identified	Identify the resources necessary to design, develop, and implement the various job-level changes specified in this phase of RIP.	The performance analyst may not have the capability to design all the changes recommended at the job level. That being the case, the analyst will need to identify the various resources (internal and external to the client organization) required to guide the next phase of the RIP.
	7. Cross-Functional Processes Specified	Specify the "should" • Process outputs or outcomes, including critical dimensions, measures, and standards • Process flow • Resources to operate and support the process • Policies • Technology	This area was not directly illustrated in the NuPlant case study, although recommendations were made to improve several processes and subprocesses.
	8. Roles and Responsibilities Specified	Determine and document the "should" roles and responsibilities of functions and individuals required to support a "should" process.	An approximation of a roles and responsibility matrix appears in appendix B (table B-5) of the NuPlant case study. Rummler and Brache (1995) offer some examples.
	9. Process PPMS Specified	Specify the "should" process-level PPMS necessary to support the execution of the "should" processes. (Refer to the discussion of management in chapter 2.)	This work is implied throughout the NuPlant case study, although there are no clear examples as such.
	10. Solution Design Resources Identified	Identify the resources necessary to design, develop, and implement the various process-level changes specified in this phase of RIP.	The performance analyst most likely will not have the capability to design all the changes recommended at the process level. That being the case, the analyst will need to identify the various resources (internal and external to the client organization) necessary to assist with the next phase of RIP.

Results Improvement Process (RIP) Phase	Serious Performance Consulting Accomplishment	Accomplishment Description	Comment
II (continued)	**(B) Changes Specified**		
	11. Super-System Monitoring System Requirements Specified	Specify the requirements of a "should" process for system-atically monitoring the components in the organization's super-system.	These areas were not illustrated in the NuPlant case study.
	12. Strategy Requirements Specified	Specify the requirements of a "should" strategy that will meet the organization's goals, given the reality of its super-system (i.e., align the strategy with the super-system).	
	13. Value Chain Alignment Requirements Specified	Specify the requirements of a "should" value chain that will implement the strategy and achieve the organization's goals (i.e., align the value chain with the strategy, goals, and customer expectations).	
	14. Organization Structure Requirements Specified	Specify the requirements of a "should" organization struc-ture that will support the value chain.	
	15. Organization PPMS Requirements Specified	Specify the requirements of a "should" organization PPMS. (Refer to the discussion of management in chapter 2.)	
	16. Solution Design Resources Identified	Identify the resources necessary to design, develop, and implement the various organization-level changes speci-fied in this phase of RIP.	The performance analyst will not have the capability to design all the changes recommended at the organization level. That being the case, the analyst will need to identify the various resources (internal and external to the client organization) required to guide the next phase of RIP.
III	**(A) Changes Designed and Developed**		
	1. Job Models Developed	Document the "should" accomplishments, critical dimen-sions, measures, standards, and performance support for key jobs.	The recommended format for this work is the job model described by Gilbert (1996). The NuPlant case study does not formally illustrate job models.
	2. Roles/Responsibility Matrices Developed	Document the "should" roles and responsibilities of func-tions and individuals required to support a "should" process.	An approximation of a roles and responsibility matrix appears in the NuPlant case study (table B-5).
	3. Performance Support Developed	Design and develop the job performance support specified in phase II. This could include training, job aids, incen-tives, feedback systems, and IT support.	The performance support might be developed by specialists in the various areas. However, the serious performance con-sultant must be sufficiently knowledgeable about the sup-port areas to properly direct and manage the development.

(continued on page 128)

Table 6-2. Serious performance consulting accomplishments (continued).

Results Improvement Process (RIP) Phase	Serious Performance Consulting Accomplishment	Accomplishment Description	Comment
III (continued)	**(A) Changes Designed and Developed**		
	4. Job Performance Planned and Managed System (PPMS) Developed	Design and develop the "should" job-level PPMS, including a planning process, measurement system, and action guidelines.	The job PPMS might be developed by specialists in the area of PPMS. However, the serious performance consultant must be knowledgeable enough of the system requirements to properly direct and manage the development.
	5. Job Solution Design Resources Managed	Direct and manage all job design and development specialists employed on the project	The resource management task will increase in complexity as the scope of the project moves up the results chain.
	6. Critical Job Issue (CJI) Evaluation System Developed	Design the evaluation system necessary to evaluate the effectiveness of the project in closing the CJI results gaps.	The complexity of the evaluation system design accomplishment increases as the scope of the project moves up the results chain. Accordingly, so must the skill of the serious performance consultant. This accomplishment was not illustrated in the NuPlant case study.
	7. Cross-Functional Processes Developed	Design and document "should" cross-functional processes to the specifications developed in phase II.	This may require working with internal cross-functional process design teams.
	8. IT Support Developed	Design and develop the "should" IT support for processes that were specified in phase II.	The IT support will most likely be provided by IT specialists. However, the serious performance consultant must be knowledgeable enough of the system requirements to properly direct and manage the development.
	9. Roles/Responsibility Matrices Developed	Document the "should" roles and responsibilities of functions and individuals required to support a "should" process.	An approximation of a roles and responsibility matrix appears in appendix B (table B-5) of the NuPlant case study.
	10. Process Performance Planned and Managed System (PPMS) Developed	Design and develop the "should" process-level PPMS, including a planning and budgeting process, measurement system, performance monitoring and action roles and responsibilities, and management action guidelines.	The process PPMS might be developed by specialists in the area of PPMS. However, the serious performance consultant must be knowledgeable enough of the system requirements to properly direct and manage the development.
	11. Process Solution Design Resources Managed	Direct and manage all process design and development specialists employed on the project.	The resource management task will increase in complexity as the scope of the project moves up the results chain.
	12. CPI Evaluation System Developed	Design the evaluation system necessary to evaluate the effectiveness of the project in closing the CPI results gaps.	The complexity of the evaluation system design accomplishment increases as the scope of the project moves up the results chain. Accordingly, so must the skill of the serious performance consultant. This accomplishment was not illustrated in the NuPlant case study.

Results Improvement Process (RIP) Phase	Serious Performance Consulting Accomplishment	Accomplishment Description	Comment
III (continued)	**(A) Changes Designed and Developed**		
	13. Super-System Monitoring System Developed	Design the "should" super-system monitoring system.	These developmental activities might be executed by specialists in the respective areas. However, the serious performance consultant must be knowledgeable enough of the solution requirements to properly direct and manage the development. These accomplishments were not illustrated in the NuPlant case study.
	14. Strategy Formulated	Formulate a "should" strategy for the organization.	
	15. Value Chain Aligned	Align the primary processes that make up the value chain.	
	16. Organization Structure Redesigned	Redesign the organization structure to support the "should" aligned value chain.	
	17. Organization Performance Planned and Managed System (PPMS) Developed	Design and develop the "should" organization PPMS, including a planning and budgeting process, measurement system, performance monitoring and action roles and responsibilities, and management action guidelines.	
	18. Organization Solution Design Resources Managed	Direct and manage all organization design and development specialists employed on the project.	The resource management task will increase in complexity as the scope of the project moves up the results chain.
	19. CBI Evaluation System Developed	Design the evaluation system necessary to evaluate the effectiveness of the project in closing the CBI results gaps.	The complexity of the evaluation system design accomplishment increases as the scope of the project moves up the results chain. Accordingly, so must the skill of the serious performance consultant. This accomplishment was not illustrated in the NuPlant case study.
	(B) Changes Implemented	• Implementation planned. • Changes installed and managed. • Changes institutionalized.	The complexity of this accomplishment increases as the scope of the project moves up the results chain. Accordingly, so must the skill of the serious performance consultant. This accomplishment was not illustrated in the NuPlant case study.
	(C) Evaluation System Implemented	Execute the evaluation system developed in phase II-B.	The complexity of this accomplishment increases as the scope of the project moves up the results chain. Accordingly, so must the skill of the serious performance consultant. This accomplishment was not illustrated in the NuPlant case study.

(continued on page 130)

Table 6-2. Serious performance consulting accomplishments (continued).

Results Improvement Process (RIP) Phase	Serious Performance Consulting Accomplishment	Accomplishment Description	Comment
IV	**(A) Performance Data Gathered and Analyzed**		
		Oversee the gathering and analysis of the performance data specified in phase II-B.	The complexity of these accomplishments increases as the scope of the project moves up the results chain. Accordingly, so must the skill of the serious performance consultant. These accomplishments were not illustrated in the NuPlant case study.
	(B) Results Analyzed and Changes Made as Required to Close Gap in Results		
		Oversee the analysis of results and guide the decisions regarding changes necessary to ensure the gap in results is closed.	The complexity of these accomplishments increases as the scope of the project moves up the results chain. Accordingly, so must the skill of the serious performance consultant. These accomplishments were not illustrated in the NuPlant case study.
Other	**(A) Project Managed**		
		Manage project resources to deliver project deliverables on time and within budget.	The complexity of these accomplishments increases as the scope of the project moves up the results chain. Accordingly, so must the skill of the serious performance consultant. These accomplishments were not illustrated in the NuPlant case study.
	(B) Engagement Managed		
		Manage a total client engagement, which might require the oversight of several improvement projects simultaneously.	The complexity of these accomplishments increases as the scope of the project moves up the results chain. Accordingly, so must the skill of the serious performance consultant. These accomplishments were not illustrated in the NuPlant case study.
	(C) Client Relations Maintained		
		• Anticipate and resolve client concerns. • Keep client continually informed of project status and issues.	The complexity of these accomplishments increases as the scope of the project moves up the results chain. Accordingly, so must the skill of the serious performance consultant. These accomplishments were not illustrated in the NuPlant case study.
	(D) Project Teams Guided/Managed		
		Instruct, guide, support, and manage client project team members.	The complexity of these accomplishments increases as the scope of the project moves up the results chain. Accordingly, so must the skill of the serious performance consultant. These accomplishments were not illustrated in the NuPlant case study.

Set up Project Teams. Collaborate with other individuals who have different performance consulting and project strengths and who are at different points in their development. A team approach ensures that the client obtains the best results while allowing individuals to continue to learn and practice their craft (ATR 6-6).

According to Rummler 6-6

As you can see from the NuPlant case study, I am partial to using pictures (e.g., process maps or flowcharts, AOP diagrams) as part of analysis and presentations to the client. Some budding analysts, though, prefer a more verbal approach. I recommend teaming a "picture" person with a "word" person to create excellent project deliverables and to provide a developmental opportunity for the (initially) nonvisual person. The same recommendation holds for presentation, project management, and client management capabilities.

Chart Your Course. Put some thought into what you ultimately need to learn about the craft of serious performance consulting. You can use the accomplishment grid in table 6-1 to help you determine your capabilities gap. Develop a set of learning objectives at the outset of each project and at its conclusion, take time to reflect on what you learned and what you need to learn next.

The Path Forward

In chapter 2, you saw how the AOP guided Bert in much the same way as knowledge of human anatomy guides a physician. The serious performance consultant is similar to a skilled physician (table 6-3). They face similar situations in that both are usually approached by someone asking for help. Their objectives are similar, and both must deliver measurable improvement (or the organization or the patient suffers). They both have a critical analytic framework.

Physicians operate with knowledge of the human anatomy. They know what every patient looks like (or should look like) under the skin. This is the basis of their diagnostic procedure and subsequent treatment. Likewise, serious performance consultants operate with knowledge of the AOP. They know what every organization looks like (or should look like) under the skin (or behind their walls), at least in respect to the factors that determine organization results. The AOP is the basis of the performance consultant's diagnostic procedure and subsequent recommendations for change.

Physicians rely on a series of diagnostic tests to make judgments as to what is required to return the patient to good health. Performance consultants apply the four views diagnostic framework (Performance Design Lab, 2004) and related templates from which they make judgments as to what is required for the client organization to close the gap in results. Both the physician and performance consultant follow a diagnostic process, and in the end, prescribe comprehensive courses of action to achieve their objectives. The performance consultant is like a medical internist, in that they both make an initial diagnosis and then consult with specialists (such as a surgeon or compensation expert) to determine and administer an appropriate "treatment." The analogy continues with the requirement that the performance consultant be professional and ethical. Finally, to be at the top of their form, both the physician and the performance consultant must continually learn and practice their crafts—learning about new ailments, new diagnostics, and new treatments or solutions.

How About You?

Are you interested in becoming a *serious* performance consultant (ATR 6-7)? Do you want to make a difference in your organization? Are you prepared to take some risks and challenge initial problem statements? Does the idea of searching for "what really killed results" appeal to you? Do you have the curiosity and diligence to dig into the detail of organization goals and measures, work processes, and the HPS to ferret out the root cause of poor results? Do you have the courage to present your findings, and do you possess the creative spirit to design effective solutions? If so, welcome to the world of serious performance consulting!

The Craft of Serious Performance Consulting

Table 6-3. Comparison of a physician and a performance consultant.

	Physician	Serious Performance Consultant
Situation	Patient feels pain. Patient enters clinic and asks for help.	Client feels pain. Client calls with request for "help" (e.g., increased customer complaints).
Objective	Relieve the pain, address the cause of the health issue, and restore the patient to good health.	Relieve the pain, address cause of performance issue, and obtain measurable improved results.
Analyst's Framework	Knowledge of human anatomy, which provides understanding of how components that make up the human body/system interact and the consequences of a failure in any one of those components. Every physician knows the factors that determine good health, the consequences of a failure in any of those factors, and what must be done to correct a failed factor and return the patient to good health. Physicians also know that symptoms in one area may result from problems in another—this requires taking a systems view of the problem.	Knowledge of the AOP, which provides an understanding of the factors that determine individual performance and organization results.
Diagnostic Tests	Basic tests include • X-ray • Blood tests • CAT scan • Magnetic resonance imaging (MRI)	Four views of an organization and related templates: • Business view • Organization system • Management system • Performer system
Diagnostic Process	1. Elicit description of symptoms 2. Interview and examine patient and conduct tests as required 3. Review test data and make diagnosis 4. Prescribe treatment/procedure or refer to a specialist	*Results Improvement Process:* I. Desired Results Determined and Project Defined II. Barriers Determined and Changes Specified III. Changes Designed, Developed, and Implemented IV. Results Evaluated and Maintained or Improved
Prescription	Corrective and preventive action prescribed to close the gap in physical well-being.	Corrective and preventive action prescribed to close the gap in results.
Treatment/ Procedure	Treatment/procedure delivered or patient referred to specialist if appropriate.	Changes designed, developed, and implemented, utilizing special resources as required.

If you are committed to performance consulting, you may wish to consider the human performance technology (HPT) certification process developed by the International Society for Performance Improvement (ISPI) and co-sponsored by ASTD. The certification process is built on 10 performance standards that closely parallel the points demonstrated by the NuPlant case study. Certification is obtained through the submission of projects (not unlike the NuPlant project) that

132

demonstrate application of the 10 performance standards. You can learn more about the HPT certification process at www.ispi.org or www.astd.org.

In the preface to this book, I explained why I still do serious performance consulting even after all these years. The work is rewarding, challenging, and fun. But, most of all, the work is important and brings value to the organizations I serve. Serious performance consulting is about better organization results, better work environments, and more effective people. I hope you are convinced, because we need you.

According to Rummler 6-7

In addition to taking the other steps described in this chapter, I'd also recommend you look into the performance consulting curriculum offered by Performance Design Lab. These workshops are designed for the individual who is serious about analyzing performance problems and identifying appropriate solutions. Whereas this case study demonstrates what a performance consultant does, the workshops address how-to aspects of the craft and present more than 30 tools for doing the kind of analysis Bert conducted at NuPlant. You can learn more about this curriculum at www.performancedesignlab.com.

CHAPTER 6 HIGHLIGHTS

1. The AOP and the RIP are scalable. They apply equally to critical job, process, and business issues. Likewise, the serious performance consultant must also be scalable, that is, able to operate on all three levels of the results chain.

2. Serious performance consulting has two dimensions:
   - scope of the project, having to do with where in the results chain the project is focused
   - rigor of effort, including application of all phases of the RIP, the depth of analysis, and the comprehensiveness of the solutions.

3. Four things contribute significantly to serious performance consulting capability:
   - knowing how business works
   - knowing your business
   - learning your craft (serious performance consulting)
   - practicing your craft

4. As you go about learning your craft, think about what you must be able to accomplish as your scope of project work moves up the results chain.

5. As you practice your craft, remember the following:
   - It helps to have a passion for what you are doing.
   - Seize opportunities for learning and practicing your craft.
   - Think of your career as a performance consultant as a journey.
   - Apply the notions and tools included in this book.
   - Consider using a buddy system with a colleague as you undertake the journey.
   - Keep a journal of all serious performance consulting projects in which you write down your initial hypotheses and project outcomes.
   - Do formal project debriefings and capture your learning with your buddy.

This appendix contains the detailed NuPlant project findings as they appeared in the project final report. Findings beginning with the letter *A* relate to production supervisor performance, and those beginning with letter *B* relate to plant performance at NuPlant and Old Plant.

```
According to Rummler

As you review these findings, note their specificity,
the detailed discussion of supporting evidence,
the crafting of an argument for change, and the use
of various graphics and displays to present the evi-
dence and argument for change. In the careful pres-
entation of these findings, Bert is trying to preempt
any of the following reactions from those who will
receive the final report and may be skeptical and
defensive:
  • "What do you mean by that? I'm not sure I
    understand."
  • "How do you know that? How did you reach
    that conclusion?"
  • "Says who? Who told you that? What evidence
    do you have?"
  • "So what? Why do you think that's a big deal?
    It happens all the time."
```

Finding A1

Production supervisors have little control over the factors critical to plant productivity. (See recommendation #4 in appendix B.)

Based on observation and extensive interviews with plant management, we compiled a list of accomplishments or conditions basic to a successfully running production line. This list appears in table A-1. In the context of this list, we were able to examine what was not being accomplished and the extent to which lack of accomplishment was a function of the production supervisors. Finally, we were able to determine the cause of the lack of accomplishment.

The accomplishments were first classified as to their relative impact on or criticality to the day's production. In other words, if the accomplishment was not done, would the day's production be disrupted? This, and subsequent classifications, were made based on interviews with all levels of production management and observation of the behavior of supervisors and general supervisors. Under the assumption that production (volume, scrap, direct labor cost) is the primary goal of the supervisor, this classification highlights those accomplishments of most concern to the supervisor. Next, the accomplishments were classified by the degree of control (considerable control, minimal control, no control) that the supervisor actually exercises over their successful completion.

The first two columns of table A-1 reveal some intriguing findings. Of the 10 high-impact or critical accomplishments, the supervisor has total control over only three—problems diagnosed, line status communicated, and line shutdown. The supervisor has no control over steel available,

Table A-1. Analysis of production line and supervisor performance.

Production Line Management Outcomes (And Outputs)	Impact (1)	Control (2)	Deficiency?	Supervisor Deficiency?	Cause (3)
1. Line started					
a. Personnel assigned	H	MC	X	X	TI, C
b. Steel available	H	NC	X		
c. Support materials available	H	NC	X		
d. Racks available	H	NC	X		
e. Piece OK'd	H	MC	X		
2. Line running					
a. Assignments followed-up	M	C	X	X	C
b. Problems diagnosed	H	C	X	X	K, C
c. Problems corrected	H	MC	X		
d. Downtime recorded	L	C			
e. Scrap recorded	M	C	X	X	C, FB
f. Manpower maintained	L	C			
3. Line status communicated	H	C			
4. Line shutdown	H	C	X	X	K, C, FB
5. Personnel reassigned	H	MC	X	X	C, TI
6. Personnel disciplined	M	C	X	X	K, C
7. Timecards processed	L	C			
8. Personnel instructed	M	C	X	X	K, FB, TI, C
9. Area clean	M	MC	X	X	TI, C
10. Absenteeism recorded	L	C			
11. Overtime assigned	L	C			
12. Worker (union) relations maintained	M	C	X	X	C
13. Hazards eliminated	M	MC			

Key:
(1) Impact on day's production: (H) high, (M) medium, (L) low
(2) Control over the outcome/output by the supervisor: (C) full control, (MC) minimal control, (NC) no control
(3) Cause of supervisor's deficiency: (K) knowledge, (C) consequences, (FB) feedback, (TI) task interference

support material available, and racks available, all of which are critical to line start-up. The supervisor has minimal control over the remaining four high-impact accomplishments. Of the 13 accomplishments over which the production supervisor exercises anything approaching considerable control, three are high impact, five are medium impact, and five are low impact.

The flow diagram in figure A-1 illustrates the general flow of the production lines and summarizes the major failures that might occur on a line. Again, the failures are classified as to the degree of control the supervisor has over them. This diagram illustrates the general plight of the supervisor, who is almost totally dependent on the operating system (the job scheduled, the die-set job, quality of steel, manpower available) and who has very few variables that he or she can manipulate to affect production directly.

The lack of control over key variables begins to explain the frustration of the production supervisor. The relative impact of the variables controlled by supervisors is a partial explanation of the priorities they assign various aspects of their job.

Finding A2

Production supervisors receive little objective performance feedback on a daily basis. They see no data on their performance over time and therefore have no objective evaluation of their effectiveness. (See recommendation #3 in appendix B.)

At the end of the shift, production supervisors turn in their down-time report (which also contains the scrap figure) and their roughly calculated direct labor/off-standard (DL/OS) cost to the general supervisor. If the figures are substantially out of line, the general supervisor will exhort the supervisor to do a better job. Unless the figures reported by the production supervisor are considerably at variance with the figures put together by production control and finance (in which case he or she must explain the differences the next day), this is the last the production supervisor will ever hear of that day's efforts.

The next day, the production supervisor will most likely be running a different line with different problems. The next time the production supervisor runs the line (perhaps in a week or in three weeks), he or she might remember the words of the general supervisor, but it is unlikely.

Production supervisors have no objective means of determining what their overall performance is over time; they cannot compare one day's performance against their normal performance. (Indeed, they may not know what normal is.) Furthermore, they can't tell whether the changes they are making regarding a particular part are having any effects whatsoever on performance. In short, it is not possible for production supervisors to evaluate whether they are having any effect at all on performance. Without this kind of information, the production supervisor must feel ineffective and very frustrated.

The problem is worse when to the lack of objective information is added the highly *subjective* information that production supervisors receive from their general supervisors and the "system." Because production supervisors cannot review any objective data on their performance, they must take the reaction of their general supervisors as the only measure of their performance and effectiveness.

Consequently, the frequent tirades of the general supervisor become very significant to the supervisor, even when the general supervisor's reaction is more a function of momentary pressures than any significant problem. The result is that production supervisors make sure they don't do whatever it was that caused that negative reaction if at all possible. Then the production supervisor's primary goal becomes to operate so as to minimize the flack he or she catches from the general supervisor because that is the only barometer of performance available. In addition, most of the heat on the production supervisor revolves around DL/OS, which has very limited value as an indicator of performance.

Still another problem occurs when supervisors (or any individual for that matter) perform in a system without objective feedback. In the absence of real data on how changes in their behavior influence performance, they begin to infer or build apparent cause-and-effect relationships between their actions and results. Because they have no real data to look at, they begin to remember that this little shortcut, that peculiar arrangement of workers and production aids, or this particular manner of chewing out hourly workers *seems* to result in more hits, lower labor costs, and so forth.

In short, production supervisors begin to develop fairly elaborate superstitions about how to do their job. Likewise, without any objective data, they fall prey to old organizational myths such as "If you have to worry about housekeeping, production will go to hell." (This myth is held only at the lowest level of plant supervision. At the upper levels, the belief is that you get good production *only* if you have good housekeeping, which is another myth.) However, if objective performance data are being fed back to the production supervisors, they can see that in fact over the past three

Figure A-1. Potential problems in the press/assembly system.

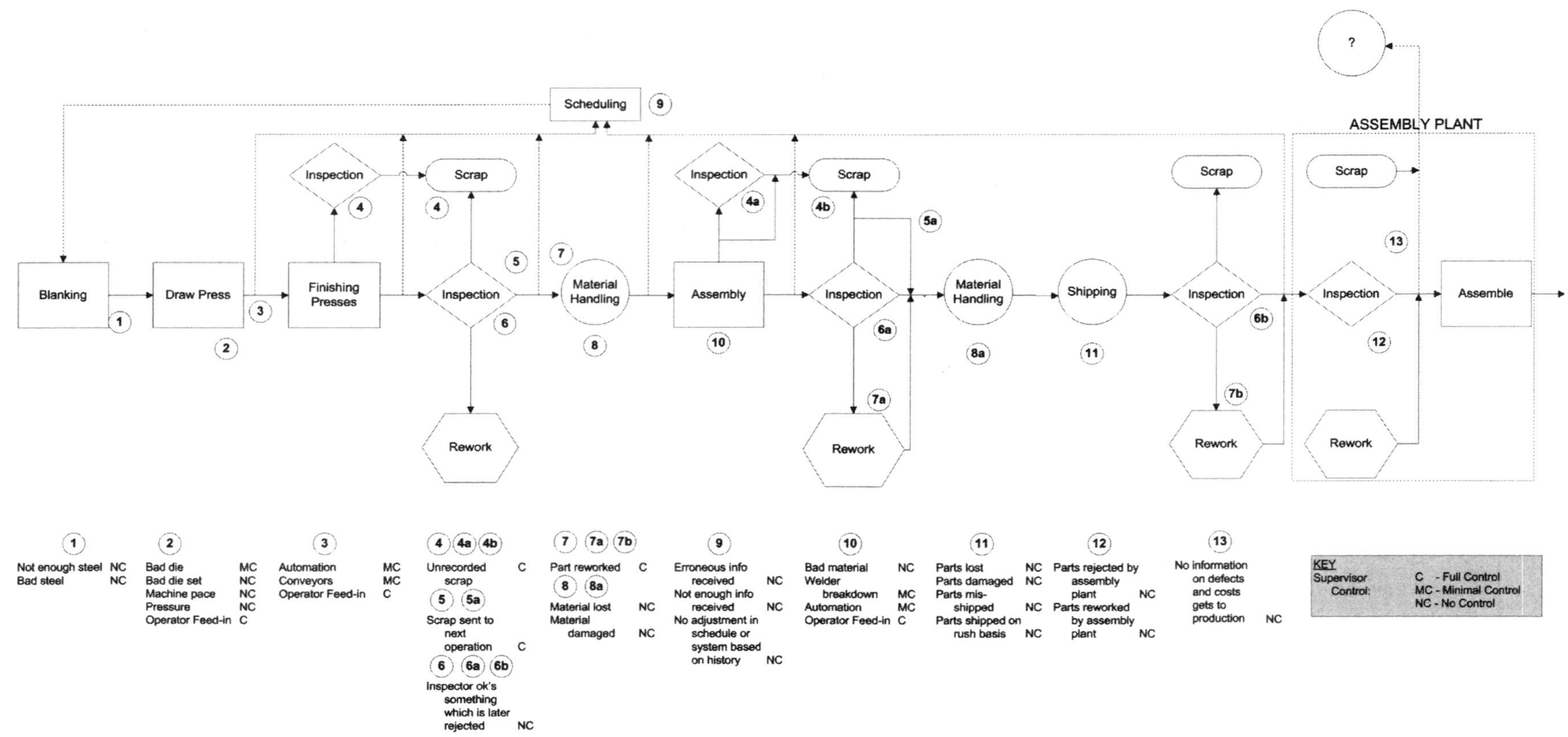

months there has *not* been a significant drop in production on the five or six days in which there were crash housekeeping campaigns, and thereby put an end to one myth.

In summary, production supervisors receive no objective feedback on the effects of their behavior and their performance. They do receive subjective feedback from their general supervisors. This feedback is generally presented in an unpleasant manner and under punishing circumstances. Based on the lack of objective data and the forcefulness of the subjective data, they begin to develop erroneous or questionable theories about what it takes to be successful in their job.

Finding A3

The productivity of NuPlant will not be significantly affected by training production supervisors. The supervisors' failure to perform has limited impact on plant productivity and is seldom attributable to lack of knowledge of what to do.

The production accomplishments that are deemed frequently deficient were identified in table A-1 and further classified as to deficiencies resulting from the supervisor's performance. The causes behind the production supervisors' failure

to perform fall into four general categories as shown in table A-2.

The assumption is that if a supervisor isn't performing properly, it is because he or she doesn't know how (K), physically *cannot* perform properly (TI), doesn't have specific enough information to improve performance (FB), or it is in their best personal interest not to perform as required (C).

In keeping with this classification, we reached the following conclusions about the supervisors' failure to perform; these conclusions are keyed to table A-1.

Ia. Workers assigned

TI: Lines may not be properly manned because not enough people are available due to absenteeism.

C: Supervisors may deliberately understaff lines (e.g., at the offal chute in the basement) to minimize their DL/OS labor costs.

2b. Problems Diagnosed

K: Many production supervisors do not know how to identify potential malfunctions or how to diagnose quickly a malfunction as to probable cause. The result is several levels of production

Table A-2. Main reasons behind the production supervisors' failure to perform.

Reason for Lack of Performance	Explanation
Lack of Knowledge (K)	The supervisor does not know how to perform or when to perform.
Task Interference (TI)	There are factors in the physical environment or in the operating system that prevent the supervisor from performing as desired.
Lack of Feedback (FB)	The supervisor does not receive information on the level of his or her performance or its effect on other systems in the plant.
Punishment or Lack of Positive Consequences (C)	The supervisor receives generally unfavorable consequences or outright punishment from management or the system. In the event there are short-term positive consequences (e.g., less "heat" from management) and potential longer-term negative consequences (low probability of getting caught), the short-term positive consequences will rule.

management in on the diagnosis or a call out to several service departments, or both.

C: Because of the emphasis on DL/OS, it is to a supervisor's advantage to ignore potential problems on the line and keep the line running. To minimize the chances of DL/OS, the press supervisor will keep the press going, recording impressions (hits), even though quality may be questionable and the machine is being damaged. A down line requires that the supervisor deal with reassigning workers (first the decision whether to reassign and then to where) and then anticipate a potential loss of pay points. For those reasons, a down line frequently results in "heat" from the general supervisor. The extent of the power of DL/OS as a consequence is illustrated by the fact that supervisors have been known to suggest to plant engineering that if a line is going to be down for some time (usually in excess of an hour), they might just keep it down. This puts the start-up problem on the supervisor on the following shift and thus avoids having to find the other workers (usually not experienced on this line) to man the repaired line.

2e. Scrap reported

C: What would seem to be a considerable quantity of defective parts is not reported (registered with quality control and tagged as scrap). The reason is that there are acceptable scrap limits and when they are exceeded, a great deal of "heat" descends through the organization and lands on the heads of the general supervisors and production supervisors. These limits and the negative consequences for exceeding them have very little effect on suppressing the amount of scrap (primarily because of the high payoff for impressions, regardless of quality). They do, however, have considerable effect on suppressing the reporting of scrap. The major result is invalid scrap data and inventory shortages with resultant extra shipping costs. Supervisors tend to dispose of unrecorded scrap by sending it to the baler (loaded on half-empty racks of already rejected parts or by

altering or stealing tags) or by managing to get it shipped (by stealing or altering tags).

FB: There is no measurement of the net parts (non-scrap, non-rework) produced on a line during a shift, so there is no feedback to the system or management on the actual net performance of a line or supervisor. Without this information, no data are available to evaluate the extent of the problem and, therefore, there is no opportunity to correct it. Likewise, no information is fed back to the production supervisors on the effect of their not reporting scrap, such as the need for recycling, extra shipping charges, and assembly plant chargebacks. In summary, there are short-term advantages in "burying" scrap and no direct long-term disadvantages.

4. Line shutdown

K: There are no clear decision rules for when a particular part should be shut down. Ideally, shut down points would vary with the extent of the defect, the cost of scrap, the cost of rework, and the demand for the part. The situation is also complicated by the fact that quality control standards frequently vary with the demand for the part (e.g., "We'll OK 4,000 in that condition, but no more").

5. Workers reassigned

C: Workers may not be reassigned as soon as might be ideal because the supervisor prefers to keep them on hand in the event the line starts up again. If the line is repaired and starts up but the workers from that line have been reassigned, the supervisor must staff that line with relatively inexperienced workers. If there is a chance the down line will start up within a certain period (usually an hour), the supervisor will keep them in the area. Some general supervisors attempt to carry open lines so they can handle unassigned workers particularly when they are running "dogs" (difficult-to-run parts, for which scrap and down time are likely to be high) and anticipate down time.

TI: Frequently workers are not reassigned because there are no places (other lines) to put them.

Also, hourly workers prefer not to be reassigned to new departments and often go to the infirmary rather than shift from assembly to press and vice versa.

6. *Workers disciplined*

K: The problem of knowing when to discipline persists despite formal contract language and general management proclamations. There always seem to be more variables to consider than are practicable for the supervisor under stress. The situation is particularly complicated at NuPlant where three members of supervision were transferred out because of their approach to discipline. Most supervisors are clear on disciplinary procedures but not clear on when it is advisable to discipline.

C: The production supervisors' disciplinary behavior is very much determined by the positive and negative consequences brought to bear by their superiors and the system. In general, the forces at play are the industrial relations group, which argues for restraint and firmness from a psychological distance of time and management level; the general supervisor, superintendent of production level where there is little distance, psychological or other, from the pressure of getting out production; and the system, which, for example, punishes the supervisor for disciplining a worker for absenteeism because that simply means sending the worker home again.

8. *Workers instructed*

K: New supervisors do not appear to have the basic skills in instructing new workers on the critical aspects of their jobs.

FB: Most supervisors are not convinced that any time spent instructing a new worker makes any difference in regard to his or her productivity.

C: The high probability of reassignment of new workers and the resultant absenteeism and turnover lead to few positive consequences to the supervisor for spending a great deal of time training a new employee. If a new worker remains for several weeks, then it might be

advantageous to take notice of him or her and make an investment in knowing and training him or her.

TI: The start-up problems and subsequent need to reassign workers in the first hour or two make it difficult for the supervisor to spend any time instructing new workers or following up on training done by utility people. The pressure to do other, more critical things is too great.

9. *Area clean*

TI: Most factors contributing to poor housekeeping are not under the control of the supervisor but are in the domain of the service departments: material handling and plant engineering. Production supervisors have little direct control over the general clutter in the work area.

C: Housekeeping generally has relatively low payoff to the supervisor, compared to scrap, productivity, and labor cost. When a supervisor is having trouble making production, he or she is going to be little concerned with housekeeping unless forced to by external pressure. At higher levels at NuPlant, a myth persists that if housekeeping can be sharpened up, high productivity and low scrap rates will result. This is nonsense. Good housekeeping is usually accompanied by high productivity and low scrap, but there is no cause-and-effect relationship. High productivity and low scrap are functions of an effective system, which allows for time to attend to housekeeping.

12. *Worker (union) relations maintained*

C: Despite all the emphasis from industrial relations, union relations are a low-priority area for the production supervisor. The consequences for low productivity—high scrap and high DL/OS—are immediate, negative, and powerful. The consequences for poor handling of union relations (within limits) are infrequent, less immediate, and not so negative.

As shown in table A-1, *the production supervisors' failure to perform as desired is attributable to lack of knowledge in only four instances,* and in each of those cases there are other factors contributing to the problem. Therefore, it is concluded that training alone will not increase the effectiveness of production supervisors.

Finding B1

The production system currently measures and emphasizes an inappropriate performance variable—direct labor cost. (See recommendation #1 in appendix B.)

Merits of the Measure of Direct Labor Cost

Because the performance of supervisors is almost exclusively gauged by direct labor/off-standard (DL/OS) variance, we sought to establish the significance of this performance variable. For this analysis, we relied on data from Old Plant because such data were unavailable at NuPlant. We believe, however, that the findings at Old Plant can be generalized to the situation at NuPlant.

First, we looked at the magnitude of DL/OS to determine whether it was in itself an economic variable of appreciable magnitude. Second, we analyzed the correlation of DL/OS and other variables (impressions and scrap) to determine if it was a useful predictor for these variables. And finally, we compared the performance of supervisors on the same lines (first and second shifts) over a period of 16 weeks to determine if a significant range of performance occurs.

DL/OS as an Economic Measure. Direct labor variances were found to be such a small part of the economy of a stamping plant that it is clear that DL/OS has no dollar significance in itself. The budgeted direct labor is less than 10% of the total budget. Variances in DL/OS amounted to so little that if one were able to make the poorest supervisor DL/OS performance match the best, savings of only a few hundred thousand dollars could be realized annually. This means that unless DL/OS is significantly correlated with more relevant measures, it is not only useless but misleading. If a supervisor can run a line to produce more doors with less scrap by using more direct labor, he or she should be encouraged to do so. However, the present system of

accounting for supervisors' performance must act to discourage any such labor-use strategies.

DL/OS as an Index. We found in a study of six supervisors over 16 weeks no correlation between DL/OS and impressions or scrap. So, not only is DL/OS useless as a measure in itself, it is of no use as an index to other, more significant reflections of productivity.

DL/OS Differences between Supervisors. To compare the performance of supervisors, we needed pairs who work under similar conditions. We obtained these pairs by taking supervisors on identical lines (doors) on the day and night (first and second) shifts. Because we had heard that the second shift performance was better than the first shift in terms of DL/OS, we sought to determine whether this was true. Statistical calculations revealed no significant difference between day and night DL/OS even during the first and second hours of start-up. This lack of significance held even when we compared in isolation the pair of door supervisors who had the greatest differences in their mean of DL/OS performance for the 16 weeks.

Variation between Supervisors on Other Measures. There were no statistical differences between several pairs of door supervisors on scrap performance or impressions made. This finding, then, supports our other, more closely made observation that supervisor differences do not have a large impact on plant production. We extended our study to general supervisors, and statistically, as we had expected from on-site observation, we found no significant differences in their productivity. Our findings for them mirrored exactly our findings for first-line production supervisors.

Comments on the Use of the DL/OS Measure

1. *Direct labor/off-standard provides a distorted view of performance.* The DL/OS figures are calculated on the basis of the number of hits and are never adjusted for the number of acceptable parts. A supervisor who manages to make a standard of 2,000 good parts (hits) per shift, with 1,600 actual good parts after

unreported scrap, reported scrap, and rework, could have a better DL/OS figure than a supervisor who managed to make only 1,800 hits but with 1,750 actual good parts.

2. *The DL/OS measure places the wrong emphasis on performance.* By emphasizing DL/OS, the production supervisor is being encouraged to run bad or marginal parts in order to record impressions. Supervisors will also overproduce a smooth-running part for the same reason. Even though this part is not in demand and the overstock causes severe inventory and material handling problems, the supervisor's DL/OS figure looks extremely good at the end of the shift.

3. *The DL/OS measure provides minimal or no control over performance.* This measure is managed as if it were a significant variable in the performance formula. The fact that direct labor makes up approximately 10% of the manufacturing budget says something about its real significance. Not only is it *not* a significant variable, but the data analysis we conducted showed that it was a poor indicator or predictor of performance.

4. *It results in poor information for decisions about performance.* Because the emphasis is on hits, there is no information on available parts. The result is major inventory discrepancies and no historical data for purposes of better scheduling. Because DL/OS is a poor indicator of performance, there are no real data on which supervisors are actually performing well.

Finding B2

There is no data storage that can function as a "memory" for the production system. (See recommendation #2 in appendix B.)

No system exists for tracking relevant history of performance in this plant. That is, there is no record of how a line has performed over time or how a part has performed over time (e.g., actual production vs. scheduled, actual cost vs. budgeted or allowed costs). Performance data are seldom retained beyond a week and generally are not available below the superintendent level. The data that are collected are not broken out by shift and line.

The result is a lack of a cumulative record, or "memory" of past performance so that trends can be noted, problems diagnosed, and results evaluated. Individuals (supervisors and general supervisors) and departments (quality control, material handling, plant engineering) remember problem parts and try to correct or compensate, often to the disadvantage of another department and the detriment of the plant.

For example, when a problem part is scheduled, the supervisor is tempted to find some excuse not to run it, the general supervisor is tempted to keep an open line so he or she can place the workers when the line shuts down, and quality control may be extra tough on clearing the job and monitoring quality so they won't get burned by subsequent (and predictable) claims of faulty parts. But, there is no *systemwide* capacity to remember (record and recall), analyze, and subsequently correct. (The only possible exception is the "10 worst parts" record compiled by finance and used to correct the worst parts. However, when a part no longer qualifies for this list, it no longer is monitored.)

Finding B3

There is little or no feedback to production supervision on the consequences to the system of its poor performance. (See recommendation #3 in appendix B.)

Information on rework costs, late shipping costs, and assembly plant chargebacks are not fed back to those members of production supervision responsible for the excess costs. The production supervisors and often the general supervisors are ignorant of the effects of their actions and are not held accountable for the results.

The only communication production and service department supervision receives on chargebacks and late shipping is in the form of announcements to general supervisors in production meetings. The information is infrequent and very general, consisting of an announcement that "last month's costs were out of line and they had better be watched."

The major cause of this problem is the lack of specific data on these costs. This would cease to be a problem if the recommended memory system were installed.

Finding B4

The NuPlant scheduling system (in contrast to Old Plant) does not have the data necessary to realistically and effectively schedule production. (See recommendation #5 in appendix B.)

The scheduling system does not have

- the data necessary to realistically and effectively schedule production
- an effective communication system with production and the service departments
- anything approximating a sound working relationship with production

Basically, two major problems exist in scheduling and production control. The first is the scheduling system itself, and the second is the failure to integrate scheduling and production management into a constructive working relationship with the shared mission of profitable productivity. There are a number of inefficiencies in daily production and scheduling operations that result from these funda-

mental problems and which are discussed in detail in finding B5.

The basic elements of the current scheduling and production control system are summarized in figure A-2. The system begins with a program need that is converted to a daily schedule. The computer records the hits, adjusts for scrap, feeds the information back, and adjusts the program need accordingly.

Unfortunately, the number of actual usable parts differs considerably from the computer count for all the reasons discussed earlier. The result is that the program requirements are altered based on highly erroneous data; consequently, parts are not available for assembly or shipping. Eventually the actual count is realized in the form of an emergency need, and the daily schedule is altered to accommodate the shortage. This situation necessarily sets back the accomplishment of the program and may require weekend work.

Because the *actual* count is never captured and fed back into the system in any orderly way,

Figure A-2. Potential problems in the press/assembly system.

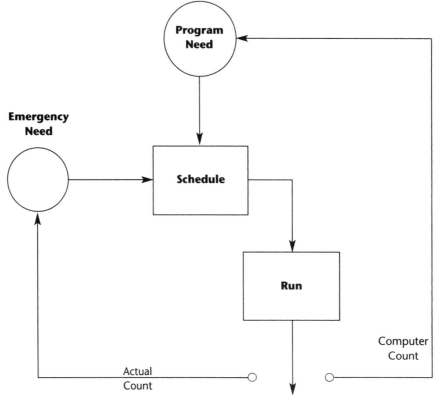

the program need is never increased to allow for a realistic output, and the cause of the low yield is never investigated or corrected. The system continues unaltered, operating on faulty information and falling further behind. The result is continuous die sets, low productivity, and the kind of anxiety among personnel described in finding B5. The problem is aggravated by the adversarial roles that seem to have been adopted by scheduling and production.

Finding B5

The NuPlant production scheduling work environment is a contributor to lack of scheduling effectiveness. (See recommendation #5 in appendix B.)

One of the critical differences we observed between Old Plant and NuPlant lies in the implementation of scheduling and material control. We are describing this difference in detail because it clearly has a bearing on the performance of production supervisors and general supervisors.

The logic of scheduling, so far as we can tell, is identical at both plants; however, the scheduling system in actual operation is so dramatically different that we spent some time observing these operations at both Old Plant and NuPlant. These observations were not limited to interviews: we sat with schedulers for several hours, night and day, and we tracked several general supervisors as they communicated with scheduling. Our observations are summarized in the table A-3.

Finding B6

The first hour line start-up is ineffective and costly. (See recommendation #7 in appendix B.)

This observation is far from profound. However, it is our belief that the cause of this generally observed problem lies outside of what is done or could be done during the first hour of production. First hour production is, by and large, outside the control of production supervisors and general supervisors, even though they frequently get burned for it.

We are sure that this problem has multiple causes. The continuing problem is most likely a manifestation of the lack of data on actual die-set time and realistic net production predictions for a run. The result is that unrealistic schedules are set (and subsequently not met), and the real problems never get corrected.

The problem will not be solved by putting heat on production supervisors. We recommend a closer look by plant management at the system causes of the problem.

Finding B7

Lines frequently run when it is more cost effective to shut them down. (See recommendation #8 in appendix B.)

The various factors encouraging a supervisor to run marginal and scrap pieces have been discussed earlier. It is also apparent that in many cases supervisors and general supervisors *just don't know* when it is most cost beneficial to shut down the line.

Finding B8

The indirect budgeting system tends to be counterproductive in times of stress. (See recommendation #6 in appendix B.)

The problems observed with indirect labor budgeting would not occur under normal circumstances. Nevertheless, the fact that these problems arise under stress indicates a basic flaw in the indirect budgeting concept.

We understand the basic rationale for budgeting indirect labor as a percentage of production. Obviously, if you are running at lower volume you should require less indirect labor. However, the system for authorizing indirect labor should be more responsive to the operating realities of production. For example, why is the volume down? If it is because of low demand, that is one thing, but if it is due to down lines because of increasing mechanical failures, then that's another problem. If lines are down for this reason, then this is the time for *more* plant engineering manpower, not less. Also, plant engineering is frequently asking to release lines for maintenance during light production times. A reduced program would seem like an excellent time to catch up on much-needed maintenance, yet manpower is not authorized.

Table A-3. A comparison of scheduling systems at Old Plant and NuPlant.

Characteristic	Old Plant	NuPlant
Atmosphere	Quiet and serene. Schedulers concentrate on work almost uninterrupted. Seldom more than one outsider in the room; more often no one else is present.	Chaotic. Locally called "the jungle" by all levels of production management. Typically, more than half the desks have a supervisor or general supervisor sitting *on* it, either using the phone or talking to schedulers or others. The area is extremely noisy and not conducive to concentration because of so much cursing and milling about. Sometimes it is difficult to make one's way through the room.
Style of Communicating with General Supervisors and Supervisors	By telephone 98% of the time. Only one telephone to the floor and that controlled by one person. General supervisors are discouraged from entering room except when called in or when telephone line not available in time. No supervisors are in room. General supervisor's office next to scheduling room never (in a two-hour period) has more than one general supervisor present. The adjoining computer room is isolated.	General supervisors spend half their time in scheduling room, going from one person to another seeking help or information. A floor telephone on each scheduler's desk is heavily used by general supervisors to communicate with supervisors on the floor. Also many supervisors are in scheduling room. The general supervisor's office is usually at least half filled. General supervisors often enter computer room seeking information.
Communication Content with General Supervisors	If general supervisors cannot place workers in their adjoining areas, they phone into scheduling. In a few minutes scheduling provides a solution. Similar means are used for problems of supply or engineering.	General supervisors are forced to use a discovery system. When they cannot immediately place their workers, they go to the scheduling room. When they state a problem, they are generally referred to someone else. They talk to everybody and may, for example, accidentally find another general supervisor who needs their workers. Or, in the scheduling room, they may stumble across a materials handling supervisor who tells them that the brackets they are due to have are not in inventory even though two scheduling people have just told them they were.
Division of Responsibility between General Supervisors and Scheduling	"When the target schedule isn't made, the fault generally lies here," we were told by two scheduling people. The scheduling room assumes responsibility for getting workers reassigned, assessing true inventory, and making many basic decisions whether to shut a line down or not. Primary responsibility for resolving conflicts between production, engineering, and material handling is taken by materials control. Scheduling manager and assistant communicated with command, acting as an extension of production manager's arm.	"I don't give a damn what material handling tells you. It says right here that they have that bracket in inventory!" This statement is typical of "passing the buck" statements we heard in scheduling. The general attitude is, "If it's on the printout, that's how it must be. It's not our fault if somebody else is screwing up." Scheduling takes no command and seems to be at odds with production management.
Reliability of Information	Schedulers are required to spend 20% of their time actually on the floor to verify the reliability of their data. They establish close relationships with stock handlers who frequently reported on inventory, down lines, etc. Cost analysts in material control check daily on the floor to ensure the accuracy of production reports.	In theory, NuPlant schedulers and cost analysts have a responsibility to go onto the floor. In practice it seems that almost never happens even though everyone knows the data are not accurate. Inventory lists are taken at face value. The general attitude is "We only know what we are told."

These problems are aggravated in times of stress and when tremendous pressure is being put on labor costs. No service department head wishes to run with labor in the red for very long (two consecutive days). This pressure causes severe problems for such departments as plant engineering (PE). Assume that the plant is running at 80% of volume on a shift with a corresponding reduction in PE personnel. If, during the first hour, the PE supervisor observes that enough lines are down and will stay down to make it unlikely to have anything close to 80% volume, he or she will begin to dump his or her labor (reassign to project work) in anticipation of the reduced authorization. If this action is not taken, labor may well be in the red for the day with the expected negative consequences. Therefore, at the very time the system needs PE help most, the PE supervisor is paid off for reducing the manpower working on the problem. (We do not mean to imply that this is standard practice in PE. The point is that it has happened and will continue to happen with this system of budgeting and labor cost pressures.)

Another problem inherent in the system is that PE knows which big lines must be kept running in order to authorize the most manpower. Naturally, these lines will receive top priority. Unfortunately, these lines may not be lines that are critical to scheduling, and conflicts over the priority of repairing lines can develop.

A second example of the unresponsiveness of the indirect budgeting system is the manner in which labor is authorized for material handling. This labor is authorized on the basis of volume and does not take into account the size or configuration of the part. Thus, for X volume parts, Y number workers are authorized. If the majority of the lines are running small parts, Y number workers can handle the job well. In fact, workers can be loaned to other departments, and material handling will be considerably in the black on labor for that shift. If, however, the majority of the lines are running large parts such as hoods and deck panels, then Y number of workers cannot handle those parts in a satisfactory way. Then, material handling must borrow workers to do the job, and, consequently, labor costs will run in the red for that shift. This situation again becomes a major problem when pressure is on labor cost, tempting material handling supervision to take shortcuts that fly in the face of good safety and quality practices.

Finding B9

The organization of responsibilities of the three lower levels of production management is inadequate for coping with the current production problems. (See recommendation #4 in appendix B.)

Production management effort is highly redundant in some areas (e.g., getting out today's production), but little effort is expended in other areas (e.g., correcting chronic problems). Obviously, part of this problem involving production supervisors, general supervisors, and superintendents is a function of the current stress on the system. However, a substantial cause is the lack of clarity of a basic mission at each level of management and the resultant distribution of responsibilities. We have noted the following:

- The production supervisor is held responsible for scrap and DL/OS on his or her line but, in fact, has little control over the factors that affect those measures. The only resource that production supervisors control in any sense is manpower and that factor has little effect on production.
- General supervisors are held responsible for the scrap rates and DL/OS of their production supervisors. They generally behave as "super-supervisors." Their job differs from the production supervisor only in the size of the physical area they patrol and additional paperwork. They have more latitude than the supervisor in the reassignment of manpower because they have more information about alternative lines. Because they supposedly control more resources, it is thought that they can bring the resources of the service department to bear on problems. It is not clear, however, that they in fact can influence the service departments and are able to manipulate those resources.
- The superintendents are held responsible for scrap rates and the DL/OS of their general supervisors. This is the first level of

management that actually has the opportunity to manage resources. But, the success of this manager depends on his or her ability to influence the management of the service units and staff offices.

In summary, the first two levels of supervision have very little to manage. All three levels of supervision have the identical, singular goal of minimizing DL/OS and scrap.

Merely establishing job definitions for these levels of management will not solve the problem. The job definitions are abstractions that do not provide a statement of mission for each level and are difficult to interpret in terms of the dynamics of the workflow.

Finding B10

Several knowledge deficiencies exist in production supervision and management. (See recommendation #10 in appendix B.)

The knowledge deficiencies are

- understanding of job responsibilities (knowledge of job definitions is compromised by what actually happens in the heat of battle).
- ability to diagnose well the operational system (including worker performance problems and their causes).
- providing adequate feedback to workers on the quality of their performance.
- providing reinforcement to workers for making constructive comments (For example, consider this exchange: Worker: "I noticed that that production aid keeps slipping away and materials jam in it." Supervisor: "Well, for Pete's sake, fix it!" or "You worry about your job, and I'll worry about the others.") The reinforcement to the worker in Old Plant for making improvement suggestions is the increase in the probability of quitting early ("early-quit" policy).

Finding B11

The introduction of new production workers into the production crews during the first hour line start-up every day is extremely inefficient and counterproductive.

As described earlier, the production supervisor's major challenge during the first hour of line start-up is to get both his or her assigned lines either up and running or officially declared down, so as to avoid being in the red regarding direct labor costs. In the event that a line is declared down, the supervisor is still charged for that labor until the crew of 20 or more production workers has physically reported to another line. This situation often results in the production supervisor and reassigned production workers literally trotting several hundred yards to the new press line.

Meanwhile, during the first 15 minutes of the shift, someone from human resources will show up on the line and introduce the production supervisor to one to four new workers being assigned to his or her line to fill openings caused by absenteeism. One of two things can happen at this point:

- One, the new employees (note that this is their first 15 minutes working for NuPlant) can join the small mob of workers who are trotting halfway across the plant to a different line and supervisor.
- Two, the supervisor says, "Nice to meet you. Please just stand out of the way for a while, and I'll be back to get you placed on the line." When the line is finally up and running, the supervisor will return to the new workers, put them somewhere on the line, introduce them to adjacent co-workers, provide minimal instruction and leave, quite possibly never to be seen the rest of the shift.

As mentioned earlier, production supervisors are reluctant to invest much time in training new production workers because they are likely to quit in a day or two. After a worker has been on the job for a couple of weeks, the supervisor will make an effort to know and train the employee. Of course, there is a Catch-22 operating here: The failure of the supervisor to know and train the new employee during the first day or two on the job contributes to the high rate of turnover. An apparent characteristic of the "new generation" workforce available to NuPlant is that they would rather be unemployed than abused or disrespected.

Finding B12

Old Plant has an "early-quit" policy that provides a significant incentive to production workers for high productivity and yield. There is no such system at NuPlant.

Old Plant has an "early-quit" policy in place that makes it possible for production workers to leave the line when that line has met the production and scrap goals for the shift. Although the workers cannot leave the plant, they may adjourn to the cafeteria for the remainder of the shift. This free time is a major incentive for these production workers to operate efficiently, alert supervision to impending problems on the line, and train and integrate new workers on the line.

NuPlant Project Recommendations

This appendix contains the write-up of the NuPlant project recommendations as they appeared in the project final report. You'll see that the recommendations are keyed to the findings presented in appendix A. For more on the organization of these recommendations see figure 3-18.

 ## Summary of Recommendations

1. **Measure performance by yield and net productivity.**
2. **Install a data system that will provide a production system "memory" function.**
3. **Provide feedback to all production supervision.**
4. **Change production supervision responsibilities.**
5. **Change the scheduling system.**
6. **Alter the basis for determining certain indirect labor budgets.**
7. **Change current start-up procedures.**
8. **Provide decision guides for supervisors and general supervisors on shutting down lines.**
9. **Train production supervision in new responsibilities.**
10. **Train production supervisors and general supervisors in selected topics.**

The objective in organizing and presenting the recommendations is to have the client take action by implementing the recommendations. The receivers of these findings and recommendations, however, are often skeptical, defensive, and wary about the work required to make the suggested changes. There will be a natural tendency on the part of the receivers to look for any excuse not to have to follow through on Bert's recommendations. To increase the odds that the recommendations will be accepted and implemented, Bert did several important things.

First, each finding was presented along with the related recommendation. They were not separated from each other, as they appear in the appendixes of this case study. (They were separated for ease of discussion in the case study.) Therefore, the need was established first (i.e., the finding), followed by the detailed recommendation to address the need.

Second, you will note that each recommendation goes way beyond a bullet point and includes substantial detail, using graphics where possible. As with the findings, Bert is trying to minimize questions along the lines of "Tell me again, why is this important?" and "What do you mean?" from the receivers of his report. This detail also continues to add to Bert's credibility because it shows that he knows as much about the business as the client—if not more, in some areas.

Third, several recommendations are accompanied by samples or suggested formats, as you'll see later in this appendix. Bert calls these solution prototypes. He has learned that if you make a recommendation like "Track and feed back production performance to supervisors," the client is likely to nod agreement, but nothing will be implemented. Why? Such recommendations sound like meaningless platitudes or business-speak jargon. Second, most likely the client doesn't know exactly what you mean but is afraid that implementing the recommendation will involve a great deal of work. When you put these two reactions together, the result is going to be inertia—no implementation.

Bert has learned to take such recommendations to another level of detail, to the point of "Let me show you what it might look like." When you do that, the response from the client is more likely to be something like "Oh, that's what you mean! That could be useful. Actually, we have some of that data already, but we don't do much with it." And, of course, the argument for the recommendation is strengthened if you can mention that you tried out the idea on several supervisors and they said such a document or process would be very helpful.

According to Rummler

Now that you know how Bert presented his recommendations by linking them to the project findings and with relevant prototypes, let's take a closer look at the recommendations themselves. These recommendations are taken directly from Bert's final project report. Note that each recommendation "headline" is followed by a full, detailed description of the changes required.

Recommendation 1

Measure performance by material yield and net productivity. (See finding B1 in appendix A.)

Based on our analysis, we recommend making several changes in the way performance is measured at NuPlant:

1. Deemphasize direct labor/off-standard (DL/OS) as a measure of performance.
2. Begin to measure material yield and net productivity.
3. Measure and manage performance by a composite of indicators including material yield, net productivity, and scrap.

All the major inputs to and outputs of the production system are identified in figure B-1. The current measures of performance are off-standard direct labor (C/D) and recorded scrap (H).

The plant would have better cost, part productivity, inventory, scheduling, and supervisor performance data if it measured steel yield, net productivity, and profitability (table B-1).

In addition to better data for subsequent performance decisions, measuring yield and net figures will result in more *accurate* data. For example, there will be little incentive for the supervisor to "bury" scrap, because the true scrap figure (J) will be D – G, and easily determined by production control. Likewise, there will be little point in manipulating C (understaffing, unwise

Figure B-1. Inputs to and outputs of production at NuPlant.

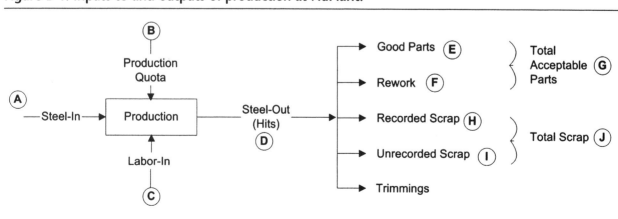

Table B-1. Recommended measures of productivity.

Proposed Measure	Description
Steel Yield	E/A and G/A, which would evaluate how the most expensive resource—steel—is being used
Net Productivity	E/B and G/B, which would indicate the parts on hand for assembly or shipping and would provide data to scheduling for realistic finished-part projections
Profitability	$\dfrac{\text{Standard Cost of a Unit of G}}{\text{Actual Cost of a Unit of G (A+C--H)}}$

reassignment) or D (producing marginal parts) because G/B, G/A, and profitability are the real measures of performance.

The current measures of scrap and DL/OS are relatively gross indicators, which are no doubt of value to the division in monitoring plants.

The recommended measures would be of greatest value in the daily internal management of the plant. Both data systems could be used. It is important, however, to understand their different functions. The recommended indices are measures of important variables that must be managed by the plant to ensure profitability. In contrast, DL/OS is a gross lagging indicator (a questionable one at that) of plant performance that merely indicates that something is wrong. Positive changes in the recommended indices will improve DL/OS figures but not necessarily vice versa.

Before any of the recommended measures are put into effect, they should be thoroughly tested and refined in some simulated plant setting or tested in parallel with the existing measures.

Recommendation 2

Install a data system that will provide a production system "memory" function. (See finding B2 in appendix A.)

Installing a data storage and retrieval system ("memory") would allow data on actual performance to be stored continuously along with data on desired performance. This system would serve as the basis for diagnosing and correcting operating problems and evaluating the performance of production and service supervision.

Specifically, we recommend the collection and storage of the information shown in table B-2, which should be available as a computer printout. The printout would provide a complete profile of the performance of a part, each time it has been run. The data can be retrieved by part (as shown) or by supervisor or by line. It would be of value in die-set meetings (predicting problems based on past runs), scheduling (data on the true yield per cycle run), programming (how long a cycle is required), budget negotiation (the actual cost of producing a part), system correction (why the difference between projected and actual), and evaluation of all supervisors (why problems persist or recur).

In addition, there should be a problem log for key parts (the format for such a log is illustrated in figure B-2). The logs would be maintained by general supervisors. They could use the document to brief the supervisors on anticipated problems with a part and to summarize their own efforts to correct problems. The logs could also serve as a record of requests for change to the superintendent and subsequent results and as a source of proposed method improvements to plant management.

Between the parts performance record and the problem log, production management would have the data necessary to improve and maintain production.

Table B-2. Part performance record.

Part Number:					
Indicators		**Runs**			
Run Number					
Date	Start:				
	End:				
Shift:					
Line:					
General Supervisor:					
Production Supervisor:					
Pieces Scheduled:					
Pieces Shipped:					
Date to Shipping:					
Date Shipped:					
Setup Time:	Standard:				
	Actual:				
Blanks In:					
Pieces to Assembly:					
Pieces to Scrap:	Code:				
	Frequency:				
Pieces Rework:	Code:				
	Frequency:				
Blanks In/Pieces to Assembly:	Standard:				
	Actual:				
Blanks In/Total Pieces to Assembly:					
First Hour Blanks In/Pieces to Assembly:	Standard:				
	Actual:				
First Hour Labor:	Standard:				
	Actual:				
First Hour Scrap:	Standard:				
	Actual:				
Press Labor:	Standard:				
	Actual:				
Press Scrap:	Standard:				
	Actual:				
$ Press Rework:	Unit:				
	Total:				
Press $ Scrap:					
Press $ Labor:					
Press Downtime:	Code:				
	Frequency:				
Unit Cost of Part through Press:	Standard:				
	Actual:				
Pieces from Press:					
Pieces to Shipping:					
Pieces to Scrap:	Code:				
	Frequency:				

Part Number:					
Indicators		**Runs**			
Pieces Rework:	Code:				
	Frequency:				
Pieces In/Pieces Shipped:	Standard				
	Actual:				
Parts In/Total Pieces Shipped (after rework):					
First Hour Parts In/Total Pieces Shipped (after rework):	Standard:				
	Actual:				
Assembly Labor:	Standard:				
	Actual:				
Assembly Scrap:	Standard:				
	Actual:				
Assembly Rework:	Standard:				
	Actual:				
Assembly $ Scrap:					
Assembly $ Labor:					
Assembly Downtime:	Code:				
	Frequency:				
Unit Cost of Part through Assembly:	Standard:				
	Actual:				
Late Shipping Charges:	Code:				
	Amount:				
Assembly Plant Chargeback:	Code:				
	Amount:				
Recycle Required?					
Unit Cost Total:	Standard:				
	Actual:				
Profitability:					

Recommendation 3

Provide feedback to all production supervision. (See findings A2 and B3 in appendix A.)

Install a feedback system that provides critical performance information to supervisors and general supervisors. To be effective, the feedback system must

1. Provide feedback *daily,* with data on today's performance available to production supervisors and general supervisors before the next day's shift begins.
2. Provide data on the critical measures of performance (i.e., yields, net productivity, scrap).
3. Be cumulative, so the recipient can see changes based on his or her actions.

4. Be easily interpreted. A visual display of curves would be more appropriate than computer printouts or columns of numbers.
5. Be reviewed jointly by the production supervisors and general supervisors to identify trends or problems and discuss corrective action (the same interaction should be held between general supervisors and their superiors).

Figure B-3 contains a proposed feedback document. This document would be displayed in a central location where it was readily accessible to the supervisors. The form would provide data on current measures (left axis) and proposed yields (right axis). It could also record accumulated delayed charges (upper left-hand corner) and downtime. The downtime designation appears

Figure B-2. Prototype of a problem predictor and elimination record.

Problem Predictor and Elimination Record			
Part no. XX-XXXX			
Critical Elements: • Special rack required • Automation after draw press critical. Needs strong grip. • Operator feed into draw press requires critical timing. • Conveyor after press #2 must be snug to press. • Steel critical. Watch during first hour.			
Operating Considerations: 1. Scrap cost is high ($X) 2. Rework on skin is costly ($X) 3. Shutdowns up to 50 minutes are tolerable due to need for part and cost of steel.			
Problem Record:			
Run Date	**Problem**	**Recommendation or Action**	**Resolution**

Figure B-3. Performance log.

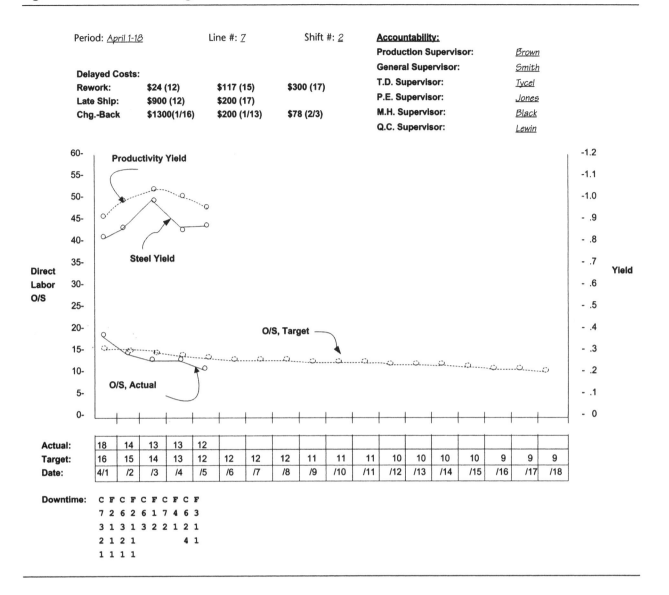

Period: _April 1-18_ Line #: _7_ Shift #: _2_

Accountability:

Production Supervisor:	_Brown_
General Supervisor:	_Smith_
T.D. Supervisor:	_Tycel_
P.E. Supervisor:	_Jones_
M.H. Supervisor:	_Black_
Q.C. Supervisor:	_Lewin_

Delayed Costs:

Rework:	$24 (12)	$117 (15)	$300 (17)
Late Ship:	$900 (12)	$200 (17)	
Chg.-Back	$1300(1/16)	$200 (1/13)	$78 (2/3)

Actual:	18	14	13	13	12													
Target:	16	15	14	13	12	12	12	12	11	11	11	10	10	10	10	9	9	9
Date:	4/1	/2	/3	/4	/5	/6	/7	/8	/9	/10	/11	/12	/13	/14	/15	/16	/17	/18

Downtime:

```
C F C F C F C F C F
7 2 6 2 6 1 7 4 6 3
3 1 3 1 3 2 2 1 2 1
2 1 2 1       4 1
1 1 1 1
```

under the date line and would include a code number (C) for the type of downtime and the frequency (F) of each type of downtime. The form would be updated and reviewed daily by production supervisors and their general supervisors.

Each general supervisor would have copies of the individual production supervisor's feedback forms, and a consolidated feedback form for all his or her production supervisors. The data on the consolidated form would function as feedback to the general supervisor to be discussed daily with the general supervisor's superintendent.

The recommended form has another capability that could be a useful management tool. The performance log can serve not only as a feedback form on the production supervisor's performance, but it can function as the feedback on the performance of the line and be distributed (upper right-hand corner) to all supervisors responsible to that line. Several management possibilities are then possible, including

- having the various service departments begin to evaluate their supervisors and general

supervisors on the performance of the production lines for which they are responsible
- providing better problem-solving data for the zone committees now being formed in the plant
- giving the plant manager a method for fixing responsibility for and evaluating results on the lines

In addition to the continuous, cumulative, daily feedback system described above, the production supervisors should have access to all or part of the parts performance record (the recommended "memory" system in figure B-2) so that they can view how their performance on a single part has been over several runs.

Recommendation 4

Change production supervision responsibilities. (See findings A1 and B9 in appendix A.)

We propose a redistribution of responsibilities for three levels of management, in keeping with the general missions recommended in table B-3.

The recommended missions, responsibilities, and evaluation criteria are summarized in table B-4. The three levels are differentiated along three dimensions: measures of performance, operating timeframe, and resources to manipulate, as shown in table B-5. The desired emphasis and information flows for the three levels are shown in figure B-4.

The recommended redistribution of responsibilities will remain valid after the current production problems are corrected, providing emphasis on running the production system at the level of the

production supervisors and general supervisors and monitoring the system at the superintendent level. The success of any such change in responsibilities depends on the plant manager's and production manager's monitoring of the changes and their consistent evaluation of the managers by the recommended criteria.

Recommendation 5

Change the scheduling system. (See findings B4 and B5 in appendix A.)

We propose a change in the basic production control system to include the elements shown in figure B-5. Again, the process starts with the program need, which is converted to a daily schedule. Then, the schedule is reviewed by a group to prepare for the run (basically the die-set meeting only with better data and supervision). This group may alter the schedule based on the status of the dies, lines, steel, and material handling. The schedule is then run. However, both the hits and the actual count are recorded, and the discrepancy analyzed. (The analysis function could be performed by an individual, a department, a taskforce, or some joint representation of production control and production.) The results are analyzed and:

1. Action is taken to correct the problem that contributed to the gap between desired and actual results.
2. The data and corrective actions are recorded on a form such as the parts performance record (table B-2). This information would be used in the run preparation reviews.

Table B-3. Aligning management responsibilities and missions.

Level	Mission
Supervisor	Get the line running and keep it running.
General supervisor	Keep the lines running.
Superintendent	See that problems do not recur.

Table B-4. Proposed distribution of responsibilities: production supervision.

Position	Mission	Responsibilities	Evaluation
Production Supervisor	Get the line running and keep it running	• Assign workers • Train workers • Monitor performance • Make adjustments of workers and equipment • Correct problems with resources provided • Make preliminary diagnosis of problems • Predict problems • Signal general supervisor (1) when having trouble (2) about changes required to avoid trouble	• Use of resources (steel, direct labor) • Value of data reported to general supervisor
General Supervisor	Keep the line running profitably	• Provide resources (service) • Make shutdown decision • Signal superintendent of problems and required changes • Carry out changes • Maintain part problem system • Clear line using part problem system and part performance record	• Use of resources (yield, profitability) • Accuracy of diagnosis of problems
Superintendent	See that problems do not occur again	• Manage the production information system • Work with service departments and front office to solve problems • Order changes implemented in production • Monitor changes and results	• Do problems get and stay fixed? • Do things get better? • Total productivity, as measured by yields, net productivity, and parts cost

Table B-5. Dimensions differentiating levels of production management.

Level	Measures of Performance	Timeframe	Resources
Production Supervisor	• Downtime • Scrap • Net productivity	Daily	Hourly workers
General Supervisor	• Yields • Net productivity • Profitability	Several days	Service departments
Superintendent	• Profitability • Cycle loss • Improvement of parts performance	Open (until the problem is corrected)	The plant

Figure B-4. Recommended emphasis and information flow.

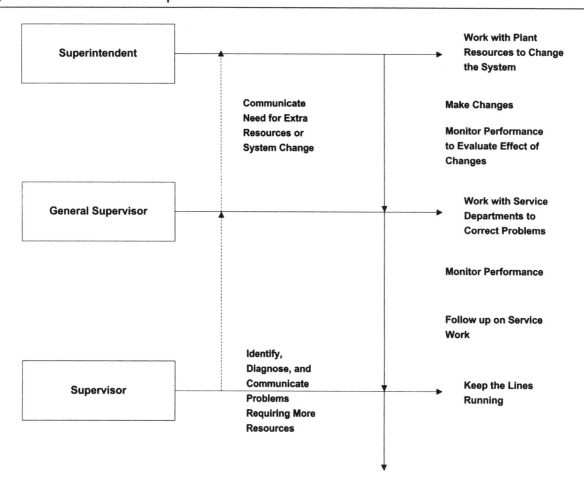

3. Any new scheduling decision factors (e.g., "Run this job for two days rather than one day because die set time has doubled due to die alteration") are fed into scheduling for more economical runs.

4. Emergency runs requested. Unlike the existing system, this action shows that steps are being taken to see that this problem doesn't occur again.

5. The desired and actual count fed into the program need, leading to an accurate reduction in the need *plus* more realistic estimates based on actual counts to predict counts next time that part is run.

Such a system provides a sound basis for production control, production, and the various service departments working toward a common goal of profitable productivity.

Recommendation 6

Alter the basis for determining certain indirect labor budgets. (See finding B8 in appendix A.)

The formula for determining indirect labor budgets should be altered so that authorization will be responsive to critical variations in production. For example, the formula for authorizing plant engineering (PE) personnel might take into account recent (two-week) downtime history. The greater the downtime, the more PE labor would be authorized (within limits, of course). There also might be a base below which the maintenance staff does not drop. Certainly, the relationship between run volume and maintenance required is not a linear one. The formula for authorizing material handling labor might well include some difficulty factor. Such a designation could easily be assigned to each part.

Figure B-5. Schematic of proposed scheduling/control system.

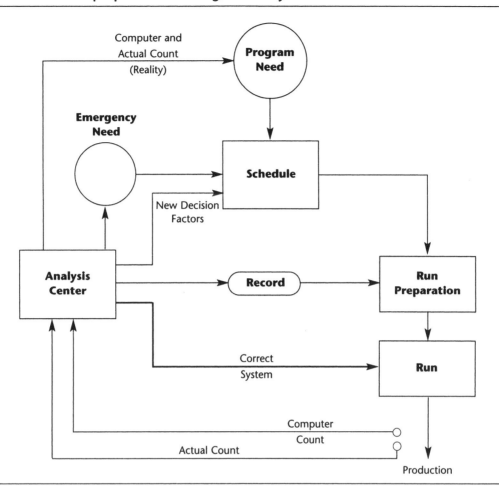

In addition, the timeframe in which indirect labor costs are reviewed might be extended for some service departments such as PE. That is, rather than holding the service department accountable for being in the black each day, require the department to net out in the black at the end of the month. This would give that department some latitude in applying manpower. By the early commitment of substantial manpower to a problem, it would get fixed rather than being jury-rigged for an indefinite time.

Recommendation 7

Change current start-up procedures. (See finding B6 in appendix A.)

This problem will not be solved by putting heat on production supervisors. We recommend a closer look by plant management at the systems causes of the problem. The investigation would be aided by, and future problems avoided by, implementing the general production control system (with the part performance record and analysis center concept) recommended above.

Recommendation 8

Provide decision guides for supervisors and general supervisors on shutting down lines. (See finding B7 in appendix A.)

Provide decision guides for selected parts on when to run and when to shut down, taking into consideration the cost of scrap and rework and the consequences of no pieces being produced. Figure B-6 shows how these data might be presented on a card for easy carrying and reference by press supervisors.

Figure B-6. Prototype decision aid for press supervisors.

Decision Aid for Press Supervisors					
Part	Cost of Steel	Cost of Labor	Cost of Rework	Acceptable Scrap (#)	Acceptable Rework (#)

Recommendation 9

Train production supervision in new responsibilities. (See finding B9 in appendix A and recommendation #4.)

Per recommendation #4, three levels of production supervision need to understand their new responsibilities, how they are to carry out those responsibilities, the resources and information available to support them, and how their performance will be evaluated in the future.

Recommendation 10

Train production supervisors and general supervisors in selected topics. (See finding B10 in appendix A.)

Training on job responsibilities should await a redefinition of relevant supervisory jobs and creation of a system for producing operational changes to make those definitions real. When training is conducted, it should be brief and directed toward specific tasks to be carried out, ways of evaluating how well each task is accomplished, and examples of particularly vague tasks, with explana-

tions of what constitutes the desired and undesired behavior of the trainees. The critical factor in the success of this change will be the subsequent monitoring of supervisory performance by top plant management.

In addition, some simple, straightforward guides should be developed to aid production supervisors and general supervisors in examining manufacturing equipment. Supervisors should receive brief training in how to use the guides. The training should be followed by frequent feedback to supervisors and general supervisors on the accuracy of their diagnoses.

Note, however, that training in feedback to hourly workers and reinforcement or acknowledgment of comments by hourly workers would probably be of little value under the present circumstances. Nevertheless, following changes in the system and a reduction of the pressure, brief training (several hours) in these areas would be fruitful. Successful application of such training depends entirely on whether general supervisors and superintendents learn to use and, in fact, practice the same concepts.

Glossary

A

Account Strategy: The strategy that an internal performance consultant develops for how he or she plans to support a client group or "account." Such a strategy might include a statement of the long-term goals for the account, a multiyear plan for how to achieve those goals, and a list of key managers whose support needs to be cultivated along the way. Each performance improvement opportunity should be assessed against the account goals and strategy.

Algorithm: A stepwise procedure for solving a problem or accomplishing some goal.

Anatomy of Performance (AOP): An "organizations as systems" framework that identifies the major factors affecting individual performance and organization results; the super-system, organization system, human performance system, and management system.

ASTD: A professional society started in 1944 that was originally the American Society for Training & Development but is now known officially by its abbreviation ASTD.

B

Business Case Template: A tool for presenting the business case for a project (as in, "Is this worth doing?"). The template can be applied to any request for help or proposed initiative an internal performance consultant is likely to receive.

C

Chargebacks: An internal accounting practice of an organization whereby the cost of certain staff activities is charged back directly to the organizational unit receiving the service. This practice is in contrast to the costs of such a staff service being absorbed as a general, unallocated overhead cost.

Critical Business Issue (CBI): A problem or opportunity that is key to the overall success of the organization. A CBI could be the need to close an actual or potential gap in a company's performance or an opportunity to make significant improvements in an area currently experiencing no performance problems. The CBI must subsequently be refined to a specific gap between current and desired results.

Critical Job Issue (CJI): A problem or opportunity related to the performance of a specific job, for example, "Sales order forms are incomplete." The CJI must subsequently be refined to a specific gap between current and desired results.

Critical Process Issue (CPI): A problem or opportunity related to the performance of a specific process. Examples include "excessive time to get new products to market" and "deteriorating customer satisfaction with time to receive orders." The CPI must subsequently be refined to a specific gap between current and desired results.

Culture: Culture can be defined on two levels: a macro, anthropological definition and a micro, behavioral definition. An example of the macro definition is the following: "A shared system of beliefs, values, and traditions that shape a person's behavior and perception of the world." This definition is sufficient for the individual who is interested in studying, analyzing, and classifying the "is" behavior of a social group. However, to alter the "is" behavior of a social system, a micro, behavioral definition and understanding of culture is required. An example of such a micro definition is the following: "Organization culture is the prevailing 'expectations-consequence' relationship (per the human performance system) that exists in a particular work environment or work social system."

Cybernetics: The theoretical study of feedback and control processes in biological, mechanical, and electronic systems.

D

Data Sweep: Performance analysis is conducted through a series of data sweeps, which involve data gathering, data analysis, recommendation generation, and planning of the next data sweep based on what was learned in the previous data sweep(s). A data sweep involves relatively short bursts of data gathering (1–3 days), followed by several days to analyze the data, generate tentative recommendations, and plan the next data sweep. A performance analysis may require two or three data sweeps, starting with an understanding of the relevant organization system and drilling down to relevant processes and jobs, as required, in subsequent data sweeps.

Die (NuPlant): A hard template or stamp that is used in stamping operation facilities, such as NuPlant, to form sheets of steel into some shape (e.g., bumpers, door frames, automobile hoods).

Die Repair Function (NuPlant): The operation in NuPlant responsible for repairing dies that have cracked or have otherwise been damaged.

Die Set (NuPlant): An operation at NuPlant whereby a die in a stamping machine is removed and replaced by another die. This operation is required every time a different part is to be run on a stamping line (e.g., converting from stamping hoods to stamping doors) or when a die is returned after repair.

Direct Labor Costs (NuPlant): The amount of time (in minutes) it takes employees on the stamping line to produce a given part (e.g., part #999, a hood for car model *X*). This is considered direct labor costs for making the part versus the indirect costs associated with the material handling, maintenance, and scheduling departments, which must eventually be allocated across all parts produced.

Direct Labor/Off-Standard (DL/OS) (NuPlant): A productivity measure used at NuPlant. It summarizes the planned versus actual labor hours required to produce a specified number of parts on a stamping line. If the number of hours actually required to produce the parts is less than planned, the line is said to be in the black. If the line requires more than the planned hours, it is in the red. The goal is to always be in the black.

Direct Labor Standard (NuPlant): The expectation or standard for direct labor costs for a specific part. For example, the direct labor standard for part #999 is 0.10 hours per unit produced. (See direct labor costs and off-standard direct labor.)

Disconnect: Any deficiency in a process that negatively affects the effectiveness or efficiency of the process.

Downtime: The time on a manufacturing line that the line is not running, for example, "Line A had 30 minutes of downtime today."

E

Engagement Models: The role of the performance consultant in the execution of the four phases of the results improvement process (RIP). The Introduction to this book presents four alternative models for executing the RIP.

Exemplar or Exemplary Performer: The best performer, which may be a company, department, plant, or individual. Exemplars can be used by the performance consultant to establish what level of performance is possible and to determine the cause of the difference in performance between exemplars and average or poor performers.

F

First Leisurely Theorem: Gilbert's (1996) formula $W = A/B$ meaning that worthy performance (W) is a function of the ratio of valuable accomplishments (A) to costly behavior (B). The theorem can be restated as $W = V$ (or R)$/C$ where the worth of doing a project (W) is a function of the value (V) or results (R) of the project divided by the cost of the project (C). The goal is for W to be much greater than one. This equation can be used to estimate a return-on-investment for a project and can serve as a useful talking point with a manager when reviewing a request for a solution.

Functions: Collections of individuals connected or bounded by some common or related area of (1) expertise, knowledge, or skill; (2) tasks; or (3) equipment. A function operates as the individual's "home room" and provides an administrative mechanism for budgetary control and career development. Also called departments.

H

Hits (NuPlant): The number of impressions recorded by the final press on a stamping line.

Horizontal Alignment: Alignment of the expectations, consequences, and measures of executives, functions, and jobs *horizontally* across all key functions in an organization. This alignment is essential if the key cross-functional processes (i.e., the value chain) are to consistently achieve their desired results.

Human Performance System (HPS): All individuals in an organization are one part of a five-part performance system. The other key components of this system are (1) performance expectations, (2) task support, (3) consequences, and (4) feedback.

Human Relations Training: Training in how to effectively supervise or manage individuals.

Human Resources: The people who perform the work in an organization.

Human Resource Function (NuPlant): The organization responsible for the recruiting, selection, training, and compensation of the human resources required to operate and manage NuPlant.

I

ISPI: International Society for Performance Improvement, a professional society for performance consultants.

J

Job or Role: The collection of tasks to be performed by an individual, presumably in support of some process. The job or the performer of the job is usually identified with a particular function. A role can be performed by different people with different jobs (e.g., team leader).

Job Level: As described in the book *Improving Performance* by Rummler and Brache (Jossey Bass, 1995), there are three levels of performance in any organization. At the highest or the organization level, there is the performance desired by the enterprise. At the next or process level, there is the performance required of all processes in order to achieve the organization-level performance. Finally, at the job level, there is the performance required of all jobs in order to achieve the process-level performance. Ideally, the performance goals of all three levels are aligned.

L

Leadership: Leadership is about setting an appropriate direction or course for the enterprise and getting the "troops" to effectively follow and implement that course.

M

Maintenance Function (aka Plant Engineering) (NuPlant): The organization responsible for maintaining the equipment on NuPlant's highly automated stamping lines.

Management Chip: The performance planned and managed system (PPMS) acts as a sophisticated guidance and control mechanism—a management chip—that is designed to optimize the performance of a job, process, or organization. A management system for an organization is a collection of these management chips inserted at key junctures in the organization.

Management Culture: How managers behave toward each other as they execute their management responsibilities.

Material Handling Function (NuPlant): The organization responsible for moving all material throughout NuPlant. In particular, this function moves the incoming steel to the press line and finished parts either to shipping (and onto rail cars) or to scrap for recycling.

Material Yield (NuPlant): The number of good parts produced from a set amount of steel by a stamping line.

Methodology: A set of practices, procedures, and rules that guides those who work in a discipline or engage in an inquiry. Phases I and II of the results improvement process described in this book constitute a performance analysis methodology.

Model: An abstract representation of reality. Models are useful in helping performance consultants understand complex organizations.

N

Net Productivity (NuPlant): The actual number of acceptable parts produced on a stamping line as a percent of the total "hits" or impressions.

O

Off-Standard Direct Labor (NuPlant): See Direct Labor/Off-Standard.

Optimization: Achieving the optimal or most favorable relationship among components of a system.

Organization Level: As described in the book *Improving Performance* by Rummler and Brache (Jossey Bass, 1995), there are three levels of performance in any organization. At the highest or organization level, there is the performance desired by the enterprise. At the next or process level, there is the performance required of all processes in order to achieve the organization-level performance. Finally, at the job level, there is the performance required of all jobs in order to achieve the process-level performance. Ideally, the performance goals of all three levels are aligned.

Organization Structure: Refers to the reporting relationships among individuals working in an organization. The organization structure is usually represented by an organization chart.

P

Pay Points (NuPlant): In the vernacular of production supervision at NuPlant, each part produced on the production line is referred to as a pay point.

Performance Analysis: A rigorous analysis methodology for improving results that identifies significant gaps in results to be closed, identifies the barriers to desired results, specifies the changes necessary to achieve desired results, and lays the foundation for determining if the desired results have been achieved.

Performance Consultant: An individual whose task is to improve the performance or results of some individual or organizational entity.

Performance Executed (PE): The performer, which can be an individual, a process, or an organization entity (e.g., a company division, plant, or department), delivers the desired performance or results prescribed in the goals and plans.

Performance Managed (PM): Actual performance is monitored against the goals and plans; and if a negative deviation is detected, a change signal may be sent to the performer or the performance planned (PP) component of the performance planned and managed system (PPMS).

Performance Planned (PP): Goals and plans (including necessary resources and processes to achieve the goals) are set and communicated to the performer.

Performance Planned and Managed System (PPMS): A framework for reviewing the management system of an organization, based on the belief that performance or results are a function of the following: performance planned (PP), performance executed (PE), and performance managed (PM).

Performance Variables: The variables or factors that determine or affect the performance of an individual, the organization, or both. The anatomy of performance provides a template for identifying the performance variables in a particular situation.

Performer: The individual who is performing tasks as part of a job or role. However, because more and more job tasks and processes are being carried out by computers, the term can be applied to computers as well.

PIPs and Stakes Analysis: Procedure developed by Thomas Gilbert for determining and evaluating the potential for improving performance. *Performance improvement potential (PIP)* refers to where there is the greatest variability in performance and, therefore, the greatest opportunity for performance improvement (e.g., variability between jobs, supervisors, shifts, districts, stores). *Stakes* refers to the economic stakes involved in the issue (e.g., scrap cost, labor cost, material cost).

Practices: Patterns of behavior. See Tosti and Jackson (1989) and Lineberry and Carleton (1999).

Primary Processes: Those processes having to do with inventing, developing, selling, or delivering products or services and which directly affect the customer.

Problem Pentagon: A preliminary analysis tool that contains questions focused on the what/where/when/who/worth of a performance problem or performance improvement opportunity.

Process: A series of planned activities that convert a given input into a desired output.

Process Level: As described in the book *Improving Performance* by Rummler and Brache (Jossey Bass, 1995), there are three levels of performance in any organization. At the highest or organization level, there is the performance desired by the institution. At the next or process level, there is the performance required of all processes in order to achieve the organization-level performance. Finally, at the job level, there is the performance required of all jobs in order to achieve the process-level performance. Ideally, the performance goals of all three levels are aligned.

Production Scheduling (NuPlant): This organization schedules how many of which parts are to be run on each press line at NuPlant.

Profile or Organization Profile: Such a profile would be developed by a performance consultant for each of the major client organizations he or she supports. A profile might consist of the performance consultant's long-term objectives or goals for the working relationship with this entity; an organization chart; an approximation of the macro anatomy of performance; a business summary of the unit; a brief history of each project undertaken with this organization, including information on accessing complete project records and deliverables.

Project Roadmap: A process map showing some recommended questions, decisions, and actions for performance consultants when working on projects.

Prototypes: When presenting recommendations for change to a client, it is frequently beneficial to include an example, sample, or prototype of what is being recommended. For example, if the performance consultant is recommending "feedback for first-line supervisors," a logical solution prototype to be included would be a sample of the form or report that the supervisor should be receiving.

Q

Quality Control (NuPlant): This organization inspects incoming steel and outgoing finished parts as they come off the press line at NuPlant.

R

Recommendation Headlines: Summary statements of recommendations, without all of the supporting detail. Recommendation headlines are easy to manage for prioritization and presentation.

Results Chain: Performance consulting is focused on delivering results—*organization* results. Therefore, it is important for the performance consultant to identify the results chain that links a critical job issue (CJI) to a critical process issue (CPI) to a critical business issue (CBI).

Results Gap: The difference between "is" or current results and "should" or desired results. For example, the desired result is market share of 60%; the current result is market share of 48%.

Results Improvement Process (RIP): A process for improving results which begins with a request for help and includes the four phases: (I) Desired Results Determined & Project Defined; (II) Barriers Determined & Changes Specified; (III) Changes Designed, Developed & Implemented; (IV) Results Evaluated & Maintained or Improved.

Root Cause: The basic or fundamental causes of a gap in results. The distinction is between surface symptoms or explanations of a gap (e.g., "Agents have a bad attitude") and the root cause of the gap ("The measures and balance of consequences for agents support their completing calls as fast as possible").

Run (NuPlant): The period of time a particular part is to be produced on a stamping line. At the end of a run, the dies are reset on the line to run a different part for a period of time.

S

Scientific Method: The scientific method is the process by which scientists, collectively and over time, endeavor to construct an accurate (i.e., reliable, consistent, and logical) representation of the world. The scientific method is based on proving or disproving a hypothesis.

Scope or Project Scope: The boundaries of a project, including the processes, functions, jobs or positions, sites, and geography to be involved.

Serious Performance Consulting: Serious performance consulting includes three things, according to Rummler: (1) It is focused on improving results; (2) It follows a systematic process; and (3) It involves a sound, rigorous methodology for performance analysis.

Standard (NuPlant): An expected result.

Strategic Assessment: A recommended initial screen or assessment of requests for help by the performance consultant. The objective is to determine the most appropriate initial response to each request.

Suboptimization Maximizing the performance of a component of a system to the detriment of the total system. The total system is suboptimized.

Super-System: The larger system in which the target system exists. If the system in question is a company, then its super-system consists of the product or service market, the shareholders, competition, resources, and general business environment. If the target system is a manufacturing plant, then its super-system consists of relevant forces within the parent company, as well as the relevant components of the parent company's super-system. The manufacturing plant has a chain of product markets, conceivably starting with a plant within the company that receives its product, to the company's distribution warehouse to the retailer and finally to the consumer.

Support Processes: Processes that support the primary processes and are typically related to human resources, finance, information technology, and so forth.

System: A group of independent but interrelated elements comprising a unified whole. For the performance consultant, the system is whatever organizational entity is the focus for improvement. It could be a total company, a division of a company, a plant, or a department.

T

Trackers or Performance Trackers: Tables or spreadsheets that display numerical results for key performance variables over time.

V

Value Chain: A chain of primary processes within an organization that produce a valued product or service to customers.

Vertical Alignment: The alignment from top to bottom of the expectations, consequences, and measures (i.e., the human performance system) of all jobs in a functional hierarchy. This is a requirement if a function is to consistently achieve its desired results.

Y

Yield or Material Yield (NuPlant): The number of good parts produced from a set amount of steel by a stamping line.

References

Adams, S. (1999). *Don't Step in the Leadership.* Kansas City, MO: Andrews McMeel Universal.

Addison, R. (2003). "Performance Technology Landscape." *Performance Improvement, 42*(2): 13–15. www.ispi.org/publications/pitocs/piFeb2003 /Addison_Four.pdf.

Burke, W.W., and G. Litwin. (1989). "A Causal Model of Organizational Performance." In: J.W. Pfeiffer (editor). *The 1989 Annual: Developing Human Resources.* San Diego: University Associates.

Gilbert, T. (1996). *Human Competence: Engineering Worthy Performance,* tribute edition. Silver Spring, MD: International Society for Performance Improvement.

Lineberry, C., and J.R. Carleton. (1999). "Analyzing Corporate Culture." In: H. Stolovitch and E. Keeps (editors). *Handbook of Human Performance Technology,* second edition. San Francisco: Jossey-Bass.

Performance Design Lab (2004). "Methodology." www.performancedesignlab.com. Accessed February 29, 2004.

Rummler, G.A., and A.P. Brache. (1995). *Improving Performance: How to Manage the White Space on the Organization Chart.* San Francisco: Jossey-Bass.

Rummler, G.A., and D. Brethower. (no year). Unpublished musings.

Schein, E.H. (1992). *Organizational Culture and Leadership.* San Francisco: Jossey-Bass.

Silbiger, S.A. (1999). *The Ten-Day MBA: A Step-By-Step Guide To Mastering the Skills Taught in America's Top Business Schools,* revised edition. New York: Quill William Morrow.

Tosti, D.T., and S.F. Jackson. (1989). *Organizational Alignment.* Larkspur, CA: Vanguard Consulting Group.

Additional Resources

The following professional organizations, websites, and books are resources you may find valuable in your quest to become a *serious* performance consultant.

Professional Societies

I have found the professional societies listed below to be valuable resources for making connections with other practitioners and for providing a way to learn about new trends in performance improvement. Each of these societies has U.S. and international chapters and holds annual conferences. Each also offers periodical subscriptions to help keep you on top of changes in the field of performance consulting.

- *ASTD:* Founded in 1944, ASTD is a leading association of workplace learning and performance professionals, forming a world-class community of practice. ASTD was formerly known as the American Society for Training & Development. In recent years, ASTD has widened the industry's focus to connect learning and performance to measurable results. For more information, go to www.astd.org.
- *ISPI (International Society for Performance Improvement):* Founded in 1962, ISPI is a leading international association dedicated to improving productivity and performance in the workplace. Leaders in the field of performance improvement present at the annual conferences, and because of the relatively

small size of the conferences, it is often possible to interact with the gurus after their sessions. For more information, go to www.ispi.org.
- *OBM Network (Organization Behavior Management):* The OBM Network is a special interest group of the Association for Behavior Analysis (ABA, www.abainternational.org). The OBM Network, founded in 1982, is a research-based organization of dedicated performance practitioners. For more information, go to www.obmnetwork.com.

Websites

The Internet can provide a wealth of information on performance consulting, including articles, case studies, workshop offerings, and newsletters. Below are listed several websites (available when this book was written) that provide information on various performance consulting topics. For each website listed, the principals of the company are included in parentheses:

- *www.performancedesignlab.com (Geary Rummler, Cherie Wilkins, Rick Rummler, Kimberly Morrill, Mark Munley):* This website provides papers, presentations, and tools on the topics outlined in the book, as well as the latest performance consulting workshops offered by PDL.
- *www.seekvalueadded.net (Dale Brethower and Karolyn Smalley):* The value of visiting this website is in signing up for the newsletters.

One is "The Moving Window," which is available free of charge and offers monthly observations of what is happening in and around the performance improvement arena. The other is "The Driving Force," which is a bimonthly newsletter for performance improvement professionals.

- *www.businessprocesstrends.com (Paul Harmon and Celia Wolf):* This website is fantastic for the keeping up on the latest information on process improvement, process management, and best practices. You can also sign up for the monthly newsletter, which provides articles on process applications and new trends. The great thing about this website is that it's not selling anything, so the information available is less biased than that offered elsewhere.
- *www.behavior.org (Cambridge Center for Behavioral Studies):* Go to the Performance Systems Analysis (PSA) section for a description of PSA, articles, and book reviews.
- *www.vectorscan.com (Bob Carleton, Eugene Drumm, Ian McGrath, Christopher Geczy, Lynne Goulding, Alan Stevens):* Visit this website for information on cultural due diligence, organization effectiveness, change management, leadership, executive development, 360-degree feedback, process reengineering, feedback, and performance management.
- *www.megaplanning.com (Roger Kaufman):* This website offers articles on performance consulting, as well as online self-assessments in needs assessment, performance improvement competencies, organizational readiness for e-learning, evaluation, culture, and performance motivation.
- *www.vanguardc.com (Don Tosti and Stephanie Jackson):* Visit this website for more information on internal branding, strategy and culture alignment, leadership, partnering, process alignment, culture alignment, customer focus, and agility.
- *www.performanceinternational.com (Danny Langdon and Kathleen Whiteside):* See this website for more information on the Language of Work model used by Performance International (conditions, input, process, output, consequences, and feedback).
- *www.train.de (Klaus Wittkuhn):* The "Train" website offers performance consulting and training resources in Germany, Switzerland, and South Africa.
- *www.binder-riha.com (Carl Binder and Cynthia Riha):* This useful web resource provides articles and resources on sales knowledge management, fluency, performance technology, results measurement, and applications in education.
- *www.partners-in-change.com (Dana and Jim Robinson):* The Robinsons' website includes papers on performance consulting and demonstration videos that show expert performance consultants performing critical aspects of the job.
- *www.franklincovey.com/jackphillips (Jack Phillips):* Visit this site for information on measuring return-on-investment for training, human resources initiatives, and performance improvement solutions.

Books

The library of a serious performance consultant is likely to include some, if not all, of the following titles:

- *The Basics of Process Mapping.* Damelio, R. (1996). Portland, OR: Productivity Inc. This title introduces process mapping tools and shows you how to use them in your organization. This is a straightforward and easy-to-use guide for those new to process mapping.
- *Human Competence: Engineering Worthy Performance*, tribute edition. Gilbert, T.F. (1996). Silver Spring, MD: International Society for Performance Improvement. Tom Gilbert is commonly known as the "father of human performance technology." Topics especially useful in the book include the focus on outputs versus behaviors, the behavior engineering model (similar to Rummler's human performance system and other individual performance models), and a job model format.

- *Mega Planning: Practical Tools for Organizational Success.* Kaufman, R. (2000). Thousand Oaks, CA: Sage Publications. Mega planning involves significant stakeholders in defining success and then identifies what each person and part of an organization must do to succeed. Kaufman covers the basics of quality management, needs assessment, gap analysis, benchmarking, reengineering, and continuous improvement. Key to Kaufman's approach is a focus on the impact of any improvement or change on society as a whole.

- *Performance Consulting: Moving Beyond Training.* Robinson, D.G., and Robinson, J.C. (1996). San Francisco: Berrett-Koehler. This book provides a conceptual framework and guidance for moving from the role of a traditional trainer to that of a performance consultant. The book includes dozens of useful tools, illustrative exercises, and a case study that threads through the book showing how the techniques described are applied in an organizational setting.

- *Moving from Training to Performance: A Practical Guidebook.* Robinson, D.G., and Robinson, J.C. (1998). San Francisco: Berrett-Koehler. This book includes chapters written by various authors and is designed to serve the growing group of training and human resource departments seeking to move from training solutions to overall performance solutions. Included is a chapter entitled "The Three Levels of Alignment" by Geary Rummler.

- *Improving Performance: How to Manage the White Space on the Organization Chart,* second edition. Rummler, G.A., and Brache, A.P. (1995). San Francisco: Jossey-Bass. With more than 150,000 copies sold worldwide, *Improving Performance* is recognized as the book that launched the process improvement revolution. It was the first such approach to bridge the gap between organization strategy and the individual. Now, in this revised and expanded new edition, Rummler and Brache reflect on the key needs of organizations faced with today's challenge of managing change. With multiple charts, checklists, hands-on tools, and case studies, the authors show how they implemented their performance improvement methodology in some 250 successful projects with clients such as Hewlett-Packard, 3M, Shell Oil, and Citibank.

- *The Ten-Day MBA: A Step-By-Step Guide to Mastering the Skills Taught in America's Top Business Schools,* revised edition. Silbiger, S. (1993). New York: Quill William Morrow. Amazon.com's description is perfect: "This accessible, step-by-step guide to mastering the skills taught in America's top business schools has been a backlist perennial since publication. It dispenses MBA skills at 1% of the cost, in all the major topics taught at America's top ten business schools. MBA applicants and students use it to prepare for entrance interviews and tests; businesspeople, lawyers, and doctors use it to gain the MBA advantage without the time or the expense."

- *Handbook of Human Performance Technology,* second edition. Stolovitch, H.D., and Keeps, E.J., editors. (1999). San Francisco: International Society for Performance Improvement and Jossey-Bass. The *Handbook* contains chapters on a collection of topics useful for performance consultants, including sections on the fundamentals of human performance technology (HPT), the process of HPT, HPT interventions, the professional practice of HPT, and the future of HPT.

- *Figuring Things Out: A Trainer's Guide to Task, Needs, and Organizational Analysis.* Zemke, R., and Kramlinger, T. (1982). Boulder, CO: Perseus Publishing. The authors outline a system for evaluating job performance, assessing training needs, improving employee motivation, and analyzing work organization. It's a very useful guide for those who want to move beyond training into more general performance consulting.

Praise for *Serious Performance Consulting According to Rummler:*

"Before there was 'lean, before there was TQM, before there was knowledge management, and before there were any one-minute cures, there was Geary Rummler preaching and practicing performance technology. His pioneering work, clear thinking, and openness to collaboration have been critical to the growth and maturation of the field. With *Serious Performance Consulting According to Rummler,* we see how important this technology can be in the right hands."

Ron Zemke, certified performance technologist, senior editor of
Training magazine, and co-author of *Service Magic: The Art of Amazing Your Customers*

"The idea behind *Serious Performance Consulting According to Rummler* is as simple as it is brilliant: Take a successful project, and let the reader follow the performance consultant through the project. Geary Rummler, a performance consultant with more than 30 years' experience, tops it off with a 'play-by-play' commentary in which he explains the consultant's reasoning and offers the reader the benefit of his experience. Novices will gain an understanding of the concepts that underpin serious performance consulting, and experts will profoundly deepen their understanding. All this is accomplished in the genuine Rummler way: by helping people learn without teaching."

Klaus Wittkuhn, certified performance technologist
and management consultant, Germany and South Africa

"At a time when performance consultants seem to be struggling with what to call themselves, Dr. Rummler's book does an outstanding job of focusing on the real issue: what they ought to be doing and why. No smoke, no mirrors, no double-talk. This is much more than a how-to book—it's an owner's manual for those who manage performance consultants, and it's a professional development plan for any performance consultant who wants to master the craft."

John Coné, former chief learning officer, Dell Computer,
and consultant in organizational learning

"Geary Rummler does it again with practical and complete guidance on how to improve individual and organizational performance. Based on science and practice, this book is the one to have."

Roger Kaufman, certified performance technologist, professor emeritus,
Florida State University, and director, Roger Kaufman & Associate

"If you are looking for a quick fix for your performance problems, this book is not for you. This book is about *serious* performance consulting. Dr. Rummler's in-depth look at the real work involved in performance consulting and what it takes to produce long-lasting, sustainable results will help you determine if you have the 'right stuff' to be a serious performance consultant."

Debbie Titus, certified performance technologist
and managing HR business partner, The Williams Companies

"If you want to make your best better and do your best more of the time, buy this book, study it, and use what you learn. Rummler draws a clear line between performance consulting 'lite' and serious performance consulting. He states in plain terms what it means to do the right thing and gives clear examples to point the way. Readers are free to disagree, but they will not be confused about what Rummler has learned in his 30-plus years as a thought leader in the field."

Dale M. Brethower, professor emeritus, Western Michigan University, and senior consultant, Performance-Based Systems, LLC

"Using a detailed case study of an actual major performance improvement project, Rummler shares a wealth of practical, down-to-earth lessons based on his decades of performance consulting experience. He fully describes a systematic process and sound, rigorous methodology that inexorably lead to solid results. He also challenges conventionally accepted views on the influence of culture and leadership as both causes of and solutions to performance issues. This is a book to be treasured by novice performance consultants and old pros alike."

Pat McMahon, certified performance technologist and Six Sigma black belt, Sun Microsystems

"*Serious Performance Consulting According to Rummler* articulates the model that sets the standard for both the internal and external organizational performance specialist. The integration of the organization super-system with the individual performance system provides a roadmap to success for improving organizational performance. The case methodology provides the means to internalize quickly these concepts and tools."

A. William Wiggenhorn, president (retired), Motorola University